The Value of Museums

The Value of Museums

Enhancing Societal Well-Being

John H. Falk

ROWMAN & LITTLEFIELD
Lanham • Boulder • New York • London

Published by Rowman & Littlefield
An imprint of The Rowman & Littlefield Publishing Group, Inc.
4501 Forbes Boulevard, Suite 200, Lanham, Maryland 20706
www.rowman.com

86-90 Paul Street, London EC2A 4NE

British Library Cataloguing in Publication Information Available

Library of Congress Cataloging-in-Publication Data

Names: Falk, John H. (John Howard), 1948- author.
Title: The value of museums : enhancing societal well-being / John H. Falk.
Description: Lanham : Rowman & Littlefield, [2021] | Includes bibliographical references and index. | Summary: "The Value of Museums makes the case that the niche museums has always been public well-being. This guide shows museums how to assess and communicate that essential public value"— Provided by publisher.
Identifiers: LCCN 2021021604 (print) | LCCN 2021021605 (ebook) | ISBN 9781538149201 (cloth) | ISBN 9781538149218 (paperback) | ISBN 9781538149225 (epub)
Subjects: LCSH: Museums—Social aspects.
Classification: LCC AM5 .F35 2021 (print) | LCC AM5 (ebook) | DDC 069—dc23
LC record available at https://lccn.loc.gov/2021021604
LC ebook record available at https://lccn.loc.gov/2021021605

™ The paper used in this publication meets the minimum requirements of American National Standard for Information Sciences—Permanence of Paper for Printed Library Materials, ANSI/NISO Z39.48-1992.

The self is our bow.
Our choices are our arrows.
Well-being is the target at which we aim unceasingly.

Contents

Preface

> In order to displace a prevailing theory or paradigm in science, it is not enough to merely point out what it cannot explain; you have to offer a new theory that explains more data, and do so in a testable way.
>
> —Michael Shermer[1]

This is a book about the value of museums. It was written for those working within or for museums, as well as those who aspire to work within or for museums. Particularly, it is intended for those who lead these institutions, whether through governance, management, curation, education, design, marketing, or visitor services. Museum leaders must continually make difficult decisions, decisions related to direction and funding. This book is intended to support those efforts by providing museum leaders with the theoretical and practical knowledge they need to effectively design quality museum experiences and to justify to stakeholders and decision makers the value those museum experiences deliver.

Although I aspired to write a timeless book on museum value, it is of course a book of its times. The fact that I was writing this book during a global pandemic—when virtually every museum in the world was closed and great uncertainty about how many would ever again reopen—influenced my thinking, so too did worldwide concerns and desires for greater social and economic justice. However, this book was influenced by more than just recent events; more than anything, this book represents the influences of a lifetime of lived experiences working with and thinking about museums.

IN SEARCH OF A PARADIGM

Paradigm (noun): In science and philosophy, a paradigm is a distinct set of concepts or thought patterns, including theories, research methods, postulates, and standards for what constitutes legitimate contributions to a field.[2]

I have been on a lifelong quest, a quest to understand and describe the museum experience. For nearly half a century, I have been thinking and theorizing about museum experiences—why people use museums, what they do during those experiences, and what they take away from these experiences, including the value they derive. Today, in this book, my explanation of the museum experience is starkly different than it was forty years ago, or even fifteen years ago.

This is not necessarily a bad thing; in fact, it is probably a good thing. Given that human knowledge and understanding are always a constructive, on-going process of meaning-making, it would make sense that ideas would evolve as new ideas and theories of the world emerge—at least it should be. In other words, like living creatures, knowledge and understanding should evolve and change if it is to remain viable and adaptive. Over the past century or so, neuroscientists and cognitive scientists have come to better understand the complex mental processes that underlie this reality. The world is chaotic and constantly changing. It comes with no boundaries or labels, but the wonder of the human mind is that it constantly strives to make sense of that chaos. Every second the mind is bombarded by a cacophony of sensations and "data." The mind transforms all this noise into patterns; the ideas, concepts, and "facts" that each of us perceives as "reality."

By correlating and combining incoming information with past information and beliefs, the brain constructs the "meanings" we call knowledge and understanding. This very individualized and constructive process is why there can, and will always be, people who hold opposing political views, varying senses of beauty and aesthetics, and yes, even differing interpretations of scientific data.

Science is supposed to be, and generally is less fickle than politics and aesthetics, but even the best-intentioned and well-trained scientists can differ in their analysis of data. This is because, as pointed out by the American physicist and philosopher Thomas Kuhn, all scientific ideas are built upon a constructed edifice of understanding, of theories of the world—what Kuhn called paradigms.[3] Scientific paradigms can and do change as more data, and presumably better understandings and new theories about the meaning of that data, become available. Scientific paradigms, and the scientific meaning-making that flows from those paradigms, are at their core just constructions of the mind; paradigms are no more "reality" than are anything else our minds construct. That is not to say science is all a fabrication, but beliefs about the nature of the world can and do change as more data and better explanations emerge.

Occasionally, new paradigms so radically change perceptions of the world that they totally displace the old ways of thinking. Such was the case with both the germ theory of medicine and Darwin's theory of evolution in the mid-nineteenth century—though it is worth noting that neither of these dramatic paradigm shifts occurred quickly or without a fight by those who still believed in the old paradigms. More frequently, new paradigms are more additive than disruptive. For example, Einstein's theory of relativity did not totally displace Newton's laws, but it did help to explain a variety of phenomenon previously discrepant with Newtonian physics. Being optimistic about the course of science, I like to think of this process as asymptotic—a case where knowledge and understanding continually change, getting closer and closer to a "true" understanding of the workings of the world without ever quite getting there.

MY ASYMPTOTIC JOURNEY

> **Asymptote** (noun)**:** A line that continually approaches a given curve but does not meet it at any finite distance.[4]

Over the course of my professional life, now over half a century, the data available for answering the fundamental questions posed above—why people choose to engage in museum experiences, what happens when they do engage in these experiences, and what value they ultimately derive from these experiences—has grown exponentially. Many in the field, including me, have offered theories about the meaning of this ever-expanding accumulation of data; however, no clear consensus exists around any of these theories. My explanations of this data, my theories, have definitely evolved over time. This book reflects that asymptotic journey.

As I will briefly also discuss in chapter 2, I spent much of the first half of my career, like the vast majority of my colleagues then and now, attempting to explain the museum experience using a learning paradigm. This approach was predicated on the assumption, whether explicitly or implicitly, that museums, first and foremost, are educational institutions, and thus the primary outcome of the museum experience was learning, broadly defined.[5] Lynn Dierking and I analyzed the available data, particularly our own efforts at mining people's long-term recollections of their museum experiences, and deciphered a clear pattern. What we found, and what tens of thousands of others since then have also seen, is that people's museum experiences are influenced by a confluence of contextual factors—personal interests and motivational factors, social and cultural factors, and factors related to the physical setting—all occurring over time. Based on these observations we developed what we called the Contextual Model of Learning. More than thirty-five years later, this theory continues to be a useful framework for making sense of how people learn, both in and beyond museums. Although the Contextual Model of Learning more than adequately helped to explain learning from museums, it failed to fully account for the totality of the museum experience. Although virtually everyone who uses a museum learns something, a learning lens is not sufficient to explain all of the various outcomes that museums afford, all the varied types of value people derive from engaging in a museum experience. Something deeper, more fundamental than learning was happening.

About twenty years ago, I began moving away from the prevailing paradigm that learning was the only, let alone the best paradigm for making sense of the museum experience. I was of course not the only person who began to move away from a learning-focused paradigm. There were others as well, some before me, who began moving in this direction.[6] But as Kuhn understood, moving away from a dominant paradigm is rarely instantaneous, particularly for those who have helped to shape the earlier paradigm—which I had. Ultimately, my transformation was catalyzed by a new set of data collected during the summer of 2003.[7] When people were interviewed years after their museum experience, the overall stories they related were strikingly similar to those I had heard numerous times before. However, what this new set of data afforded me was a more complete picture of the museum experience, and that fuller picture compelled me toward embracing a different paradigmatic lens.

In the past, all I had were fragments of the museum experience—individuals sharing their entry motivations or individuals observed within the museum or individuals recalling over time what they recalled about their museum experience. This time, I had a longer vantage point with data for the same individuals for all three of these critical time periods, and this data helped me to realize that something deeper and more fundamental was driving people to use museums. Indeed the public was coming to museums in order to learn, but more importantly, the public was primarily using museums as vehicles for accomplishing their own (identity) self-related needs and priorities.[8] I hypothesized that sometimes these self-related needs related to learning but not always and was able to demonstrate, through a major in-depth hypothesis-testing study,[9] that most people come to museums primarily to satisfy a handful of specific self-related needs. Over the past two decades, hundreds of institutions of all types from all over the world have further validated these findings.[10] The public uses museums in order to satisfy their curiosity and their general intellectual interest-related needs (explorers), their socially driven needs (facilitators), and their psychic and emotional escape-related needs (rechargers). There are also people who use museums to directly and specifically extend their sense of self (affinity seekers), and at least at some museums, use the institution as a vehicle for paying homage and respect to a site or to others (respectful pilgrims). Like the Contextual Model of Learning, I believe this theory is true and useful, but I also now believe, that like the proverbial onion, there is still another layer lying below self-related needs, a still deeper set of reasons that explain why people use museums and what value they derive from those experiences.

How I came to this position is an interesting part of my intellectual journey, one worth sharing. My interest in identity and sense of self did not begin in the early 2000s. I actually had become quite interested in this topic more than twenty years earlier, in parallel with my earliest work in museums. The way I attempted to approach the question of self was not from a social science perspective but rather from a biological, evolutionary perspective. Many may not be aware, but I actually did doctoral research in two separate disciplines, one in education and the other in ecology. For years, I pursued research in both areas simultaneously. In the early 1980s, I became fascinated with trying to understand and explain the origins of self-perception and the role this ability played in the evolution of life on earth. The upshot of those early efforts were a series of unpublished articles and a never-finished book on the topic. In 2012 I decide the time had finally come to finish what I had started and actually complete a book on the evolution of self. Although I have written a number of books, this book proved particularly challenging, involving numerous false starts and countless drafts over many years. The title of the final product, *Born to Choose: Evolution, Self and Well-Being* (2018), well encapsulates my journey. What began as a book about the evolution of self, which is still part of the book, ended up as a book on choice, and more specifically a book on the role that self and well-being play in choice. As I discovered over the course of this intellectual odyssey, choices are a means to an end, driven by perceptions of self, but self is not the endpoint. Self, too, is but a means to an end, and that end is well-being.[11]

This brings me again to this book. As I have continued to review and interpret the data on the museum experience, I now believe that I have, at last, a way of describing the ultimate core of the "onion." The "theory"—dare I suggest the new paradigm—that I have arrived at clarifies and explains why people engage in museum experiences. I believe it also parsimoniously explains the data about why people behave in the ways they do in museums. Perhaps most importantly, the theory that I am about to put forward in this book provides a far more consistent and inclusive depiction of the value people derive from their museum experiences. In other words, it is a theory that allows for a more complete, and I believe conceptually grounded, explanation of why people describe their museum experiences in the ways they do. The theory I will put forth in this book builds on the ideas of well-being I first laid out in *Born to Choose*.

As I will describe more fully in the pages that follow, I do not conceptualize well-being in quite the same way many now do. Rather than framing well-being, as most "positive psychologists" do in terms of happiness, or any of the other myriad New Agey ways that currently are in vogue, I use the term well-being to describe a biological process, a mechanism for achieving balance and homeostasis. (Homeostasis is the process that cells, tissues, and organisms use to maintain and regulate their condition to ensure the stability and constancy needed to function properly.) All living things continually strive to attain this kind of balance in their lives, not merely in a single dimension but across thousands and thousands of dimensions. This pursuit of well-being forms the core of ALL human experience; in fact, it is at the core of ALL life. No living thing ever, once-and-for-always, attains well-being. Every minute, living things must work to maintain their balance, their well-being. The struggle is ongoing and never ending because the forces of nature always push things out of balance. When they get pushed too far out of balance, the result is death. However, despite the challenges, all the millions of different kinds of living things on earth have evolved to be highly successful at this balancing act; living things are, if nothing else, highly skilled "well-being machines." Life has achieved this success through the trial-and-error process called natural selection. Those living things best able to achieve and sustain well-being are the ones most likely to survive and pass on their genes; and in the case of humans, they are the ones best able to pass on not merely their genes but their ideas and beliefs as well.[12]

I assert that it is the pursuit of enhanced well-being, a complex and multidimensional process with deep evolutionary roots, that motivates people to engage in museum experiences. I further assert that it is the successful creation of feelings of well-being that best explains why most users find their museum experiences both so satisfying and so memorable. These feelings of well-being also make people want to replicate the experience and share it with others. The pursuit and achievement of enhanced well-being lies at the heart of all aspects of the museum experience.

I of course may yet change my mind and propose yet another explanation for what I believe lies at the core of the museum experience. For now, though, I think this is unlikely. I believe the model I propose in this book gets as close to the line of "truth" about the nature of the museum experience as I am likely to get.

THE VALUE OF MUSEUM EXPERIENCES

I have divided this book into three major parts and ten chapters. Each chapter is designed to build the case for how museums can, do, and should enhance the public's personal, intellectual, social and physical well-being. I will show that museums have long had success at supporting enhanced well-being, that the benefits of enhanced well-being are worth millions of dollars, and finally, that the goal and practice of enhancing the public's well-being provides a tangible foundation on which to build a new generation of sustainable and relevant museum experiences.

Part I, "Value Revealed," states the problem and how I suggest approaching the solution of that problem. Chapter 1 begins by stating the obvious. For more than a quarter century, museums were one of the fastest growing, most successful institutions in the world. Over the past decade or more, though, the museum community has been bumping up against the limits of its success. The community currently faces significant challenges to its future on multiple fronts. One clear approach to dealing with the serious challenges now facing the museum community is to better understand what it was about museums in general, and museum experiences in particular, that made them so popular and successful in past, that defined the value they delivered.

Chapter 2 introduces a solution, or at least how I would suggest approaching a solution, to defining the value of museum experiences. The essential value of the museum experience, a value long intuitively understood but never fully articulated, was the notion that these experiences delivered enduring and important benefits for users. For most of the history of museums, the nature of these enduring "benefits" were always defined by the people who worked *inside* the museum, by museum professionals, and not by the people on the *outside*, the publics who actually used and presumably derived these benefits from the experience. As a consequence, all previous attempts to describe and define the value of the museum experience, including those made by me, variously missed the mark, frequently focusing on the means rather than the ends. At best, these "insider" efforts to define the value of the museum experience captured some of the parts, for example learning or social cohesion, but rarely, if ever, the whole value these experiences supported, the value of enhanced well-being.

The third and concluding chapter of this introductory section provides a brief but thorough description of what I mean when I talk about enhanced well-being. Unlike the way most social scientists today conceptualize well-being, my framing of well-being—and what it means to have enhanced well-being—is built on not one but two equally important conceptual foundations. Obviously, like other social scientists, my theory of well-being is based on what is known about the ways people process and make sense of the world; but unlike most social scientists, my theory of well-being is equally anchored in biology and evolutionary theory, what is known about the ways all living organisms utilize perceptions of well-being in order to maximize their longevity and survival.[13] Although there are multiple dimensions to well-being, and myriad ways in which the public can and does achieve enhanced well-being as a function of their museum experiences, for practical as well as theoretical reasons I have collapsed all these various dimensions into four basic categories—personal well-being, intellectual well-being, social well-being, and physical well-being.

The next section of the book, part II, "Value Achieved," is divided into four chapters. Each chapter provides concrete examples of what museum experience–derived well-being looks like in each of the four unique but overlapping categories of well-being—or at least what it looked like for much of the past half century, up until the beginning of 2020.

Chapter 4 focuses on *personal well-being*, that uniquely human desire for transcendent identity-building experiences. These can be perceived emotionally as awe, amazement, and joy; or they can be framed more intellectually as self-actualization and personal growth. For centuries, museums have been one of the few places that consistently delivered these types of experiences to a broad public. Museum experiences regularly create for people those once-in-a-lifetime moments, those memorable life markers that are remembered as the time "I was there and saw that," those life events that people say they will never forget for as long as they live.

Chapter 5 describes *intellectual well-being*. Humans, more than any other living creature, have the ability to use their previous experiences to both explain their past actions and to plan and organize how to positively shape their future. Museums have long provided a broad public with tangible ways to support these intellectual needs, perhaps doing so as well as any educational institution ever devised.

Chapter 6 documents the critical *social well-being* outcomes museum experiences support. All humans exist within a cultural milieu of social relationships that suffuse virtually every aspect of their lives. People eat, work, play, learn and even sleep socially. Despite the importance of other needs, no need is more fundamental to overall human well-being than the need to belong to, and feel respected by, one's social group. Museums are social-cultural constructions, and the overwhelming majority of museum use happens socially. The content and nature of the resulting social-cultural interactions form the heart of not only most people's actual museum experiences but also the core of why they chose to use the institution and what they will remember and value about their museum experiences in the future.

Closing out this section, chapter 7 focuses on *physical well-being*. Basic human needs such as eating, staying warm and sheltered, feeling safe, and remaining free from injury and disease are essential to survival, and humans worldwide have evolved complex and often highly pleasurable, culturally specific ways for insuring these needs are met. The rapid rise in the popularity of museums over the past several decades can be explained by museum professionals' growing appreciation of the value of coupling the historic personal, intellectual, and social benefits of museum-going with the benefits of having one's physical well-being-related needs also satisfied. Particularly notable, was the ability of museum experiences to reduce stress. Increasing numbers of museum users report that the primary benefit of their museum experience was that it provided a short-term, readily accessible "fix" for tamping down the stresses of modern life.

This brings me to the final section of the book, part III, "Value Applied." As suggested in the chapter epigram, any paradigm worth its salt provides not just explanation, but also testable predictions. In the final three chapters, I put this new museum experience paradigm to the test by addressing, in turn, how to measure the well-being-related value of museum experiences, how to apply the idea of enhanced well-being to the challenge of inventing the next generation of museum experiences, and finally, how to design more engaging and effective museum experiences.

Chapter 8 focuses on how to apply this new theory to the problem of convincing funders and policy makers of the importance of museum experiences, of the value these experiences deliver to the community. Validly and reliably measuring something as inherently ephemeral and internal as well-being has long challenged social scientists, but by building on years of research related to why people use museums, I was able to devise a way to measure the well-being museums deliver. Pilot results from six diverse museums from three countries are presented. However, this data, in and of itself, is not sufficient as it does not credibly answer the value question.

Value cannot be assessed in isolation; value is always made by comparing one thing to another. For better or worse, the way most people make this type of comparison (i.e., determine value) is monetarily. Specifically, funders and policy makers want to know whether the benefits that accrue from a particular museum experience, or even collection of experiences, is worth the cost it takes to create and deliver them. Historically, efforts to monetize the museum experience have been virtually nonexistent; and those few that have been attempted have suffered from a host of flawed assumptions, not least being a poor understanding of the actual benefits museum experiences provide the public. Again, using data from my pilot research, I describe the impressive, financial return on investment these six museums were able to generate through their museum experiences.

Chapter 9 addresses the future of museums, a future most agree is quite uncertain, and not just for museums but for all institutions. In this final chapter I speculate on what museums could and potentially should look like, how the once thriving museum community must now attempt to reconcile how their institutions, built on a foundation of twentieth-century traditions and assumptions, can best adapt to an uncertain future. I believe museums can survive and become even more popular and relevant in the coming years, but to do so will require making enhanced well-being not merely an incidental outcome but central to their missions and their practice. Clearly, the realities of the twenty-first century demand that museums invent new ways of working and thinking, but the public's need and desire for enhanced well-being, and the museum community's long-standing track record for supporting it, represents a strong foundation on which to build and launch a whole new generation of successful museum "products" and "services."

The final chapter, chapter 10, focuses on strategies for creating quality museum experiences. Perhaps I flatter myself, but I think I have learned quite a bit over my half century's musings about what motivates people to use museums, what quality of museum experiences result in high levels of user satisfaction, and what post-use experiences best support and extend the value of earlier experiences and increase the likelihood of future satisfying museum experiences. With support from a host of talented and knowledgeable museum colleagues, I consolidated these various understandings into a set of ten "principles" for designing better museum experiences.

Like most books, the various sections and chapters of this book were organized with the assumption, and hope, that the ideas logically flowed from beginning to end, but of course no one is required to read it that way. One could read the first chapter and skip to the final section and get the high points. For that matter, some might be content with reading just the chapter on measurement or just the final chapter. Regardless of how one engages with the ideas presented, hopefully all will find at least a few things worthy of further thought and use.

Given that the majority of this book was written during the "plague" year of 2020, the future well-being of museums, let alone the well-being of the publics they seek to serve, seems far more daunting now than it did even a year ago. What is clear, though, is that there will always be a niche for institutions capable of supporting the public's long-term personal, intellectual, social, and physical well-being-related needs. What is less clear is what those experiences should look like and who in the future will emerge as best able to support those needs. I have tried to make the case that museums currently are ideally positioned to be that "who," but doing so consistently and sustainably will require considerable vision and innovation. Unfortunately, those wanting a detailed blueprint for how to accomplish this task will be disappointed. This book does not provide those details, which given the diversity and complexity of museums is arguably an impossible goal anyway. Hopefully, though, the new paradigm proposed in this book provides a useful compass, a way-finding tool that can help museums better navigate within, around, and through the volatile and uncertain future they now face.

NOTES

1. Brainy Quotes. https://www.brainyquote.com/topics/paradigm-quotes. Retrieved March 21, 2021.

2. Wikipedia. (2021). https://en.wikipedia.org/wiki/Paradigm. Retrieved March 21, 2021.

3. Kuhn, T. (1962). *The Structure of Scientific Revolutions.* Chicago: University of Chicago Press.

4. Oxford Dictionary (n.d.). https://www.lexico.com/en/definition/asymptote. Retrieved October 18, 2020.

5. See Falk, J. H., and Dierking, L. D. (1992). *The Museum Experience.* Washington, DC: Whalesback Books; also Falk, J. H., and Dierking, L. D. (2000). *Learning from Museums.* Lanham, MD: Rowman & Littlefield.

6. Some notable examples of this movement are cited below, but note, that even as many of these scholars began moving away from learning, most still clung to some aspect of the earlier paradigm: Silverman, L. H. (1995). "Visitor Meaning-Making in Museums for a New Age." *Curator* 38(3), 161–70. McLean, F. (1998). "Museums and the Construction of National Identity: A Review." *International Journal of Heritage Studies* 3(4), 244–52. Pekarik, A. J., Doering, Z. D., and Karns, D.A. (1999). "Exploring Satisfying Experiences in Museums." *Curator* 42: 152–73. Leinhardt, G., Crowley, K., and Knutson, K. (Eds.). (2002). *Learning Conversations in Museums.* Mahwah, NJ: Lawrence Erlbaum Associates Publishers. Rounds, J. (2004). "Strategies for the Curiosity-Driven Museum Visitor." Curator 47(4), 389–410. Packer, J. (2006). "Learning for Fun: The Unique Contribution of Educational Leisure Experiences." *Curator* 49(3): 329–44.

7. Falk, J. H. (2006). "An Identity-Centered Approach to Understanding Museum Learning." *Curator* 49(2), 151–66.

8. See Falk, J. H. (2009). *Identity and the Museum Visitor Experience.* Walnut Creek, CA: Left Coast Press.

9. See Falk, J. H., Heimlich, J. E., Bronnenkant, K., and Barlage, J. (2005). "Assessing the Impact of a Visit to a Zoo or Aquarium: A Multi-Institutional Research Project." *Proceedings of the 6th International Aquarium Conference, Monterey, CA.* December 2004. Also, Falk, J. H., Heimlich, J. and Bronnenkant, K. (2008). "Using Identity-Related Visit Motivations as a Tool for Understanding Adult Zoo and Aquarium Visitor's Meaning Making." *Curator* 51(1), 55–80.

10. See review in Falk, J. H. & Dierking, L. D. (2019). "Learning from Museums," second edition. Lanham, MD: Rowman & Littlefield.

11. As suggested in the poem I wrote, derived from an ancient Hindu prayer, that serves as the frontpiece for this book.

12. For a deep dive into these ideas, see Falk, J. H. (2018). *Born to Choose: Evolution, Self and Well-Being.* London: Routledge.

13. Falk, J.H. (2018). *Born to choose: Evolution, self and well-being.* London: Routledge.

Acknowledgments

Where does one begin in thanking all of those who have contributed to my nearly fifty-year, asymptotic pursuit of the museum experience? Without question, the place I need to begin is by acknowledging and thanking my intellectual and life partner over the vast majority of these years, Lynn D. Dierking. Without her support—and equally important, critical feedback—these ideas and those that preceded them would never have happened.

There is an immense list of colleagues that have been influential to my ideas and activities over the years, with many of them referenced in the text and dozens and dozens more cited in my references. However, I want to give a particular shout-out to the select and smaller set of individuals who specifically contributed ideas to this volume, most notably I want to thank Martin Brandt Djupdræt for helping me regain my focus on what was really important. Thanks also to Barry Van Deman and Annalisa Banzi for their immensely helpful comments and suggestions. Thanks also to a host of individuals who contributed suggestions for the final chapter. In no particular order, thanks to: Elaine Gurian, Barry Van Deman, Benjamin Dickow, Sarah van Haastert, Charlie Walter, Amina Dickerson, Amparo Leyman-Pino, Ida Brændholt Lundgaard, Carol Stapp, Lynn Dierking, Nik Honeysett, Daniel Spock, Judy Koke, Des Griffin, Diane Miller, Francois Mairesse, Robert Griesmer, Kate Livingston, Erik Jacquemyn, Jessica Luke, Jim Hakala, Marianna Adams, Marsha Semmel, Martin Brandt Djupdræt, Mikko Myllykoski, Paul Martin, Paul Orselli, Shari Werb, Silvia Singer, Spencer Crew, Tom Owen, Tonya Matthews, Tengku Nasariah, Derek Fish, and Zhou Jingjing.

As always, I am deeply indebted to all of my colleagues at the Institute for Learning Innovation, with specific thanks to Judy Koke, Stacey Sheehan, Dave Meier, Elysa Corin, and Kimberly Young for supporting this particular effort. Also, thanks to ILI board members Joe Cone, Tom Owen, Larry Johnson, Meena Selvakumar, and again Nik Honeysett and Tonya Matthews. Special thanks to Nicole Claudio for her help with references.

A very special thanks to the directors and staff at my six pilot monetization research sites for not only being willing to take a flyer on this new approach but actively supporting these efforts by relentlessly striving to collect the necessary data. Again in no particular order, thanks to David M. Simmons, executive director, Billings Farm and Museum; Dolf DeJong, chief executive officer, and Kevin Kerr, manager of species recovery and program assessment, Toronto Zoo; Barry Van Deman, former president, and Laurie Reinhardt, vice president for external relations, Museum of Science and Nature; Mikko Myllykoski, chief executive officer, and Tyystjärvi, project manager, Heureka, the Finnish Science Centre; Maureen Marshall, founding director, and Nadine Villasin Feldman, director of programming, Myseum of Toronto; and Trevor Jones, director and CEO, History Nebraska.

I also want to acknowledge and thank the several economists with whom I had very helpful conversations as I muddled my way through figuring out how to monetize well-being. In particular I want to thank Kreg Lindberg but also Brent Never, Margaret Ray, and Kelly Biedenweg. Also my good friend and trusted expert on psychometrics Mark Needham.

I would be remiss if I did not thank my publisher Charles Harmon for his unflagging support and commitment to this project—so, too, my book editors Erinn Slanina and Meaghan Menzel and copy editor, Rae-Ann Goodwin.

I humbly and gratefully acknowledge Mikko Myllykoski, Ganigar Chen, Lori Fogarty, Silvia Singer and Trevor Jones for their kind statements about this book.

Finally, I want to express my sincere thanks to the many funders, organizations, and publishers who, over all these many years, have made it possible for me to investigate and explore these ideas and provided me with a forum for sharing my ideas through books, articles, and countless talks and presentations.

I

VALUE REVEALED

1

We Have a Problem

The opposite of a problem would likely be the correct solution.

—Joey Lawsin[1]

On April 13, 1970, an onboard explosion rocked the Apollo 13 command module as it was returning from its mission to the moon. With Earth still more than two hundred thousand miles away, everything went dark. The astronauts radioed mission control:

Astronaut Swigert: "Houston, we have a problem."

Mission control: "This is Houston. Say again, please."

Astronaut Lovell: "Uh, Houston, we've had a problem."

Within minutes, everyone understood the immediate challenge the astronauts faced, how to return power and water to the command module again. Everyone also understood the consequences of not resolving this issue, the three Apollo 13 astronauts were going to die. No one knew exactly what the problem was that caused the command module to lose power, and no one knew how to solve the problem, but, most importantly, everyone knew that the problem needed to be fixed soon.

Over the ensuing hours, engineers worked furiously on trying to devise a solution. The challenges were many, and ultimately, the engineers on the ground did indeed devise a way to get the Apollo 13 crew home safely, but doing so required out-of-the-box thinking. The craft could not just be brought down and put into drydock, using "appropriate" spare parts to make repairs. The solution needed to utilize whatever resources, tools, and skills already existed on board; the solution needed to build on existing assets. The ultimate lesson that can be learned from this historic event is that, in real life, it is not always possible to solve a problem by just fixing things in traditional ways. Sometimes, one needs to step back and look at problems from a new angle, figuring out how to reassemble one's assets to remake the craft while moving. That, it seems, is the situation in which museums find themselves today.

Museums are currently in crisis, rocked by repeated explosions from outside and implosions from within. Meanwhile, the professionals who support and run museums, the analog of mission control engineers and on-board astronauts, are scrambling to diagnose and fix the problem. Too often, though, there is no clear consensus on exactly what the problem is or how to solve it. Everyone seems to accept that major "fixes" will be difficult because the organization cannot just be stopped and figuratively put in drydock. Though the timeline is longer, the ultimate consequences of not resolving the current crises the museum community faces is no less existential than that faced by the Apollo 13 mission. If not resolved, museums will not survive.

I believe that, like the solution engineers devised to resolve the crisis that faced the Apollo 13 mission on April 13, 1970, the challenges museums now face require, first and foremost, a willingness to think in new ways about existing realities. Paraphrasing the opening epigram by Joey Lawsin, an engineer and educator, the place to start is not with what is wrong but rather with the opposite, what is right about museums. What is right about museums is that, currently and historically, millions of people have perceived that they derive real value from using museums. What is wrong is that no one has been able to really determine exactly what that value is nor how much that perceived value is actually worth. That is what this book seeks to do.

The purpose of this book is to help museum professionals fully appreciate and understand, perhaps for the first time, what the verifiable value is that they create for the public. If one truly understood the value that makes so many people want to use museums again and again, then it would be much easier to know how to enhance that value so that more people, including more different people, could receive those benefits. Equally importantly, if one had the ability to convincingly, and authoritatively, describe that value to the decision makers and policy makers who support and fund museums, then it would be much easier to convince them to make that support available.

What is that value? The answer is enhanced well-being. Millions of people have determined that museum experiences were beneficial to them because they resulted in a discernable and tangible increase in their personal, intellectual, social, and physical well-being. As I will describe, enhancing personal, intellectual, social, and physical well-being is neither easy to accomplish nor trivial once accomplished. The enhanced well-being that museums support has real value; real financial worth. The fact that museums have for years been successful at this task represents a significant asset and needs to be the foundation on which museums build their future purpose and stake their claim to being a necessary and valuable community resource.

However, for this book to be useful, for me to convince you the reader that the true value of museums lies in enhanced well-being, I will need to clearly define what I mean by enhanced well-being—what it looks like and why it is so important. I also will need to demonstrate that this value can be accurately measured and monetized. Finally, I will need to clearly describe how enhanced well-being can be used to support more successful and sustainable future practices, both long-term organizational purposes and missions, as well as the short-term development and implementation of improved museum experiences. All of these things I will do, but first, I need to make clear the nature of the problems that this solution of enhanced well-being is designed to solve.

CLARIFYING THE PROBLEM

Although the last quarter of the twentieth century was an amazing time for museums, with near exponential growth in both the number of users and resources generated, the first decades of the twenty-first century have been considerably rockier. In the early years of the new millennium, usage flattened out for most and declined for many. Then the Great Recession created significant financial challenges for all cultural institutions, with both public and private sources of support declining. After a brief respite and modest recovery, the COVID-19 pandemic struck. Virtually all museums across the world were shuttered.[2] For many, the closing was temporary but not for all. Hundreds of museums never reopened. Reopening proved to be only part of the challenge, as institutions of all types and sizes experienced reductions in financial support. Meanwhile, thousands of museum professionals lost their jobs, and with these layoffs the community lost years of social and intellectual capital. Many want to believe these challenges represent just a short-term blip, but most in the museum world appreciate that this is likely just the beginning and not the end of the crisis.

Not surprisingly, the sector has not been passive in the face of these challenges. Museum leaders have intuitively understood the essence of the threat they face. Neither the policy makers who fund museums nor the public who museums depend upon for support see museums as essential in these troubling times. In most communities, museums are, as suggested by Stephen Weil some twenty years ago, perceived as nice but not necessary.[3] When times are good, everyone is eager to support the niceties of life, but when times are tough, only the necessary can be prioritized. This is the difficulty museums find themselves in at the moment. Few argue that the museum experiences are bad, but few see these experiences as essential to the health and prosperity of the community.

The lack of status engendered by this perception of museums as nice but not necessary has been much discussed and debated and museum leaders have long argued that museums are indeed essential, cornerstone civic organizations that deliver genuine value to their communities and thus worthy of support. However, it is not clear how many within the public and positions of authority believe these assertions. Museums have not enjoyed the same funding status as other presumably, comparable cornerstone civic institutions such as libraries, and few policy makers think of museums as being in the same "essential" category as schools, hospitals, and law enforcement.

Over the years, considerable efforts have been made to define and variously measure the value of museums.[4] Arguably, the most concerted efforts, as well as among the most challenging, have been efforts to measure the intrinsic, often intangible value museums support.[5] Far and away the greatest energy has been within the area of educational impact. To date, literally hundreds of studies have demonstrated that the educational value of museum experiences is large and uncontestable, arguably even being equal to or in some cases, even greater than that made by schooling.[6] Although these measures of impact come close to what a measure of value should be, and despite the overwhelming amount of evidence now available, at least as judged by the ongoing challenges within the sector, these measures of value too have gained only minimal traction amongst policy makers and the broader public.[7]

(RE-)ASSESSING THE PROBLEM

All can agree, both those within and without the museum community, that the essence of the difficulty is that museums have yet to convincingly make the case for the value of the experiences they create.[8] Despite years of efforts to solve the problem of defining and measuring the value of museums, as judged by the current predicament museums face, the community has made little if any real headway on alleviating its public perception problem. Perhaps it is time to admit that, as Albert Einstein once quipped, "we cannot solve our problems with the same thinking that created them."[9] It is time to step back and rethink how to define the value of museum experiences, and then, and only then, think how best to document this value.

At its core, the problem museums face is not a lack of high-quality collections nor the ability to create engaging exhibitions and programs that attract legions of users, most of whom spend real money on these products and services. In other words, the problem is not that the people who work in museums have not been doing their job, that they have not been creating valuable experiences for the public, at least as they define valuable. As documented in the end notes, a wealth of research provides compelling evidence that museum professionals have in fact done quite a good job in doing what they themselves define as important and valuable work. The problem, appears to be that there is a gap between the ways museum professionals and researchers themselves have historically attempted to define and measure their value and the ways users and funders understand the value of museum experiences.

How else to explain why the people who use and support museums have not been persuaded by all the evidence cited above? Clearly, people do think museum experiences have value, otherwise why would millions of people use them, and why would government and private funders continue to support them, albeit at diminished levels? However, the following is equally clear: the value the public and policy makers currently see in museum experiences is neither as great nor necessarily even the same as the value museum professionals themselves see in these experiences.

So, what happens if one does go into the community to ask people to describe what they like about their museum experiences? In particular, why do people say museums are so memorable and satisfying? The default answer will converge around a statement similar to: "It was a really good experience." When asked to be more specific, to describe what they mean when they say museums provide "good experiences," people answer:

> "Well, I was able to see things that I can't see anywhere else."
>
> "[The museum] allowed me to find out more about who I am and how I relate to other peoples and societies."
>
> "[The museum experience] was special because my children and I got to better understand our people; where we come from."
>
> "I don't know, it was just nice, you know, stimulating."
>
> "I was just amazed by that airplane – it was something I had heard about, something I really wanted to see, and then I saw it."
>
> "[The museum] was such a safe, family-friendly, clean, and welcoming place. We had a great time."
>
> "I found it awesome, inspiring."
>
> "[Museums] are really important institutions in our community. We need more places like this. These places are really good for attracting and retaining a vibrant business community."
>
> "I take my children to [this museum] every week. I want them to stay curious, engaged. I want to give them a leg up in the world."

It would be easy, and very tempting, to want to interpret these responses in the same old ways; that is, to look at these data and say, "see, people do want to learn, people do enjoy the things we exhibit." However, I would argue that these responses, in fact, reveal a deeper purpose; one consistent with how museums have created experiences, but not completely consistent with how museums have historically defined their purpose and achievements. The above data only partially support the contention that museums primarily enhance the learning or even the aesthetics of art, history or science. A better interpretation of these data would be to see museum experiences as supporting four broad, well-being-related outcomes:

1. Personal Well-Being—catalyzing wonder, interest, and a sense of identity; creating feelings that foster a sense of belonging and stronger sense of self.

2. Intellectual Well-Being—facilitating curiosity and learning and the ability to utilize improved understanding in the service of solving personal and societal challenges.
3. Social Well-Being—making it possible for individuals to feel stronger linkages with their family and friends, building shared life experiences and forging deeper coherence with others.
4. Physical Well-Being—providing opportunities for people to gather (physically or virtually), interact, explore, and learn within a safe, healthy, anxiety-free, and restorative environment.

To put it plainly, if the public's concept of what they feel differs from what the museum profession perceives is important, no amount of evidence for the value of this thing the profession asserts is important is likely to change the public's perceptions of value. This, I believe, is the essence of why virtually all the "solutions" to the "museum value" crisis described above have failed to solve the problem. Virtually all, including my own efforts, have begun from an "insider's" definition of the importance and value of museums and the experiences they create rather than starting with how those outside the institution—the users and policy makers—define the importance and value of museum experiences.

If we are to be successful, we must begin with how the public and policy makers themselves define the outcomes of museum experiences, and then help these same people appreciate just how much value those outcomes are worth. That is because *users, not producers define value*. Something is not valuable just because the people who created it assert it is. Value begins with a subjective perception of value, followed by tangible and observable actions. Whether or not something is perceived as valuable can be readily judged by how people use something, and the importance and worth they ascribed to that use—things are valuable when they are treated as valuable. There is nothing intrinsically more valuable about gold than aluminum, both are durable, shiny, malleable metals. Obviously, the difference is that people widely perceive gold as more valuable than aluminum, and perceiving it so makes it so. People vote with their pocketbooks as well as their feet. These truisms get to heart of the museum community's problem. What is needed is not a measure of value that makes sense to museum professionals but rather a precise and persuasive accounting of the value of museum experiences that rings true to nonprofessionals, to users and would-be users. What is needed is a way to define and measure the value of museum experiences that decision makers and the broader public find not only believable but significant, a way that is consistent with users' own sense of what is important in their lives.

ACCOUNTING FOR THE VALUE OF MUSEUM EXPERIENCES

In this book I will attempt to provide an accounting of the value of museum experiences. Accounting actually has two meanings. As part of a panel discussion on the value of community arts programs, Harvard public value guru Mark Moore highlighted these dual meanings.[10] Most people these days immediately think of accounting as an assessment activity, the process of collecting, summarizing, analyzing, and reporting of data and transactions. Accounting, in this sense, is the empirical process that allows individuals and organizations to evaluate and make sense of their activities. This is clearly an important meaning and many museums have focused of late on trying to provide this kind of empirical accounting of their value. But there is a second, equally important definition of accounting, one that is in fact older. That definition is the telling of a story, to provide a compelling explanation of one's activities. This latter definition of accounting is what historically all museums relied on, and many still do, when attempting to justify their value. To be successful in today's world, museums need to do both types of accounting—they need to tell a good story, and they need to back up that story with real data, real evidence of accomplishment. Achieving both of these meanings of accountability is essential, but historically museums have not been particularly good at this. In the past museum professionals have either provided great data in support of a flawed story or told great stories without any credible data to back up those stories.

My goal in this book is to account for the value of museum experiences in both senses of the word. I will provide what I believe is a compelling story about the benefits users of museums perceive they derive from their museum experiences, and I will also describe how to validly and reliably measure the tangible value these benefits deliver. In the process I seek to demonstrate not only how and why museums experiences create both substantial and fundamental value but how a newfound understanding of the value museum experiences can create might be leveraged to insure a more successful and sustainable future for museums.

Let me be clear: I do not believe that the way I account for the value of museum experiences in this book is the only possible way to define and solve the current crisis museums face nor do I believe that the approach I offer here, by itself, will resolve all of the many difficulties museums now face. What I do assert is that if museums are to successfully extricate themselves from the current accountability crisis they face, then new ways of describing and quantitatively demonstrating their value are required; all of which need to start by understanding how the public themselves define the value of their museum experiences. In this way, my definition of the nature of the problem significantly differs from those that have come before. Appropriately, this is also where my story, my accounting, begins.

NOTES

1. https://www.goodreads.com/quotes/tag/problem-solving. Retrieved May 9, 2021.

2. Battaglia, A. (2020). "Museums in Crisis, Art Spaces Lobby New York State, and More: Morning Links from October 13, 2020." ArtNews. https://www.artnews.com/art-news/news/museums-in-crisis-morning-links-1234573525/. Retrieved November 3, 2020. See also, Pogrebin, R. (March 18, 2020). "Met Museum Prepares for $100 Million Loss and Closure till

July." *New York Times*, March 18, 2020. https://www.nytimes.com/2020/03/18/arts/design/met-museum-coronavirus-closure.html Retrieved March 19, 2020. Yilmaz, E., and Zipsane, H. (Ed.). (2021). *The European Museum Academy Reports on The Museum Temperature by the End of 2020.* http://europeanmuseumacademy.eu/wp-content/uploads/2021/02/210222-EMA-National-Museum-Reports-2020.pdf. Retrieved May 9, 2021.

3. Weil, S. (2002). *Making Museums Matter.* Washington, DC: Smithsonian Institution Press.

4. For a review of different approaches, compare, Scott, C.A. (2011). Measuring the immeasurable: Capturing intangible values. Marketing and Public Relations International Committee of ICOM (International Council of Museums) Conference Keynote Brno, Czech Republic 19th September 2011. https://citeseerx.ist.psu.edu/viewdoc/download?doi=10.1.1.1058.3671&rep=rep1&type=pdf. Retrieved February 18, 2020).

5. Educational examples include the following:

ArtsCouncil UK. (n.d.). "Generic Learning Outcomes." https://www.artscouncil.org.uk/measuring-outcomes/generic-learning-outcomes. Retrieved February 25, 2020.

Bonnette, R. N., Crowley, K., and Schunn, C. D. (2019). "Falling in Love and Staying in Love with Science: Ongoing Informal Science Experiences Support Fascination for All Children." *International Journal of Science Education,* DOI: 10.1080/09500693.2019.1623431.

Crystal Bridges. (2013). "Crystal Bridges Museum of American Art and University of Arkansas Department of Education Reform Announce Results of a Study on Culturally Enriching School Field Trips," September 16, 2013. https://crystalbridges.org/blog/crystal-bridges-museum-of-american-art-university-of-arkansas-department-of-education-reform-announce-results-of-a-study-on-culturally-enriching-school-field-trips/. Retrieved March 19, 2020.

CASE: The Culture and Sport Evidence Programme. (2010). *Understanding the Impact of Engagement in Culture and Sport: A Systematic Review of the Learning Impacts for Young People.*

Falk, J. H., and Dierking, L. D. (2010). "The 95% Solution: School Is Not Where Most Americans Learn Most of Their Science." *American Scientist* 98, 486–93.

Falk, J. H., Dierking, L. D., Swanger, L., Staus, N., Back, M., Barriault, C., Catalao, C., Chambers, C., Chew, L.-L., Dahl, S. A., Falla, S., Gorecki, B., Lau, T. C., Lloyd, A., Martin, J., Santer, J., Singer, S., Solli, A., Trepanier, G., Tyystjärvi, K., and Verheyden, P. (2016). "Correlating Science Center Use with Adult Science Literacy: An International, Cross-Institutional Study." *Science Education* 100(5), 849–76.

Falk, J. H., and Needham, M. (2011). "Measuring the Impact of a Science Center on Its Community." *Journal of Research in Science Teaching* 48(1), 1–12.

Falk, J. H., and Needham, M. D. (2013). "Factors Contributing to Adult Knowledge of Science and Technology." *Journal of Research in Science Teaching* 50(4), 431–52.

Falk, J. H., Pattison, S., Meier, D., Livingston, K., and Bibas, D. (2018). "The Contribution of Science-Rich Resources to Public Science Interest." *Journal of Research in Science Teaching* 55(3), 422–45.

Hull, D. (2011). "Assessing the Value and Impact of Museums." Technical Report. Belfast: Northern Ireland Assembly Research and Library Service Research Paper. http://www.niassembly.gov.uk/globalassets/Documents/RaISe/Publications/2011/Culture-Arts-Leisure/2911.pdf. Retrieved February 20, 2020.

Powell, R. B., Stern, M. J., and Frensley, B.T. (2020). "Identifying Outcomes for Environmental Education Programming in National Parks." In J. Thompson and A. Houseal (eds.),

America's Largest Classrooms: What We Learn from Our National Parks, pp. 245–58. Berkeley, CA: University of California Press.

Stein, R. (2018a). "Museums and Public Opinion: Exploring Four Key Questions about What Americans Think of Museums." American Alliance of Museums. Technical Report, January 20, 2018. Washington, DC: American Alliance of Museums. https://www.aam-us.org/2018/01/20/museums-and-public-opinion/. Retrieved February 18, 2020.

Social examples include the following:

Ashton, S., Johnson, E., Nelson, K. R., Ortiz, J., and Wicai, D. (2019). "Brace for Impact: Utah Is Conducting a Pilot Study to Show the Social Impact of the State's Museums." *MUSEUM*, May-June 2019, 26–31.

Australian Expert Group on Industry Studies (AEGIS). (2004). *Social Impacts of Participating in the Arts and Cultural Activities: Stage Two Report—Evidence, Issues and Recommendations.* Sydney, AU: University of Western Sydney. https://www.stategrowth.tas.gov.au/__data/assets/pdf_file/0003/160833/Social_Impacts_of_the_Arts.pdf. Retrieved February 25, 2020.

Dafoe, T. (2020). "Attendance Has Always Been a Narrow Way to Define Success. That's Why This Museum Is Using Data Science to Measure Its Social Impact." Artnet News, February 19, 2020. https://news.artnet.com/art-world/oakland-museum-social-impact-1780698#.XlEnYoZUia0.twitter. Retrieved February 23, 2020.

Fristrup, T. (Ed.) (2019). *Socially engaged practices in museums and archives*. Jamtli Forlag. Fornvårdaren Serie No. 38.

Maas, K. (2008). "Social Impact Measurement: Towards a Guideline for Managers." https://www.erim.eur.nl/fileadmin/default/content/erim/research/centres/erasmus_centre_for_strategic_philanthropy/research/publications/social_impact_measurement_voor_sso_nieuwsbrief%5B1%5D.pdf. Retrieved February 25, 2020.

Museums, Libraries and Archives Council. (2008). "Generic Social Outcomes." http://nia1.me/5pf. Retrieved February 18, 2020.

Wood, C., and Leighton, D. (2010). "Measuring Social Value." http://www.demos.co.uk/files/Measuring_social_value_-_web. Retrieved February 18, 2020.

Intellectual examples include the following:

Bradley, R. D., Bradley, L .C., Garner, H., and Baker, R. (2014). "Assessing the Value of Natural History Collections and Addressing Issues Regarding Long-Term Growth and Care." *BioScience* 64(12), 1150–58.

National Academies of Science, Engineering and Medicine. (2020). *Sustaining the Future of the Nations' Biological Collections*. Washington, DC: The National Academies Press.

Suzrez, A.V., and Tsutsui, N. (2004). "The Value of Museum Collections for Research and Society." *BioScience* 54 (1), 66–74.

Te Papa National Services. (2001, June). "Valuing Collections." Technical Report. Wellington, NZ: Museum of New Zealand Te Papa Tongarewa. https://www.tepapa.govt.nz/sites/default/files/13-valuing-collections_0.pdf. Retrieved February 18, 2020.

Physical examples include the following:

Djupdræt, M. B. (2018). *Historiebevidsthed hos demente. Erindringsforløb, velvære og identitetsdannelse på museer, Kulturstudier nr.* 1. https://tidsskrift.dk/fn/article/view/106574.

Falk, J. H. (2018). *Born to Choose: Evolution, Self, and Well-Being.* New York: Routledge.

Fristrup, T. (Ed.) (2019). *Socially engaged practices in museums and archives*. Jamtli Forlag. Fornvårdaren Serie No. 38.

Fujiwara, D., Kudrna, L., and Dolan, P. (2014, April). "Quantifying and Valuing the Wellbeing Impacts of Culture and Sport." Technical Report. London: UK Department for

Culture, Media and Sport. https://assets.publishing.service.gov.uk/government/uploads/system/uploads/attachment_data/file/304899/Quantifying_and_valuing_the_wellbeing_impacts_of_sport_and_culture.pdf. Retrieved February 18, 2020.

Hansen, A. (2016). Learning to feel well at Jamtli Museum: A case study. *Journal of Adult and Continuing Education*, 22(2), 168–83.

Packer, J. (2008). "Beyond Learning: Exploring Visitors' Perceptions of the Value and Benefits of Museum Experiences." *Curator: The Museum Journal* 51 (1), 33–54.

Packer, J., and Ballantyne, R. (2012). "Comparing Captive and Non-Captive Wildlife Tourism." *Annals of Tourism Research* 39(2), 1242–45.

Packer, J. and Bond, N. (2010). "Museums as Restorative Environments." *Curator: The Museum Journal* 53(4), 421–56.

6. For example, ArtsCouncil UK. (ND). "Generic Learning Outcomes." https://www.artscouncil.org.uk/measuring-outcomes/generic-learning-outcomes. Retrieved February 25, 2020.

Bonnette, R.N., Crowley, K., and Schunn, C. D. (2019). "Falling in Love and Staying in Love with Science: Ongoing Informal Science Experiences Support Fascination for All Children." *International Journal of Science Education,* DOI: 10.1080/09500693.2019.1623431

CASE: The Culture and Sport Evidence Programme. (2010). *Understanding the Impact of Engagement in Culture and Sport: A Systematic Review of the Learning Impacts for Young People.*

Falk, J. H., Dierking, L. D., Swanger, L., Staus, N., Back, M., Barriault, C., Catalao, C., Chambers, C., Chew, L.-L., Dahl, S. A., Falla, S., Gorecki, B., Lau, T. C., Lloyd, A., Martin, J., Santer, J., Singer, S., Solli, A., Trepanier, G., Tyystjärvi, K., and Verheyden, P. (2016). "Correlating Science Center Use with Adult Science Literacy: An International, Cross-Institutional Study." *Science Education* 100(5), 849–76.

Falk, J. H., and Needham, M. (2011). "Measuring the Impact of a Science Center on Its Community." *Journal of Research in Science Teaching* 48(1), 1–12.

Falk, J. H., and Needham, M. D. (2013). "Factors Contributing to Adult Knowledge of Science and Technology." *Journal of Research in Science Teaching* 50(4), 431–52.

Falk, J. H., Pattison, S., Meier, D., Livingston, K., and Bibas, D. (2018). "The Contribution of Science-Rich Resources to Public Science Interest." *Journal of Research in Science Teaching* 55(3), 422–45.

Hull, D. (2011). "Assessing the Value and Impact of Museums." Technical Report. Belfast: Northern Ireland Assembly Research and Library Service Research Paper. http://www.niassembly.gov.uk/globalassets/Documents/RaISe/Publications/2011/Culture-Arts-Leisure/2911.pdf. Retrieved February 20, 2020.

Powell, R. B., Stern, M. J., and Frensley, B.T. (2020). "Identifying Outcomes for Environmental Education Programming in National Parks." In J. Thompson and A. Houseal (eds.), *America's Largest Classrooms: What We Learn from Our National Parks*, pp. 245-58. Berkeley, CA: University of California Press.

Stein, 2018b.

7. For example, Kelley, R. (2014). "The Emerging Need for Hybrid Entities: Why California Should Become the Delaware of 'Social Enterprise Law.'" *Loyola L.A. Law Review*, 47, 619–55.

Barrero, J. M., Bloom, N., and Davis, S. J. (2020). "COVID-19 Is Also a Reallocation Shock." University of Chicago, *Becker Friedman Institute for Economics Working Paper No. 2020-2059*. https://ssrn.com/abstract=3592953. Retrieved June 1, 2020.

Walker, D. (2020). "Extraordinary Times, Extraordinary Measures." Ford Foundation, June 11, 2020. https://www.fordfoundation.org/ideas/equals-change-blog/posts/extraordinary-times-extraordinary-measures/. Retrieved June 11, 2020.

8. Compare, Ashton, S. Johnson, E., Nelson, K. R., Ortiz, J., and Wicaj, D. (2019). Brace for Impact: Utah is conducting a pilot study to show the social impact of the state's museums. *MUSEUM*, May–June 2019, 26–31.

Berger, K., Penna, R. M., and Goldberg, S. H. (2010). The battle for the soul of the nonprofit sector. *Social Innovations Journal*. http://www.philasocialinnovations.org/site/. Retrieved February 18, 2020.

Dafoe, T. (2020). Attendance has always been a narrow way to define success. That's why this museum is using data science to measure its social impact. *artnet news*. https://news.artnet.com/art-world/oakland-museum-social-impact-1780698#.XlEnYoZUia0.twitter. Retrieved February 23, 2020.

Davies, S. (2008). Intellectual and political landscape: the instrumentalism debate. *Cultural Trends*, 17(4), 259–65.

Fujiwara, D., Kudrna, L., and Dolan, P. (2014). Quantifying and valuing the wellbeing impacts of culture and sport. *Technical Report*. London: UK Department for Culture, Media & Sport. https://assets.publishing.service.gov.uk/government/uploads/system/uploads/attachment_data/file/304899/Quantifying_and_valuing_the_wellbeing_impacts_of_sport_and_culture.pdf. Retrieved February 18, 2020.

Holden, J. (2006). Cultural value and crisis of legitimacy. *Demos*. https://www.demos.co.uk/files/Culturalvalueweb.pdf. Retrieved July 2, 2020.

Hull, D. (2011). *Assessing the Value and Impact of Museums*. Technical Report. Belfast: Northern Ireland Assembly Research and Library Service Research Paper. http://www.niassembly.gov.uk/globalassets/Documents/RaISe/Publications/2011/Culture-Arts-Leisure/2911.pdf Retrieved February 20, 2020.

Jacobsen, J. W. (2016). *Measuring Museum Impact and Performance: Theory and Practice*. Lanham, MD: Rowman & Littlefield.

Scott, C. (2008). Using "values" to position and promote museums. *International Journal of Arts Management*, 11(1), 28–41.

Scott, C.A. (2011). Measuring the immeasurable: Capturing intangible values. Marketing and Public Relations International Committee of ICOM (International Council of Museums) Conference Keynote Brno, Czech Republic 19th September 2011. https://citeseerx.ist.psu.edu/viewdoc/download?doi=10.1.1.1058.3671&rep=rep1&type=pdf. Retrieved February 18, 2020.

Sheppard, S. (2014). Museums in the neighborhood: the local economic impact of museums. In F. Giarratani, G., J. D. Hewings, and P. McCann (eds.) *Handbook of Industry Studies and Economic Geography*, 191–204. Cheltenham: Edward Elgar Publishing.

Teasdale, P. (2018). Go figure: How to measure the value of museums? Frieze, 194. https://frieze.com/article/how-measure-value-museums. Retrieved February 18, 2020.

Weil, S. (2002). *Making Museums Matter*. Washington, D.C.: Smithsonian Institution Press.

Weil, S. (2003). Beyond big & awesome outcome-based evaluation. *Museum News*, November/December, 40–45, 52–53.

9. https://articulous.com.au/problem-solving/. Retrieved February 6, 2021.

10. See, NA. (2013). "Show Me the Value—a Discussion about Public Value and the Arts." Panel discussion sponsored by QPAC, Queensland, Australia. https://www.youtube.com/watch?v=_4Aw0pCDmHg. Retrieved February 13, 2021.

2

Why People Value Museum Experiences

Sometimes you never realize the value of a moment until it becomes a memory.

—Dr. Seuss[1]

I have spent a lifetime thinking about and researching the museum experience, seeking to answer three fundamental questions: Why do people seek out museums and choose to engage in the experiences they offer? What do people do during their museum experiences? And what is it that people take away from these museum experiences? Over the past, nearly half a century, I have read thousands of research papers—many specific to museums, many more not. I have led or participated in hundreds of studies, which have collectively observed and interviewed tens of thousands of museum users, in order to make sense of the museum experience and answer these three fundamental tightly interconnected questions in the hopes of understanding the value people derive from engaging in museum experiences.

Multiple times over the years, I thought I had figured things out; I thought that I could provide a reasonable answer to each of these basic questions. After even further thinking, observing, and listening, I reevaluated my answers and came to different conclusions. Thus, when I say that I think I finally have it figured out, even I am inclined to be a bit skeptical and totally understand if others too might be a little dubious. That said, I now believe that I have come up with a way to describe why and how people use museums, that I can now describe the value people get from engaging in museum experiences.

Critical to my approach now, as well as in the past, has been my focus on the public rather than the museum. By this I mean that my goal has always been to understand the museum experience from a user's perspective rather than from a museum professional's perspective. Not that the two perspectives are necessarily different, but often they are. I aspired to understand how users *authentically* experienced the museum, what benefits, if any, they themselves perceived they gained. By contrast, museum professionals have typically been primarily interested in knowing whether the public gained the benefits they hoped they would. In other words, whether the museum was successful in creating experiences that yielded specific, typically pre-proscribed outcomes.

Despite this goal, alas I fear that for much of my career, I too was guilty of the problem raised in the previous chapter. The user outcomes I disproportionately focused on were too strongly influenced by own preconceptions about what the nature of the museum experience should be about. Too often, I bowed to the desires and assumptions of the other professionals I worked with and for and allowed myself to be swayed by what we collectively hoped and assumed would be the outcomes of a museum experience. Not surprisingly, these preconceptions influenced how I interpreted and made sense of the data I and others collected.

As I now look back over this multitude of data, I am struck by how consistently people described their museum experiences. The data I collected on people's recollections of their museum experiences forty years ago could just as easily have been collected yesterday—people then, and now, talked about the things they saw, the people they were with, the spaces they encountered, and most importantly, the feelings they had as a consequence of all these experiences. The outcomes people describe, and the benefits people ascribe to these outcomes, has changed little over the past forty-plus years. What has changed is how I, and others, have tried to make sense of this data. Today, my explanation of the value of the museum experience is starkly different than it was forty years ago, or even fifteen years ago.

For much of the first half of my career, I believed that museums were first and foremost educational institutions, and thus learning must be the essence of the museum experience.[2] Not surprisingly, when looked at through this lens, the results seemed to conform to that perspective. Then, starting about twenty years ago, I changed my perspective, appreciating that something deeper, and more fundamental was driving people to use and value museums—that museums were merely the vehicles people used for accomplishing their own (identity) self-related needs and priorities.(Starting in 2012, I began appreciating that "self" rather than "identity" was actually a more fundamental and basic framing for what I was talking about.)[3] Over the past two decades my colleagues and I, and increasingly dozens of other museum professionals around the world, have documented that people do indeed come to museums primarily in an effort to satisfy roughly a half-dozen specific types of self-related needs—needs such as curiosity/general intellectual interest-related needs (explorer); socially driven needs (facilitator); psychic and emotional escape-related needs (recharger); and/or the need to pay homage and respect (respectful pilgrims).[4] As I further reviewed these data, I once again began to have second thoughts about my interpretation. Again, as before, it was not the data that changed but my interpretation of what the data meant.

The more I thought about the answers people were giving to why they used museums and what value they derived from their experiences, the more I began to appreciate and understand that for many people, learning—or for that matter social interactions, recharging, paying homage, or any one of the other self-related reasons people gave for their visits—were important but were not the ultimate basis for their use. Deep below the surface was a still deeper, more fundamental purpose. I came to believe that things like learning, social interactions, and mental recharging were merely mechanisms for building and supporting a person's self/identity, but that self/identity too was merely a means to an end, a vehicle for achieving an even deeper life-purpose.

It is this deeper purpose that I will describe here. It is a purpose revealed by the hundreds upon hundreds of interviews I have conducted over nearly fifty years. Allow me to share just one example, one data point, which I believe will provide a useful springboard to understanding the value people derive from their museum experiences.

FRANK'S MUSEUM EXPERIENCE[5]

It was Friday, February 9, 2021. Frank, his wife, and his nine-year-old daughter Chloe[6] arrived early that day, around 10:30 a.m., eager to visit the California Science Center. Frank is a well-educated, African American male in his late thirties / early forties working as a traffic department scheduler for a large entertainment company in Los Angeles. Frank's wife also works full time. This happy threesome spent a little over two hours at the science center that day, trailed throughout their visit by my colleague Martin Storksdieck.[7] Two years later, Martin and I recontacted Frank and asked if he would be willing to allow us to talk with him again about his visit.[8] Frank agreed and we set up a time to visit him at his work place in Anaheim. What follows is an excerpt from that interview.

> Q: What did you see or do [at the science center] that was memorable?
>
> A: Nothing that stands out. On that particular day, I was more of a follower [laughs], watching my daughter going from exhibit to exhibit. That was her goal, to get all of her stamps [there was a "passport" activity provided by the science center designed to encourage children to visit exhibits throughout the museum]. I tried to get her to slow it down a little bit to learn about all of the different things that were going on in the exhibit at that particular time. That was a little difficult; she was just happy to be somewhere. We concentrated on food groups for humans, because to me that's important—making sure she understands a balanced meal and things of that nature. My daughter was also fascinated by *Tess* [a theater-type experience featuring a fifty-foot animatronic female].
>
> Q: So you saw the show?
>
> A: Yes, but mostly I was just trying to keep up with my daughter.
>
> Q: Do you remember anything about the show?

A: I remember what my daughter's reaction was. She was fascinated with seeing something this large and understanding something about the heartbeat. I think she [a featured girl in the show's movie] was playing soccer.

Q: Did you learn anything from the show?

A: I'm not sure. I was really focused on watching my daughter.

Q: Whose idea was it to go to the science center?

A: It was my idea for a family outing. We became members that same day. I've taken my niece and nephew once who are seventeen and fourteen, and they've gone with my daughter on their own.

Q: You said you were a follower that day. What was the purpose of that visit when you were a follower?

A: Having an activity for my daughter to do for a day. My wife had the day off. It's possible that it was a weekday and we both had the day off and we wanted to do something interesting, and the museum was one of the first choices.

Q: Do you take your daughter other places to do something interesting?

A: No, she's so involved on the weekends with ice skating, ballet for a while, now volleyball and in a dance class. She's pretty active on the weekends so we don't have as much time to visit other places.

[Later in the interview]

Q: Can you give me some examples of what you or your daughter saw?

A: We saw the Human Miracle and the baby chicks. The first was where the fetuses are. We went in and talked about it. It was fascinating for her and to see the process of being small and growing. She got a kick out of the baby chicks. That part of the exhibition is always fascinating to her[;] even when we've gone back again, she'll stop and look at that exhibit. She loves to see the eggs, some of which are whole, some of which are empty and some of which are in the process of having a chick emerge from them. It makes the process so real.

Q: Is it fascinating for you too?

A: It's always fascinating, the process of life, even though we've seen it over and over again. I've seen it at the old science center, since I was almost her age. Actually, when we were having breakfast one day and opened up an egg and she saw red specks and she asked questions about that, I used the exhibit as a teaching tool. I said that's where chickens come from, remember the science center.

[Later in the interview]

Q: So did you have a good time?

A: Yes, absolutely. We had a great time.

Q: How do you know?

A: I bought a membership! [laughs] It wasn't just for the discount in the store! It is a valuable experience to go to the science museum at least every six months, if not more. If [my daughter] didn't have so many other things going on, I'd probably keep better track of what's going on at the museum, like seminars, things for kids.

[Later in the interview]

Q: But this particular science center visit was not for you, it was for your daughter?

A: Yes. Definitely for her. . . . As long as she's having a good time, I'm happy. . . .

Q: What would you characterize as the single most satisfying characteristic of that visit?

A: That I did something good for my daughter, because she enjoyed it and she took some things with her. If I went by myself, I'd look for a higher level of understanding, but that was not the purpose of this visit. . . . Being exposed to different elements at the museum was a major plus [for my daughter]. It's important to get kids interested [so they can] pursue that which they find interesting.

Q: So if you had to summarize why this science center experience was so memorable for you, what would you say?

A: It was a really good experience. It made me feel good because I knew I was doing something special for my daughter.

As suggested above, like most people who have studied museums, I initially assumed that what made museums so successful was their ability to allow people, large numbers of people, to see and interact with real, often rare and unusual things—objects and exhibitions—in an engaging and educational way. After all, museums are widely known to be places with "cool stuff" organized into complex and compelling exhibitions expressly designed to convey information and foster learning. At one time, the question of whether people learned from museums was challenged but no more. Today, a vast body of research, including my own, convincingly and unequivocally shows that museums are critical contributors to the public's education, places where people can and do learn many things.[9] However, after repeatedly listening to people like Frank talk about their museum experiences, my views on museums bumped up against a painful reality. Yes, museums do support learning through objects, but for many people, this outcome was not the true value their museum experiences provided them.

Learning is important, but it is not the sole reason that people visit museums—nor is it necessarily what brings them satisfaction. People also go to museums in order to feel a sense of awe and wonder, or like Frank above, many museum users find social aspects of the experience to be what really matters. Frank was there as a parent, as someone who felt the need to support his daughter's growth and development. His stated goal was not really learning *per se*. Frank was much more concerned with nurturing his daughter's *interest* in science than he was in any actual changes in her science knowledge or her specific understanding of any particular aspect of the world. Again, for Frank, the value of the museum experience, and there can be no doubt that Frank perceived this experience to be valuable, lay in something deeper than just learning.

Beyond opening the box up on museum experience outcomes, this brief interview with Frank serves another important purpose. Although the particulars of Frank's experience, like everyone's museum experience, are unique, one aspect of this interview stands out as totally generalizable and emblematic of museum experiences worldwide. Despite roughly two years having elapsed since he visited this museum, an experience that lasted only slightly more than two hours, he was still able to vividly recall much of what happened that day. He could still talk, literally for over an hour, about the things he and his daughter saw and did those many years previously. He could not only share with us his recollections of what he did, he could even talk about how he felt on that day. In fact, he was even able to recall how he perceived his daughter felt that day. Woven throughout his conversation with us were examples of how the events of that day subsequently permeated his thoughts and impacted his life over the following years.

There are precious few two-hour experiences that create such lasting memories! Museum experiences are clearly special events in people's lives—they must be, or they would not be so salient and so memorable.

This is a fundamental observation! By better understanding what it is about museum experiences that makes them so important, so valuable to people that they remain entrenched in long-term memory, is key to understanding the how and why of their value.

MEANING AND MEMORY

In order to understand why a museum experience creates such long-term and indelible memories for people, we need to begin with a statement of the obvious—memory is always highly selective. Only a tiny subset of the things experienced in our lives are truly memorable; most are soon forgotten. This is obvious, but the question is whether it is possible to predict which things will be selectively remembered, and why these things and not others? The key to understanding what is memorable hinges around understanding something about the biological basis of memory and the highly personalized "experiential filters" every individual uses in life to determine what to attend to and what to ignore, what to remember and what to forget. These filters evolved for a singular purpose, to enhance the ability of humans and other senescent creatures to survive and thrive. Or as research has shown, our memory systems are optimized to process and retain survival-relevant information.[10]

Starting with first principles, everyone is constantly bombarded by stimuli, so much so that no one could possibly accommodate, let alone remember, all they are capable of perceiving. People apply mental filters to determine not only what to attend to, but what of all the things attended to are worth hanging onto in memory? In recent years we have come to increasingly explain this filtering process using the concept of *meaningfulness*. By definition, we attend to that which we find *meaningful* and ignore that which we find *meaningless*. But what is meaning? According to anthropologist Clifford Geertz, meaning is our mind's way of making sense of the world, the translation of existence into conceptual form.[11] Meaning provides a framework for helping us assess what is important and supports our understanding and actions. Obviously, things that have the potential to affect our long-term survival and well-being are perceived as meaningful.

Humans, in particular, are extremely adept at meaning making; it is arguably one of the things that sets humans apart from other life forms. A skill that humans have gotten ever better at over time. Starting some million or so years ago, the pace of human cultural evolution increased—at first slowly and then ever more rapidly—ultimately supplanting biological evolution as the main vector of change and adaptation of our species.[12] Over the past several millennia, improvement in this capacity has become ever more rapid, so too has selection pressures for individuals capable of sifting through ever greater quantities of information and sorting out that which has meaning for them and that which does not.

Putting these two ideas together—that people actively filter the myriad events in their life, selectively remembering only the most meaningful things, and that the most likely events to be memorable, and thus perceived as meaningful, are those that support and enhance survival—we can conclude that, for some reason, people find museum experiences meaningful because they are somehow related to their survival. The question then becomes this: what is it about museum experiences that make them meaningful, that is, supportive of enhanced survival?

We know that the meaningfulness of museum experiences differs between users, that it is always a personally constructed, highly individualized reality. Each visitor's reality is only loosely tethered to the actual, fixed realities of the museum's space, exhibitions, and/or events. Not only can and will two visitors have different visitor experiences despite ostensibly doing and seeing the same things at the museum, but even the same individual on two different days will almost certainly have a different visitor experience because he or she is not the same person on those two days.[13] This is why for some the meanings they seek and find during their museum experience are intellectual, while for others it is social, and for still others spiritual or experiential.

We also know that each and every museum user's meaning making, whether they are visiting a physical museum or engaging in some type of virtual experience, is fashioned through the lens of prior knowledge, experience, interests, values, and expectations. In order for someone to actively, though not necessarily consciously, determine which parts of the museum experience are worth focusing on, these kinds of pre-visit framings are essential.[14] It is a truism but important to say, every museum user selectively attends to only those aspects of the experience that they find most meaningful to *them*. In fact, it is this "free-choice" aspect of museums that has, in large part, made museums, and the experiences they support, such powerful cultural institutions.[15] Each user's *reality* is determined by what they selectively pay attention to not what is there.

Selective attention turns out to also be something that has been extensively studied. The key to selective attention is the neural-chemical process we generically call "emotion."

IT ALL STARTS WITH EMOTIONS

All enduring long-term memories involve emotion-rich experiences.[16] A critical reason that Frank, or you, or for that matter anyone can remember anything about a long-past museum experience, including and particularly those parts remembered in any detail, is because this was an emotionally saturated experience. When talking about something being emotionally rich or saturated, I am not suggesting that Frank was so moved by his science center visit that he broke down and wept when we talked to him. Rather, what I am referring to is the fact that it was clear that Frank's visit experience and his subsequent memories of that experience involved not just cold, "rational" descriptions of what he saw and did but expressions of strong feelings, attitudes, and beliefs.

Arguably, one of the most startling findings of the last quarter century of research on the brain has been the critical role played in all memory by the brain areas known as the limbic system. The limbic system is evolutionarily one of the oldest parts of our brain. Located in the middle of the brain and made up of a number of discrete structures (for example, the amygdala, hippocampus, and thalamus), the limbic system probably first evolved among reptiles, but it is well developed in all mammals, including us humans. Appropriate to its ancient lineage, very early in the history of brain research the limbic area was recognized as a major component of emotional and geographical memory.[17] However, these functions are not "localized" in this region of the brain, as previously thought. Most functions are not restricted to just one part of the brain but highly integrated and interconnected throughout the brain.[18] Significantly, the limbic areas of the brain appear to play a critical role in all brain functioning, and the limbic areas of the brain have been found to be extensively interconnected in looped circuits with every part of the brain as well as to all of the body's organs and systems. Limbic system input appears to be involved in virtually every aspect of human functioning, every thought, every need, every demand of every bodily function and cycle.[19] The various parts of the limbic system not only help regulate emotions and geography, but they have been discovered to be the focal point for regulating all actions, including memory.[20]

Before any perception begins the process of being permanently stored in memory, it must first pass through at least two appraisal stages involving the limbic system.[21] All incoming sensory information are given an initial screening for meaningfulness and personal relevance by structures in the limbic system. These bits of "information" are also filtered for their relationship to our internal physical state (e.g., I'm hungry, so I guess I'll focus on things related to food rather than Shakespeare). This filtering and interpretation of incoming sensory information, though centred in the limbic system, involves virtually every part of the brain and the body. In essence, this process both determines *what* is worth attending to and remembering (i.e., Will this be important information in the future? Does it relate to something I already know, feel, or believe?) and *how* something is remembered (e.g., That object reminds me of an interesting experience I once had. I saw that beautiful painting at the same time I was having a good time with my spouse.). In this way, in fractions of a second, our mind separates, sorts, combines, and judges perceptions occurring both inside and outside of us based on how important they are to our past and potentially our future life. Is this something that will improve my health, my security, my social status, or my intellectual capabilities (i.e., my well-being)? This key role of the limbic system has made cognitive scientists come to more fully appreciate just how important emotions are in the entire meaning-making process.

Historically, emotions were thought to be a set of stereotyped and automatic expressive behaviors. Now it is understood that not only are emotions an integral part of brain functioning, but they are surprisingly nuanced, variable, and continuously "constructed."[22] As psychologist Richard Lazarus explains, "[E]motion recruits cognitive and affective components in order to assess the import of events in the environment for a person's key goals, such as a key relationship, survival, identity, or avoiding moral offence. The brain makes an initial judgment of whether the information it has received bodes 'good' or 'bad' for such goals."[23] Neuroscientist Jonathon Turner explains it this way: "Emotions give each alternative a value and, thereby, provide a yardstick to judge and to select alternatives. This process need not be conscious; and indeed, for all animals including humans, it rarely is. . . . One can't sustain cognitions beyond working [i.e., short-term] memory without tagging them with emotion."[24] Thus we can see that our brains store memories in networks of meaning and that emotions play a big role in whether an event is experienced as meaningful and thus whether and how it is remembered. What a person remembers is thus largely determined by their state of emotional arousal, with the most emotionally rich memories becoming the most memorable.[25] So the fact that virtually every study ever conducted on museum users has found that users find the experience highly enjoyable and satisfying helps to explain, at least in part, why museum memories are so long-lasting. Enjoyable experiences are memorable!

But museum users typically only remember selected parts of the museum experience. What makes some parts of an overall enjoyable experience particularly memorable and not others? My own research has pointed to the memorable "bits" being those that the individual found unusually emotionally salient, with high emotional salience often being things perceived as either highly unusual and novel or things that directly connect back to and reinforce the person's initial motivations for visiting/using in the first place.[26] Evidence in support of these assumptions came from a study Katie Gillespie and I conducted, again at the California Science Center.[27] Our research showed that museum experiences that were specifically and particularly emotionally arousing resulted in the strongest and longest-lasting memories. And as predicted, in general, the experiences most likely to be perceived as emotionally arousing were those that involved instances of something being particularly stimulating and/or novel, and/or an event that was personally relevant and agenda-reinforcing.

A careful reading of the transcript at the beginning of this chapter clearly reveals that emotion played an important role in Frank's science center visit and no doubt significantly contributed to the memorability of his experience. For example, "On that particular day, I was more of a follower [laughs], watching my daughter going from exhibit to exhibit. I tried to get her to slow it down a little bit to learn about all of the different things that were going on in the exhibit at that particular time. That was a little difficult, she was just happy to be somewhere." In another passage, Frank says, "She got a kick out of the baby chicks." The joy that Frank derived from this visit was clear throughout our interview with him; his daughter's joy was his joy—"I remember what my daughter's reaction was. She was fascinated with seeing something this large and understanding something about the heartbeat. . . . That part of the exhibition is always fascinating to her[;] even when we've gone back again, she'll stop and look at that exhibit." In other words, the experiences Frank's daughter had that day totally fulfilled his hope and expectations; in fact, they reinforced and supported ideas about the role that he as a father should be playing in his daughter's life. He hoped that his daughter would become more engaged with, and excited by the science phenomenon she saw. At least in Frank's mind, this is exactly what happened. Thus, Frank found his museum visit very, very satisfying, and thus emotionally salient, and thus highly memorable.

SOMETHING IS GOING ON HERE!

As my and many other people's research have shown, the vast majority of museum users find their museum experience very satisfying.[28] As the above evidence would suggest, at least some if not a large part of the satisfaction users derive from their museum experience is the ability to use the museum as a vehicle for fulfilling their personal needs and agenda. Virtually all museum users enter into the experience with some kind of pre-use, self-related, visit agenda,[29] and virtually all figure out a way to fulfill that agenda. That closed cycle—develop an agenda, fulfill that agenda—turns out to be very emotionally satisfying.[30] Clearly, the fact that museums are great places for people to have their self-related needs met is important, as is the fact that museums are also great places to see and do interesting and novel things, but there needs to be more to the story than just that. After all, museums have not traditionally been viewed as *the* place to go if you want to experience an emotional high, nor even settings that are particularly emotionally rich. In the former category we typically might think of theme and amusement parks or perhaps films or sporting events. In the latter category, we typically think about life events such as weddings, funerals, and graduations. But perhaps we've underestimated the emotional impact of museum experiences. Perhaps there is something going on here that is more important than previously assumed.

I believe that something else is that museums do not just make people feel good, they make them feel good in a particularly important, highly emotion-rich sort of way. The "good feelings" that museums satisfy transcend those offered by most forms of modern-day leisure, including theme and amusement parks, movies, and sporting events. After all, in today's cluttered leisure environment, it is easy to fill one's times with all sorts of experiences. These days, the offerings available on television and through streaming services is almost inexhaustible. In addition, there are restaurants to go to, movie theaters and concerts, thousands of books and magazines to choose from, and of course the aforementioned theme and amusement parks, and sporting events. All are satisfying in their own ways, all support our short-term expectations, and most are at least fleetingly memorable. Few, however, directly match the salience and persistent memorability of museum experiences. Few it turns out, as directly and successfully support the public's most deeply cherished and most fundamental needs.

Places such as art, history, natural history, and children's museums, science centers, zoos, aquariums, nature centers, arboretums and botanical gardens are the venues people utilize in order to achieve such critical needs as learning about one's self and one's place in the world, as well as critically shaping one's sense of social, civic, and cultural belonging. Museums are also notable because many, though not all, people have historically found these settings to be socially supportive and welcoming. Museums are one of those rare settings where people, or at least some people, can find something of value.[31] Perhaps most striking, is the fact that museums have come to be widely seen as places people willingly and proactively go to with their children, friends, and relatives. Research has shown that doing these fundamental, soul-enhancing types of things—things that make you feel like you have done something worthwhile with your time, things that enhance your and your loved one's chances of leading a satisfying and successful life, things that make you feel safe and secure—are all things perceived to be particularly valuable and worthwhile.[32]

The term that I believe best captures these diverse positive perceptions of benefit is *well-being*. In particular, these feelings, albeit often ephemeral, are indicative that the person has experienced something they believe is deeply significant, that consciously or unconsciously they appreciate that what has transpired contributes to their life balance, their "success" as a person, in other words their biological and cultural "fitness." They perceive that somehow, in some way, for some reason, they are experiencing something that has appreciably boosted their, and/or their loved ones', state of intellectual, social, and/or physical equilibrium with the world, something that will increase their status, enhance the quality of, and perhaps even the longevity of, their life.[33] Although rarely thought of this way, these feelings of enhanced well-being correlate with an array of factors associated with greater survivability.

The public chooses to utilize museums in the hopes that these experiences will enhance their well-being. When people engage in museum experiences, they use the museum in ways designed to satisfy their well-being-related needs. And when people reflected back on their museum experiences, days, weeks, and even years later, the benefits they describe receiving can best be summarized as feelings of enhanced well-being.

ENHANCED WELL-BEING

Coming back to our example of Frank, Frank was definitely hoping to have an enjoyable time with his daughter. He even hoped to have his daughter learn a few things. Fundamentally, though, his main goal that day was to enhance his sense of well-being by being a good father.

For Frank, being a good father meant being someone who cared about his daughter and spent quality time with her. It meant not just spending time but spending time in ways that increased the likelihood of her having a successful future. When we interviewed Frank, we also asked him about his own childhood, about the kinds of museum experiences he had had early in his life. Frank did go to museums as a child, but it was always his mother who brought him to the museum. His father, according to Frank, was always too busy with work to spend that kind of time with his children. Frank did not want to be that kind of father.

As revealed in other parts of his interview, Frank made clear that he was determined to be the kind of father he never had, a father who invested time in his daughter, who wished to support her in ways that transcended money and stern lectures about being successful in life. Frank had vowed that he would become a better kind of father; he would be a father who made the time to take his daughter to museums. Frank aspired to be a father who proactively and measurably contributed to the likelihood that his daughter would achieve a better, healthier, more secure, and potentially more successful life. Frank's desires for his daughter are not unique, virtually all parents have this desire for their children. Significantly, though, many today also share Frank's view that museums can be used as an effective tool for helping them to achieve this desired outcome.

During the visit, Frank sublimated his own interests in deference to the interests of his daughter. Although he states that he did try to talk with his daughter about what she was seeing in order to help her think further about those exhibits she found particularly intriguing, ultimately, he allowed her to go wherever she wanted to go, even when he perceived that she was just running all over the museum. Years later, not only were his memories of the experience quite positive, they also tended to follow this same basic narrative. He talked about trying to slow down his daughter so that she would be able to pick up a few important things. He specifically remembered attempting to focus her attention on certain subjects and specific exhibits, "We concentrated on food groups for humans, because to me that's important—making sure she understands a balanced meal and things of that nature." But he ultimately was quite comfortable with the reality that most of his "educational" efforts seemed to fall on deaf ears.

He certainly could see that his daughter was enjoying herself, and enjoying herself in a science-rich environment, and that she was eager to come again. In fact, Frank deemed the visit was such a success that it prompted him to become a member of the museum, which in turn provided the needed incentive to repeat the experience of visiting the science center with his daughter again and again. This experience struck a very deep and fundamental chord in Frank, helping Frank to satisfy a very fundamental and important well-being-related need.

Yes, Frank's expectations for his visit helped to create a self-fulfilling prophecy. His visit to the museum was not accidental; it was a visit designed to accomplish something specific. Although Frank may not have ever specifically articulated to his wife or even himself this goal, his desire to enhance his personal and social well-being, it was clear he used the museum as a tool for accomplishing this goal, a goal operationalized through the act of being a good father. Wonderfully, for Frank, he also perceived, perhaps consciously but equally likely mostly unconsciously, that he accomplished this goal. As we talked with Frank, he let us know that this "good parent" goal was one of his highest life priorities, and in thinking back upon his museum experience that day, he attributed the California Science Center to being a place that allowed him to satisfy this goal. Consequently, he perceived that this museum experience created a very tangible and memorable marker for him, an indelible marker in his life that confirmed for him that "yes, I really am a good father." These feelings precipitated not only positive feelings and memories but also the desire to continue doing this and other things like it.

Supporting people like Frank—those with the ability to enact their role as caring, nurturing parents—is just one of the many ways museums help users achieve a sense of well-being. As outlined in the previous chapter, museums are perceived by the public as supporting their efforts to achieve a sense of well-being in four distinct areas:

1. *Personal Well-Being*—museums catalyze wonder, interest, and curiosity; all of which foster a sense of personal power and identity. They also support feelings that foster a greater sense of personal connectedness, appreciation, belonging, and harmony with the human and natural world, all in ways that people find fun and enjoyable.
2. *Intellectual Well-Being*—museums help people more clearly comprehend how past understandings and activities have affected their present circumstances; they inspire awe and appreciation for the best of human and natural creation; and under the best of circumstances, even serve as guides to a better, more informed and creative future
3. *Social Well-Being*—museums enhance many user's sense of belonging to family, group, and community and do so in ways that bestow the user with a high degree of status and respect.

4. *Physical Well-Being*—museums (at least historically) are perceived as safe, healthy, and restorative environments that allow people to gather (physically or virtually), interact, explore, and thrive without fear or anxiety.

Museums have always recognized and prided themselves in helping the public achieve well-being in several of these areas, particularly, the first two areas—those of wonder and appreciation—and enhanced knowledge, understanding, and creativity. In fact, as I will describe more fully in later chapters, the majority of self-related needs the public visits museums to satisfy fall within these first two domains. Still, beginning a generation or more ago, it became widely understood within the museum community that the social benefits of museum-going were also important to the public. Despite the fact that some hard-liners, to this day, reject the validity and importance to museums of these benefits, most museums make a considerable effort to support family and other types of groups use of museums. The fourth and final set of well-being-related needs—the needs of physical safety, security, and sustenance—have long been the stepchild of the museum world, with concerns about these needs largely delegated to the facilities and marketing folks. Most within the museum community, until recently, considered these needs clearly secondary to or even incidental to the core mission of the organization. Obviously, recent events, such as the COVID-19 pandemic, have made it abundantly clear that these physical and security needs were always important, if unspoken, needs that museums fulfilled.

Historically, the public has long perceived, again sometimes somewhat unconsciously, that they were selecting from this menu of well-being-related benefits when they utilized a museum. Sometimes they only sought one of these benefits, or more frequently, some mix of these benefits, but rarely more and never less. These are the "good" things, the inherent value, the public and many in the museum profession have long intuitively understood but historically poorly accounted for as the essential value museums deliver, in whole or in part.

For much of human history, for most people achieving any of these well-being-related benefits, let alone several or all at the same time, was challenging and rare. Until recently, the vast majority of people had to spend all of their time exclusively focused on satisfying the last of these four sets of needs—*physical security*—and if they were lucky, maybe also *social cohesion* and *esteem*. However, with greater affluence and discretionary time arose a concomitant desire, arguably a need, among an ever-larger segment of the population for more personal, spiritual, and intellectual pursuits.[34] Enter the modern museum, one of those rare and amazing entities where it was possible to actually achieve not just a limited dose of well-being but a healthy and long-lasting sense of well-being-related benefits across not just one but all four domains of well-being-related need—personal, intellectual, social, and physical.

The fact that museum experiences became seen as vehicles for conveniently and affordably achieving some measure of well-being in each of these four important domains helps to explain not only the salience and memorability of museum experiences, but it also helps to explain, at least in part, the exponential growth and success of museums during the last quarter of the last century. But that was then, and this is now. All of sudden, only a couple of decades into the twenty-first century, museums find themselves poised on a precipice. Many question whether the pre-COVID-era success of museums will be sustainable in a post-COVID world.[35]

What lies over the horizon is of course uncertain, but I believe that critical to whether museums continue to flourish and thrive or wither and disappear depends upon how they negotiate and serve the public's well-being. One thing that is certain, the public's desire to achieve enhanced well-being is not going to go away any time soon. In fact, the current pandemic and the other insecurities of our time—economic, social, political, and environmental—have only served to heighten the public's desperate need for feelings of well-being. This longing for well-being is not some fad that will quickly pass; the need for well-being never disappears. The need for well-being is very deeply rooted in our biological and psychological makeup, and the pursuit and (always fleeting) achievement of well-being turns out to be nothing short of fundamental to what it means to be human, to be alive. In fact, so fundamental is the need for well-being, I believe it might well be considered the Secret of Life!

To understand why this is so requires delving more deeply into the reality of this phenomenon I call well-being; where the desire for well-being comes from, and what purpose achieving a sense of well-being serves. That is where we will go next.

NOTES

1. Quotepark.com. (n.d.). Dr. Seuss. https://quotepark.com/quotes/1490624-dr-seuss-sometimes-you-will-never-know-the-value-of-a-momen/. Retrieved July 19, 2020.

2. See Falk, J. H. and Dierking, L. D. (1992). *The Museum Experience*. Washington, DC: Whalesback Books. Also, Falk, J. H., and Dierking, L. D. (2000). *Learning from Museums*. Lanham, MD: Rowman & Littlefield.

3. See Falk, J. H. (2009). *Identity and the Museum Visitor Experience*. Walnut Creek, CA: Left Coast Press.

4. See recent review in Falk, J. H. (2018). *Born to Choose: Evolution, Self and Well-Being*. London: Routledge.

5. Frank is a pseudonym.

6. Chloe is a pseudonym.

7. See Falk, J. H., and Storksdieck, M. (2005). "Using the Contextual Model of Learning to Understand Science Learning from a Science Center Exhibition." *Science Education* 89, 744–78.

8. Falk, J. H., and Storksdieck, M. (2010). "Science Learning in a Leisure Setting." *Journal of Research in Science Teaching* 47(2), 194–212.

9. See Falk, J. H., and Dierking, L. D. (2019). *Learning from Museums*, second edition. Lanham, MD: Rowman & Littlefield.

10. Naime, J. S., and Pandeirada, J. (2016). "Adaptive Memory: The Evolutionary Significance of Survival Processing." *Perspectives on Psychological Science* 11(4), 496–511.

11. Geertz, C. (1973). *The Interpretation of Cultures*. New York: Basic

12. Roberts, A. (2018). *Evolution: The Human Story*, second edition. New York: Penguin Random House.

13. Falk, J. H. (2018). *Born to Choose: Evolution, Self and Well-Being*. London: Routledge.

14. For a more detailed explanation, see Falk, J. H., and Dierking, L. D. (2019). *Learning from Museums*, second edition. Lanham, MD: Rowman & Littlefield.

15. Falk, J. H., and Dierking, L. D. (2019). *Learning from Museums*, second edition. Lanham, MD: Rowman & Littlefield.

16. McGaugh, J. L. (2013). "Making Lasting Memories: Remembering the Significant." *Proceedings of the National Academy of Sciences U.S.A.*, 110(Suppl 2), 10402–407.

17. Eagleman, D. (2015). *The Brain: The Story of You*. New York: Pantheon.

18. Eagleman, D. (2015). *The Brain: The Story of You*. New York: Pantheon.

19. [19] Damasio, A. (2011). *Neural Basis of Emotions*. Scholarpedia 6(3), 1804. http://www.scholarpedia.org/article/Neural_basis_of_emotions. Retrieved December 8, 2016.

20. Damasio, A. (2011). *Neural Basis of Emotions*. Scholarpedia 6(3), 1804. http://www.scholarpedia.org/article/Neural_basis_of_emotions. Retrieved December 8, 2016.

21. Eagleman, D. (2015). *The Brain: The Story of You*. New York: Pantheon. Damasio, A. (2011). *Neural Basis of Emotions*. Scholarpedia 6(3), 1804. http://www.scholarpedia.org/article/Neural_basis_of_emotions. Retrieved December 8, 2016.

22. Barrett, L. F. (2017). *How Emotions Are Made: The Secret Life of the Brain*. New York: Houghton Mifflin Harcourt.

23. Lazarus, R. S. (1966). *Psychological Stress and the Coping Process*. New York: McGraw-Hill, 16.

24. Turner, J. H. (2000). *On the Origins of Human Emotions: A Sociological Inquiry into the Evolution of Human Affect*. Stanford, CA: Stanford University Press, 59.

25. McGaugh, J. L. (2013). "Making Lasting Memories: Remembering the Significant." *Proceedings of the National Academy of Sciences U.S.A.*, 110(suppl 2), 10402–407.

26. Falk, J. H. (2009). *Identity and the Museum Visitor Experience*. Walnut Creek, CA: Left Coast Press.

27. Falk, J. H., and Gillespie, K. L. (2009). "Investigating the Role of Emotion in Science Center Visitor Learning." *Visitor Studies* 12(2), 112–32.

28. See reviews by the following:

Bounia, A., Nikiforidou, A., Nikonanou, N., and Matossian, A. (2012). "Voices from the Museum: Survey Research in Europe's National Museums." EuNaMus Report No. 5. Linköping: Sweden, Linköping University Electronic Press.

Faerber, L. S., Hofmann, J., Ahrholddt, D., and Schnittka, O. (2021, June). "When Are Visitors Actually Satisfied at Visitor Attractions? What We Know from More Than 30 Years of Research." *Tourism Management* 84. https://doi.org/10.1016/j.tourman.2021.104284. Retrieved March 29, 2021.

Preko, A., Gyepi-Garbrah, T. F., Arkorful, H., Akolaa, A. A., and Quansah, F. (2020). "Museum Experience and Satisfaction: Moderating Role of Visiting Frequency." *International Hospitality Review* 34(2), 203–20.

29. See Falk, J. H. (2009). *Identity and the Museum Visitor Experience*. Walnut Creek, CA: Left Coast Press. Also, Falk, J. H., and Dierking, L. D. (2019). *Learning from Museums*, second edition. Lanham, MD: Rowman & Littlefield.

30. See Falk, J. H., and Storksdieck, M. (2010). "Science Learning in a Leisure Setting." *Journal of Research in Science Teaching* 47(2), 194–212. Also, Falk, J. H., and Dierking, L. D. (2019). *Learning from Museums*, second edition. Lanham, MD: Rowman & Littlefield.

31. Smith, J. K. (2014). *The Museum Effect.* Lanham, MD: Rowman & Littlefield.

32. For review, see Falk, J. H. (2018). *Born to Choose: Evolution, Self and Well-Being.* London: Routledge.

33. Falk, J. H. (2018). *Born to Choose: Evolution, Self and Well-Being.* London: Routledge.

34. Falk, J. H., Ballantyne, R., Packer, J., and Benckendorff, P. (2012). "Travel and Learning: A Neglected Tourism Research Area." *Annals of Tourism Research* 39(2), 908–27. Freysinger, V. J., and Kelly, J. R. (2004). *21st Century Leisure: Current Issues.* State College, PA: Venture Publishing. McLean, D. (2015). *Kraus's Recreation and Leisure in Modern Society,* tenth edition. Burlington, MA: Jones and Bartlett Publishers.

35. Ulaby, N. (2020). "One-Third of U.S. Museums May Not Survive the Year, Survey Finds." National Public Radio, July 22, 2020. https://www.npr.org/sections/coronavirus-live-updates/2020/07/22/894049653/one-third-of-u-s-museums-may-not-survive-the-year-survey-finds. Retrieved July 30, 2020.

3

Well-Being

> Everything should be made as simple as possible, but not simpler. —Albert Einstein[1]

Since the premise of this book is that the value of museum experiences is enhanced well-being, it stands to reason one must understand what is meant by this key term—"well-being." That is the purpose of his chapter. Importantly, I need to be clear up front that my definition of well-being differs considerably from the way most today define this term. Most writers and researchers have defined well-being exclusively as a human, psychological phenomenon associated with the pursuit of

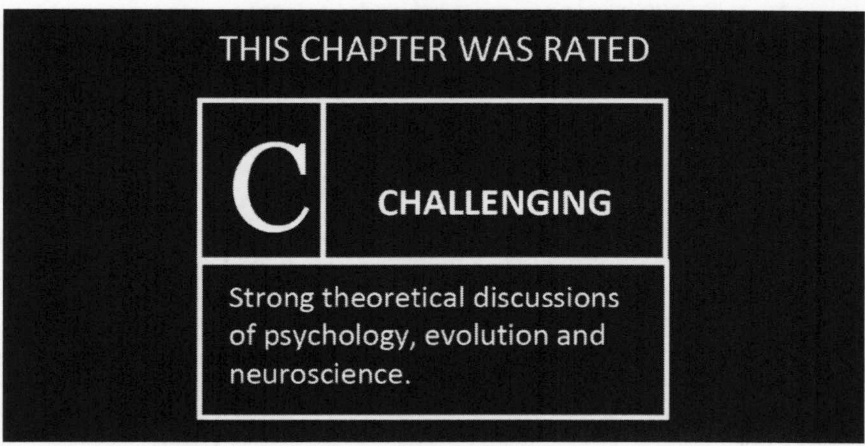

THIS CHAPTER WAS RATED
C
CHALLENGING
Strong theoretical discussions of psychology, evolution and neuroscience.

Source: John H. Falk

happiness.[2] By contrast, I define well-being as first and foremost an evolutionary phenomenon associated with the pursuit of biological fitness and survival.[3] As you will see, this distinction is essential. However, before proceeding further, be forewarned that this chapter comes with a warning; reader discretion is advised.

THE DESIRE FOR ENHANCED WELL-BEING

The essence of well-being is balance and for thousands of years, people all over the world have been concerned with achieving appropriate balances in their life. This constant and never-ending search for personal, intellectual, social, emotional, spiritual, and physical balance and equanimity with the world is something that all humans do. Being in balance feels good, being out of balance feels bad. People often find it difficult to describe what well-being feels like, but they know what the *symptoms* of well-being, both positive and negative feel like. They know when they are in balance, they feel healthy, secure, confident, valued, and vital. Similarly, people know what it feels like to be out of balance. They feel angry, frightened, ill, neglected, and insecure.

This desire for balance and wholeness is a universal human desire, but every culture has viewed and described this idea differently. Culture—a system of ideas, an integrated pattern of beliefs, behaviors, and shared ways of life of a people—always shapes the beliefs and concerns of a people, as well as the language they use to describe those beliefs and concerns. People all over the world have been concerned with the desire for *well-being*, each in their own unique way. For example, central to the Maori of New Zealand's philosophy of life is something they call *hauora*, which is the balance a person needs to strive for between their physical, social, emotional, and spiritual life.[4] Native American communities talk about "finding balance in chaos . . . an ever evolving point of balance, perpetually created and perpetually new."[5] Australian aboriginal peoples talk about well-being as a desire to be spiritually connected to the past, to ancestors and the values that they represent. It is a state of being that brings balance to their thoughts and relationships and engenders calmness, acceptance and tolerance, focus, inner strength, cleansing, and inner peace.[6] Hindu philosophy and traditions also emphasize the importance of well-being, believing that a life of wholeness, balance, and life equilibrium is the pathway to obtaining *sukha*—spiritual bliss and well-being.[7] While many African cultural communities place balance and equanimity, that is, well-being, at the center of their daily lives, the well-being focus of many sub-Saharan communities is on the role of the individual within his or her social group. In this scheme, social relationships are paramount, and every individual must constantly maintain balance in his or her actions and relationships—first as a person, second as a member of a group, and third as a member of a community.[8]

The Chinese have two ancient spiritual/philosophical traditions—the Taoist and the Confucian—and both of these traditions emphasize balance. In the Taoist tradition, the idea of balance, the yin and the yang, is a central concept with the core idea of harmony—or *Héxié*—typically thought of as the goal of trying to find balance with the forces and events in the natural world.[9] Confucianism also emphasizes balance, as best exemplified by the central "Doctrine of the Mean" or *Zhongyong. Zhongyong* is the title of one of the "Four Books" of Confucian philosophy.[10] By contrast with Taoism, though, this Confucian focus on balance and harmony, much like what was suggested above for many African societies, is primarily focused on the need of the individual to achieve balance within and between one's various social relationships.

Western societies also speak about and emphasize the importance of balance. For example, the Classical Greeks were quite fixated on the concept of the "Golden Mean." Aristotle believed a good life, eudaimonia, was achieved by maintaining well-being, a way of life that required a balance between virtue and vice so as to insure good health, positive social relationships, and moral and intellectual achievement.[11] More recently, these ideas have variously become embedded within constructs such as the Anglo-American idea of well-being, the Danish notion of hygge, or the German concept of gemütlichkeit. Unfortunately, today many Western societies have replaced these historically rich ideas about balance and equanimity in all of life's practices with a variety of overly simplistic ideas such as happiness, prosperity, and/or comfort. This does a supreme disservice to the real underlying complexity and holistic principles at work here. Neither the idea of happiness, prosperity, nor comfort fully encapsulate the deeper, more visceral, realities of daily human strivings, the realities I have chosen to capture with the term well-being.

DEFINING WELL-BEING

Despite the pervasiveness of these well-being-related ideas in all world cultures, it is surprising to discover how poorly this idea of well-being has been defined and studied by scientists. Beginning several decades ago, a group of Western psychologists resolved to remedy this situation by applying both theoretical and experimental rigor to the understanding of what it means to cultivate and live a satisfying life.[12] Often referred to as "positive psychologists," in response to the fact that psychology was, and in large measure still is, primarily concerned with the study of human dysfunction and malaise, these researchers focused on better understanding and measuring well-being.[13]

In the ensuing years, hundreds of books and even more articles have been written on well-being-related topics, all however have begun with the assumption that well-being and its related states are a uniquely human, almost exclusively psychological phenomenon.[14] Although it has long been understood that well-being can be framed in many ways, and encompasses many facets of life-balance, such as in health, social welfare, and emotional outlook,[15] over the years, Western science has disproportionately defined human well-being from a deficit perspective. From this perspective, well-being is an achievable end state, one that most people currently lack due to the absence of one or some combination of elusive but achievable set of missing attributes, values, or possessions. A classic example of this approach is revealed in the way physical well-being, or health, has been defined.

In theory, there are three possible ways one can define physical well-being.[16] The first is that physical well-being is the absence of any disease or impairment. The second is that physical well-being is a state that allows the individual to adequately cope with all the demands of daily life (implying also the absence of disease and impairment). The third definition states that physical well-being is a state of balance, an equilibrium that an individual establishes both within himself and between himself and his social and physical environment. Disproportionately, rather than taking the more holistic approach suggested by the third definition, Western science has chosen to primarily utilize the first or occasionally the second of these definitions, presumably because each of these first two make it relatively easy to measure the presence or absence of physical well-being, for example, you either have a disease or you do not. However, what has been lost, and not just in public health but in all facets of life, by eschewing the third, more holistic approach is an appreciation of just how relative and organic life is. Life is not static, either "good" or "bad"/ healthy or sick, but rather always somewhere in between. Life is about becoming not arriving! Perhaps more importantly, in their zeal to identify and concretely measure the outward manifestations of well-being, researchers have sought specific, measurable "indicators" of well-being. For example, medical researchers have focused on things like body mass index or cholesterol level as indicators of physical well-being. Social scientists have determined social well-being though metrics such as the size of one's social network. Economists have measured financial well-being through measures of net worth and Psychologists have framed personal well-being through measures of happiness. In all of these examples, the relatively static nature of these indicators of well-being has served to obscure the highly dynamic nature of well-being and thus has failed to robustly reveal the true function that perceptions of well-being serve in humans.

Perceptions of well-being, such as feelings of health, social connectedness, prosperity, and happiness, are indeed indicators of how modern, mainly Western, educated people perceive well-being.[17] But well-being is not reducible to some simplistic, easily describable, outward set of generic feelings—presumably culturally neutral but in fact not neutral—feelings such as "good health," "financial wealth," or "happiness." Nor, for that matter, is well-being something one can "attain," once and for all time. Quite the contrary, feelings of well-being are neither rare nor ever permanent. Neither are perceptions of well-being something unique to humans. A formal definition might be something like the following:

> Well-being is the on-going, always ephemeral process of trying to maintain an appropriate balance with one's physical, social, intellectual, and personal/spiritual world. It is a holistic feeling that arises from the integration of a vast array of biological and

cultural survival-oriented perceptions. Collectively, these perceptions evolved as part of a complex system designed to support the persistence of the individual and the species over time.

The goal of this chapter is to more fully explain why I define well-being this way. Taking my cue from the Albert Einstein quote at the beginning of this chapter, I will do my best to make my explanation as simple as possible, but not simpler.

My definition includes three key parts, descriptions of (1) WHAT the human perception of well-being "feels" like; (2) HOW well-being functions in general and in humans in particular; and most importantly, (3) WHY the ability to feel a sense of well-being is important. I will address each of these topics in turn, starting in reverse order by addressing the most fundamental question first, WHY it is that humans have evolved this amazing ability to perceive well-being, when this capability first emerged, and for what purpose.

THE WHY OF WELL-BEING: THE ORIGINS AND "PURPOSE" OF PERCEIVED WELL-BEING

So, what is this thing called well-being? As suggested above, most people, including most researchers, typically define well-being-like states as a human-centric process whereby people consciously experience feelings of health, happiness, prosperity, and life satisfaction—or even more specifically, as the ability to manage stress and find purpose in life.[18] Yes, these are all consequences of well-being, but well-being is actually much more basic than this.

Fundamentally, well-being is about being able to sense when things are going well, and equally importantly, when things are going poorly. Well-being is not just about feeling happy, it is equally about feeling like one has a full belly and is physically comfortable, that one is not feeling ill or threatened. These are not things that only humans worry about, nor are they things that only humans are capable of perceiving. Your dog or cat has the ability to perceive these things too. So too, in their own ways, can every plant in your garden; even the bacteria in your gut can recognize these states. All of these creatures, like us, use their perceptions of well-being to manage their life pathway. Of course, how a dog, a plum tree, or bacterium actually perceives well-being and then responds to those feelings is by necessity very different from how a human perceives and responds to well-being, but perceive and respond they do.[19]

The perception of the quality-of-life processes and events—both those internal and external to the organism are not mere niceties, they are necessities of life. Every living creature has evolved the ability to sense these indicators of well-being. The ability to perceive and manage well-being turns out to be central to what it means to be alive, hence my assertion at the end of the last chapter that well-being is the secret of life!

Well, perhaps it is only the *perceptible* half of the secret of life. The other half, which is always there but generally not perceptible, is the need and desire to survive—to persist in time and space beyond the present moment. More than a century and a half ago, as part of his theory of evolution, Charles Darwin postulated—and hundreds of thousands of scientific observations since Darwin have confirmed—that all life forms spend their days focusing their energies on surviving.[20] Either directly through, for example, the taking in and processing of energy and nutrients, or indirectly, for example, through reproduction. Living things live their lives in ways that to the best of their abilities help them ensure that they will live another day, and another day, and on and on.

Every form of life, each in its own way, endlessly strives to live forever. Over time, and on average, the fittest members of each species do survive and persist; this maxim has popularly been referred to as "survival of the fittest." What makes an organism "fit" depends upon the nature of that organism and the realities it encounters. For a gazelle, the fittest might mean the fastest, the one best able to outrun a predator. For a lion, it might mean the smartest and strongest, the one best able to ambush and then bring down a prey with a single swipe of its paw. For virtually all, it means the most fecund, those most able to produce numerous, healthy offspring. Whatever adaptation makes an organism more fit, evolution has seen to it those traits, those organisms, on average, not only live longer individually than do those who are less fit, but they also live longer over time, able to transmit their genes, their cellular materials, and in the case of humans, also their influence and ideas, across generations.[21] This is the essence and brilliance of Darwin's insight and his theory of evolution by natural selection.[22]

That is the big picture, but what Darwin's legion of followers have been trying to figure out ever since is exactly how living things enhance their fitness. Since fitness is not really something that is readily perceivable, can a living thing actually influence its own survival? How does an organism "know" whether any particular choice or action it takes today is going to enhance its genetic or cultural fitness tomorrow; in other words, does life have the ability to directly act in ways that enhance survivability and ultimately persistence? *Enter the perception of well-being.*

Although fitness, *per se*, is not perceivable by living things, perceptions of well-being are.[23] Long before the evolution of consciousness, or even the evolution of a central nervous system and brains, I have argued that life evolved perceptions of well-being as a way to fill this vital "fitness feedback" function.[24] Perceptions of well-being, feelings related to health, safety, and security, all evolved as mechanisms for judging fitness—not a perfect judgment, but ones that were, on average, and over time, a reasonably accurate proxy for fitness.

In other words, very early in the evolution of living things, life evolved the ability to "perceive" conditions within and around itself. Even the most rudimentary "perceptive" ability would have been adaptive, since even a minimal ability to determine when conditions were better or worse would have increased the chances of survival. So early on, and initially very grossly but over evolutionary time with ever-increasing acuity, the perception of well-being came to be the way living things threaded the fitness needle. Perceptions of well-being evolved as tangible mechanisms for enabling life to gather information about, and manage its relationship with, both the internal and external world. These perceptions of well-being led to the evolution of a sense of self, the ability to distinguish that which is "me" from that which is "not me." And in turn, the need to make these self/non-self distinctions resulted in the evolution of learning, the ability to avoid making the same self/non-self mistakes again and again, such as consuming something that made one sick. In this way, by virtue of being able to perceive and behave in ways that maximized a sense of well-being, life evolved the ability to perceive and behave in ways that maximized its chances for survival. And this is exactly what every form of life that has ever existed on earth has persistently done, and continues just as assiduously to do, every moment of every day.[25]

Every human alive today is the descendent of a long line of survivors, an unbroken chain going back billions of years. The only reason all those ancestors survived was that they were, on average, the ones that most successfully were able to perceive the presence or absence of well-being and then act in ways that enhanced their well-being. From this perspective, then, it should be clear why well-being is the secret of life. Maximizing one's well-being is the key to survival; it is the ability to effectively adapt one's behavior to current realities, and in so doing, live longer and more successfully. The perception of well-being is the "secret trick" that has sustained and perpetuated life on earth for nearly four billion years.[26]

THE WHAT OF WELL-BEING: HOW WELL-BEING WORKS

After billions of years of evolution, the perception of well-being has morphed into an almost limitless set of inter-related processes, but everything has to start somewhere. So, the question arises, how and when did the perception of well-being arise? Along with numerous others, I believe the oldest and most rudimentary form of well-being was the biomechanical "sensing" process all cells use to regulate their chemical balance.[27] Cells after all, are just bags of chemicals—but not random chemicals, very special chemicals organized in very specific and distinct ways. For a cell to survive, whether it be a free-living bacterial cell sloshing around in the ocean or one of the trillions of communal cells that make up the human body, every cell needs to maintain an optimal balance of the chemicals within itself. Cells achieve this balance through an active process of monitoring and managing the chemical concentration of each chemical within itself.[28] Without this ability to maintain chemical conditions different from that of its surroundings—both the bringing into the cell of scarce but beneficial chemicals, generically referred to as "food," as well as the removal of toxic, unbeneficial chemicals, generically referred to as "waste"—the cell could not survive. This ability is so fundamental to life that every living cell on earth today possesses this ability to appraise the chemical composition of its insides relative to its outside, to judge when things are positively balanced (going well) and when they are out-of-balance (going poorly). More striking though, is the fact that every cell alive on earth today, from the simplest to most complex, possesses virtually identical, biologically and genetically, versions of this well-being machinery.[29] This suggests that the origins of well-being must be very ancient indeed, likely arising from a common ancestor, sometime at the dawn of life itself. [30]

These earliest forms of well-being acted much like a thermostat, helping to gauge and regulate current conditions. Much as we use thermostats in our houses, offices, and automobiles to help us ensure an optimal air temperature (e.g., turning on a heater when things get too cold or an air conditioner when things get too hot), every cell possesses a series of biochemical "thermostats" that help it regulate the balance of its internal chemical environment. As long as conditions fall within an acceptable range, all is well, but when conditions fall below or above some acceptable range, the "thermostat" sends a signal indicating that corrective action is required. These thermostatic-like processes ensure that corrective action(s) continue until an appropriate balance is restored, at which point, another signal is sent indicating that corrective actions should cease. However, unlike a mechanical thermostat, life's thermostats possess an amazing degree of variability and adaptability. Perceptions of well-being can and do change over time as the organism moves through the world. Arguably, it is this dual ability to both perceive and act when things are "optimal" or "sub-optimal," and the ability to adjust these processes in response to changing conditions, that has made life as we know it possible.

The perception of well-being evolved as a tool for judging fitness. Over billions of years, life has evolved the ability to perceive a wide variety of things as "positive well-being." These include being able to identify and mate with the most "attractive" members of one's species, the ability to recognize the warning signs of danger, and the ability to react to those warning signs with a range of protective strategies (e.g., hiding, fleeing, or fighting). Perceptions of well-being have also supported the evolution of selectivity in what one eats, with living things preferentially only eating the most "nutritious" foods available at any given moment in time. In social organisms like us, the perception of well-being has also supported such highly adaptive behaviors as awareness of social status and sensitivity to the ways one's actions influence others in our group. All of these behavioral well-being-related preferences, on average, have resulted in positive survival outcomes. Meanwhile, life also benefited by evolving the ability to perceive as "negative well-being" things that diminished survival chances, things like the "taste" of rotten or toxic food, the "feel" of being injured or sick, or the "fight or flight response" that arises when something big and potentially harmful suddenly appears. The living things best capable of perceiving and acting upon positive perceptions of well-being were the living things most likely to survive. Perhaps even more importantly, the living things able to perceive and act upon negative perceptions of well-being, were particularly likely to survive. This is because bad things are often much more consequential than good things. For example, eating a particularly delicious meal may be satisfying, but eating something toxic is likely to be disastrous.

The ability to use perceptions of well-being to boost chances for survivability proved so successful that over evolutionary time these thermostat-like well-being mechanisms proliferated and diversified. As living things became more complex, so too did the various well-being feedback systems that evolved to support this complexity.[31] As is the nature of life, most of these new well-being systems elaborated on or repurposed bits and pieces of older well-being systems. Over the history of life on earth, billions if not trillions of these well-being systems have evolved.[32] Some persist into the present, though most have vanished along with the organismic capsules in which they first evolved and functioned. Again, as is the nature of life, those living things possessing the best adapted well-being systems, those that allowed their owners to accurately perceive and adjust their relative fitness to an ever-changing environment, were the living things most likely to survive. Some superlative examples of successful and highly evolved well-being systems include the digestive system; the immune system; sensory perception systems such as sight, hearing, touch, and taste; and of course, the vertebrate brain that evolved to synthesize and coordinate all of these various systems. Although life has evolved countless well-being feedback strategies, many unique to the particular lifeforms in which they exist, what is critical to remember is that all retain the same fundamental, survival-related purpose as those original chemical thermostat-like systems that first evolved in the warm, Precambrian seas some 3.8 billion years ago.

Fast-forward to the present day and the human perception of well-being. As this very brief history of life makes clear, the perception of well-being is certainly not a uniquely human capability. Nor are perceptions of well-being restricted to just the most "elevated" perceptions of wealth or a life "well-lived." For simplicity, I have separated the deep underlying causes/needs of well-being into seven major modalities, which again for simplicity, I have grouped together into four broad categories—personal well-being, intellectual well-being, social well-being, and physical well-being. I may have chosen to limit the total number of categories and modalities, but my decision was anything but arbitrary. Drawing equally from research and theory in evolutionary biology, the social sciences and philosophy, these seven basic modalities emerged as clearly distinguishable clusters of human need, each representing a critical burst of development during the long history of life on earth, in particular, the history of the branch of life represented by humans. Each of the seven modalities represents a cluster of loosely related well-being-related needs; each the by-product of a major transitional event in evolutionary history, each of which left an especially noticeable strong footprint on our human behavior and psyche.[33] Below, listed in reverse order, from most recently evolved to most ancient, are humanity's core well-being modalities:

Personal Well-Being

1. *Creativity/Spirituality/Actualization* (originating more than 350 thousand years ago)—needs associated with abstract thought and fulfilment, the satisfaction

of which enables humans to purposefully and imaginatively project their sense of self into situations, both good and bad, unfettered by immediate realities. Often the main goal of these needs are personal fulfilment and the building of identity.

Intellectual Well-Being

2. *Reflectivity* (originating more than 5 million years ago)—needs that harness the power of conscious awareness to consider one's situation beyond immediate bounds of time and space. These abilities allow people to improve their understanding and actions in the present and future by considering and explaining what happened to them and others like them in the past.

Social Well-Being

3. *Relationality* (originating more than 16 million years ago)—needs that harness the power of conscious awareness in order to appraise one's relative standing as compared with others within one's social group. These abilities allowed individuals to understand relationships and proactively influence their social status.
4. *Sociality* (originating more than 600 million years ago)—An entire suite of needs associated with maintaining and fostering small and large group associations and cooperation. These abilities allow people to expand their self beyond the individual and become part of a group, with all the benefits and strengths that larger entity can provide.

Physical Well-Being

5. *Sexuality* (originating more than 2 billion years ago)—Needs that prime the individual to recognize and respond to others, either positively or negatively depending upon cultural and biological determined sexual characteristics. Although from an evolutionary perspective, the main goal of sexuality is reproductive success, sexual relationships are intrinsically pleasurable and humans have evolved complex cultural framings around both courtship, mating, and sexual relations.
6. *Individuality* (originating more than 3.5 billion years ago)—This is the whole range of needs associated with the recognition of the self as singular entity, distinct from the rest of the world and needing protection from others. Those others can be microorganisms that cause disease, potentially injurious macroorganisms such as snakes or lions, or more often than not among humans, other humans. Obviously, the main goal of these abilities is to ensure the health and longevity of the individual.[34]

7. *Continuity* (originating more than 3.8 billion years ago)—These are not only the oldest but also the most basic of needs that all people share, including the need for food, water, shelter, and warmth. Although a person may become aware of these needs, particularly when they go awry, most function well below the level of conscious awareness and as in all living things, the main goal is to ensure the continuous functioning and stability of all the physiological systems that allow a person to stay alive.

Each of these seven categories of need arose in response to specific environmental events and selective pressures. Within each of these seven modalities, in particular those that are most recently evolved, it is also possible to identify entirely modern and uniquely human types of needs. But whether ancient or modern, all the well-being-related needs within a particular modality converge on supporting suites of behaviors we would recognize as related, for example, the need for physical health, or the need to be recognized and approved by one's social group. However, it is critical to appreciate that these categories are not as distinct nor hierarchical as might first appear, at least not fundamentally.

The needs of *Reflectivity* and *Creativity/Spirituality/Actualization* or *Continuity* and *Individuality* are all biologically homologous. They may not be identical psychologically, but they all share a high degree of biological similarity, even in the ways they are neurologically processed.[35] This is because later evolving systems of well-being arose from the foundations of earlier evolved systems of well-being, with each new system repurposing, or at times merely borrowing, earlier evolved biological pathways and processes in order to adapt to new challenges and opportunities.[36]

All the different ways present-day humans have of achieving well-being arose through biological and cultural evolutionary elaborations of earlier systems of well-being; and thus, all share a common origin. This process of evolutionary complexification has been going on for a long time, starting long before there were humans, in fact, starting long before there were even such things as brains.

No doubt, many readers may immediately see that a similarity exists between my seven modalities of well-being-related need and Abraham Maslow's hierarchy of needs.[37] That is reasonable and appropriate as Maslow's insights about human needs have been widely utilized and regularly hailed as one of the greatest achievements of modern social science.[38] However, as outlined in detail in my book *Born to Choose: Evolution, Self and Well-Being*,[39] there is not a one-to-one relationship between the well-being-related needs I have defined and those defined by Maslow. Like Maslow, my categories are reflective of human behavior, but I have modified and extended Maslow's categories based on additional data, particularly data from biology, anthropology, psychology, and the neurosciences.[40]

Importantly, unlike Maslow, I have not thought of these seven modalities as hierarchical, since functionally that is not how they seem to operate. People are capable of achieving well-being through satisfaction of the needs associated with any of the seven modalities of well-being, in any order and at any time. Achieving well-being

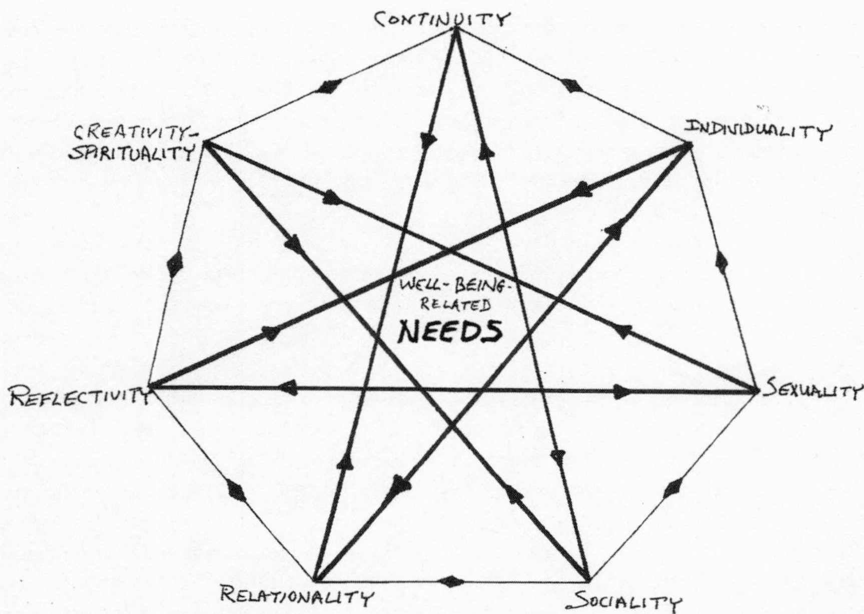

Figure 3.1. Falk Well-Being Model. *Source:* John H. Falk

by satisfying *Creativity/Spirituality/Actualization*–related needs does not result in a higher state of well-being than satisfying *Continuity*-related needs. Well-being feels good, whether achieved by listening to a Beethoven sonata or eating a satisfying meal. Reinforcing the fundamental "sameness" of these seemingly disparate activities, data from brain research is showing that these seemingly different experiences arise from activation of nearly identical brain regions and virtually identical neural processes.[41] Similarly, one can feel a depressed sense of well-being just as acutely whether one has the flu or one has had one's book proposal turned down, yet again, by another publisher. A way to visualize this non-hierarchical array of well-being related needs is shown in figure 3.1.

As suggested by figure 3.1, at any given moment, well-being is typically a blending of needs rather than a hierarchy. The demands of life are normally just too complex to allow an individual to focus her energies for any length of time on just one modality of well-being-related need. Imagine being faced with a thousand or more equally compelling, but potentially contradictory needs, each demanding action right now! This is what is actually happening, every moment of every day. Fortunately, our minds have evolved the ability to triage all those competing demands, integrating the demands of these thousands of well-being-related needs, and then directing the body to act in ways designed to simultaneously satisfy the greatest number of important needs as possible. As outlined in the previous chapter, the emotional centers of the human brain play a major role in this triaging process, helping to prioritize the most important, most meaningful, most survival-related perceptions and actions.

In complex organisms like humans, it turns out to be possible to react to not just one important need at a time but rather to "blend" one's needs and act in ways that satisfy multiple purposes at the same time. This "blending" process turns out to be one of the ways life has evolved to accommodate the overwhelming complexity of the world, and complex creatures like us humans are particularly adept at this strategy. This blending process is also what accounts for the amazing flexibility and diversity of human actions; we humans can generate an almost infinite number of ways to respond to and act upon the events in our lives. The possible variability created by this process is truly enormous and never totally predictable. Taken together, this immense flexibility coupled with individual difference helps to explain why there can be so much variability in behavior within even a single species, including and particularly, us humans.

To understand how an almost limitless variability can arise from a quite limited starting point, I have found a useful analogy to be the way paint companies today have made it possible for us to individualize the color of the walls of our houses. Once upon a time paint only came in a few basic colors but not today. The range of paint colors we can choose from now seems almost limitless, but not because the paint store keeps thousands of different colors in some warehouse waiting for a customer to decide to select one. No, the process is at once much more complicated and at the same time much simpler. Today's paint store offers up an enormous palette of colors, but mainly only stocks one color of paint: white.

Anyone who has ever gone to the paint store to buy house paint knows how this works. Typically, a large chunk of wall space in the paint store is devoted to racks full of hundreds upon hundreds of little cards, each card containing a dozen or so different colors on it. After spending some time narrowing down one's choices, a person selects the paint color they like best. Next to the color on the card is a number. That number is actually a code representing a specific ratio of four pigments—red, blue, yellow, and black. When the customer hands this color card with the selected color and specific number code over to the paint store employee, she uses a large paint-mixing machine to create that custom color. The machine makes it possible for the paint store employee to add just the right amount of each of the four primary pigment colors to a can of white paint, as specified by the formula, to create the chosen color. Voilà ! From out of the thousand or more initial color choices, the customer's specific color paint was created, all by just mixing together four core pigments into a white base.

Now imagine how many more options there would be if instead of just four pigments, there were seven pigments.[42] But of course, in reality, the starting point is not seven identically manufactured pigments but hundreds of thousands of options that get mixed together. Each of the seven modalities of well-being I have described are actually just conceptual placeholders for entire suites of well-being systems; within each modality are tens of thousands or more evolutionarily and culturally related well-being systems, each system designed to support thousands upon thousands of well-being-related needs—the result would be a number with more than 250 zeros behind it.[43] Further, adding even more complexity to the system, none of these well-being-related systems are ever totally static, each is constantly morphing and adapting to changing circumstances.[44] Also, since each human is a genetically, culturally, and experientially unique individual, the specific details of how each of these well-being systems within us works is also unique, with even slight variations resulting in enormous differences in expression. The possible "combinations" of all these highly unique and variable well-being-related human perceptions and actions is astronomically large. So vast is the number of possible combinations that it far exceeds the number of the stars in the universe; in fact, the possible variability exceeds the bounds of human imagination.

This blending process not only influences human actions, but equally the ways we perceive well-being. Since our survival depends upon ensuring the continuous and ongoing satisfaction of the needs associated with all seven modalities of well-being, we are constantly aware of and monitoring the state of each modality. Although we clearly are capable of singularly focusing on only one type of need at a time, such as hunger, companionship, or creating a work of art, such focus, as suggested above, is actually quite infrequent and difficult. Awareness and focus on these modality-specific needs only occasionally filters up to our conscious minds; more typically, what we are aware of, if we even are aware at all, is of just a single, blended, general sense of well-being—or not. This brings us to the third, and final key part of my definition of well-being, how well-being is perceived.

THE HOW OF WELL-BEING: THE WAYS IN WHICH HUMANS PERCEIVE WELL-BEING

Starting with first principles, it is clear from all of the above, that the general perception of well-being is neither a rare nor unusual activity. The perception of well-being is something that every human does at some level, and in some way, all of the time.[45] In other words, every second of every day, the mind is flooded with myriad "signals" related to well-being. These signals emanate from both within and without the body—signals from the gut, signals from the feet, signals from eyes, ears, and nose, and lots and lots of signals from the brain itself. The mind takes in and processes all these signals and determines, based on a combination of long-ago evolved and recently learned pathways, which of these signals are inconsequential and thus ignored and which are likely to be of consequence and thus attended to. Then, based on this assessment, our minds and bodies determine how best to act.

Although our brains "perceive" and "process" a huge number of well-being-related signals every second, most of this activity happens below the level of conscious awareness. Just to provide a sense of the scale of this discrepancy, it has been estimated that every second, the human brain processes around 11 million bits of information, but only about thirty to forty of those bits of information ever filter up to the conscious mind.[46] In other words, what a person is consciously aware of at any given moment represents only the tiniest fraction of events going on inside and outside of them, which is not the same as saying that only a tiny fraction of events are perceived and acted upon by the brain; just that only an infinitesimally small percentage of these perceptions ever rise to the level of conscious awareness.

At its most basic level, consciousness has been defined as the "sentience or awareness of internal or external existence."[47] Despite centuries of analyses, definitions, explanations, and debates by philosophers and scientists, consciousness remains puzzling and controversial.[48] Countless books have been written on this topic too, and clearly it is well beyond the scope of what is needed here to delve into this fascinating, complex, and still evolving topic. However, what is important to know is that although when awake we perceive that we are actively attending to and fully aware of the events in our world, in reality, what we are aware of at any given moment is actually quite limited, always selective and frequently distorted.[49] The problem is, at any given instant, we are only consciously aware of that very tiny fraction of events going on around and within us; at least as far as our conscious minds are concerned, functionally, all else in the world ceases to exist. The psychologist Julian Jaynes described this phenomenon well. "Consciousness is a much smaller part of our mental life than we are consciously aware of, because we cannot be conscious of what we are not conscious of. . . . It is like asking a flashlight in a dark room to search around for something that does not have any light shining upon it. The flashlight, since there is light in whatever direction it turns, would have to conclude that there is light everywhere. And so consciousness can seem to pervade all mentality when actually it does not."[50] As we move through the world, as we move through life, most of what is transpiring within and without us is in the dark, unrevealed by the flashlight of our conscious awareness.

The reality is that people do not consciously think about most of the things going on inside and outside of them over the course of the day.[51] A person's conscious intentions are at best vague and undeveloped, or more often, entirely nonexistent. This lack of clear intentionality or even unawareness, though problematic for social science researchers, is actually not a problem for "real" people most of the time, since it rarely prevents them from processing billions of bits of information every day and making thousands of choices in an effective and "typical" manner. Of course, that is not how we perceive what we perceive. Like Jaynes's flashlight, we are highly aware of what our conscious minds illuminate and presume that is all there is.

Because of the limitations of conscious awareness, people are only capable of consciously perceiving one or at most two or three things at a time.[52] For example, although most of the time people are oblivious to their breathing or heart beating, it is possible to focus conscious awareness on one of these physiological processes. However, when one does focus on such physiological processes, one's heartbeat for example, one cannot simultaneously add up a list of numbers (if you doubt this is true, give it a try).[53] This tendency of the conscious mind to concentrate on a single track clearly distorts one's perception of all that is going on in one's mind, but the ability to focus and have a singular frame of reference has clearly had great survival benefits for humanity.

Experience has taught us, as humans, that those things that do rise to the level of conscious awareness are important. Arguably, one of the big adaptive advantages the evolution of conscious awareness made possible for our human ancestors was a heightened awareness of cause and effect, and subsequent learning that this awareness made possible.[54] Although, contrary to how consciousness has been widely believed to function (by both the general public and social scientists), it is highly unlikely that conscious awareness evolved as a way of directing current actions.[55] Rather, consciousness primarily appears to have evolved as an effective device for helping people evaluate the importance of immediate past events and actions in their life. This is because the events and actions that rise to the level of conscious awareness are, by definition, events and/or actions that are highly salient and potentially important to one's life—the big decision, the near miss, the met gaze with the attractive person across the way. Noticeable events/actions are more likely to be events/actions worth remembering since they represent events/actions worthy of repeating or avoiding in the future.

However, merely being noticeable does not make something memorable. As touched on in the previous chapter, only the tiniest fraction of all the events/actions we are consciously aware of in any given day is likely to be remembered. Only the most highly salient and important life experiences are the ones we find truly memorable, experiences likely to be retrievable days, weeks, and years later. What this means, by the numbers, is that roughly one in a million well-being-related perceptions bubbles up to conscious awareness, and likely only one in a million of these ever becomes sufficiently important as to be indelibly etched in memory and readily retrievable, let alone describable months and years later. After all, it is possible for a significant well-being-related event or action to be "memorable" but not "describable," since this is what myriad life forms achieve every day. But for humans, being able to transform a memory into language, to be able to describe that event/action to someone else, represents the highest of the high; an event/action that was truly extra-especially salient and memorable.

Humans are uniquely capable of being able to recall and verbally communicate, both to themselves and to others, these rare, important, and salient life events. These autobiographical narratives, as they are labeled by psychologists, are how people make sense of not only their world but their place in that world.[56] Humans are certainly not the only species to communicate their well-being-related feelings through some kind of sound or behavior, but humans are truly unique in their ability to use language to ascribe meanings to these well-being-related events. Both the verbal descriptions people use to make sense of the feelings bubbling up to conscious awareness, and the verbal descriptions they use to describe these feelings to others, make humans very special indeed. And all of these words, all of these descriptions a person might think about and speak, are constructs of that person's social-cultural milieu.

And all of the interpretations of what those spoken words mean, are equally molded by and through the culture of the individual listening to those words.

By socially-culturally constructed I mean that neither the ongoing perceptions of well-being nor how someone might make sense of and describe those few, critical, seminal well-being-related events a person might feel uniquely distinguishes their life derive from some universal set of biological or neurological clues waiting to be "revealed." There is no "well-being center" in the brain; not even any specific parts of the brain from which well-being derives. Rather, every person constructs their sense of well-being based on how they were taught to interpret those various signals emanating from their brain and body. Quite literally, humans learn to make sense of, and linguistically label, their perceptions of well-being based on the implicit or explicit cues they receive from their parents, peers, and social environment. For example, when a parent says, "Oh, look at that smile; what a happy baby," or says, "What's the matter darling? You are acting funny; are you sick?" That parent is framing for that child how to interpret and describe those feelings. In the absence of this kind of explicit, verbal framing, these sensations would be just that—sensations.

So, although every human is born with the ability to register the well-being-related signals coming from their bodies and environment, every person needs to learn what those signals *mean*, what to call them, which are really important, and which are not. There is no universal feeling of well-being. All perceptions of well-being derive from a person's individual, social, and culturally lived experience. There are no exceptions. Even the way someone perceives and responds to such seemingly fundamental biological well-being-related needs as hunger and pain avoidance turns out to be culturally dependent.[57] Thus, although it is possible to describe the kinds of well-being-related experiences most of the people likely to read this book would find highly salient and memorable, it should not be assumed, as most well-being researchers have,[58] that these perceptions of well-being, or their meanings, are in any way universal to all humans everywhere.[59] Although 99 percent of all people alive today share many similar cultural beliefs, it must be remembered that these 99 percent of people today represent less than 1 percent of the cultural diversity in the world.[60]

So what types of experiences or events do most people today consider as truly memorable and important indicators of well-being? For starters, it is fair to surmise that much of what constitutes a memorable, well-being-related experience for people living today is highly likely to be quite different from what would have been considered a memorable, well-being-related experience to a human living a thousand years ago. As the bulk of humanity transitioned from a hunter-gatherer to an agrarian, and then to an industrial, and today to an information/knowledge-based lifestyle, so too at each stage did the perceptions of what constituted survival-related well-being. Whereas once it was critical that every male be able to read the signs of game, by agrarian times these skills were replaced by other, more situationally important types of knowledge, such as the best time to plant and harvest. Today, no longer salient is the presence and quality of animal spoor or the slant of the sun at noon at different times of year, but highly salient is the ability to utilize a wide range of knowledge-based tools, including and particularly digital technologies. As a consequence of these shifting needs, an ever-larger percentage of the public now ascribes great value to such exclusively personal and intellectual well-being-related attributes as creativity and scientific and systems thinking. Those few individuals in our society widely acknowledged as highly creative, the Stevie Wonders, Frank Gearys, and Steve Jobses of the world, are richly rewarded and widely admired, so too are spiritual leaders and gurus like the Dali Lama and Pope Francis. Even at more modest levels, opportunities to express one's creativity satisfy a long-desired goal such as seeing one of the wonders of the world, or experiencing a moment of spiritual tranquility and bliss are all highly valued today, particularly so when these accomplishments are shared with and appreciated by others.[61]

One of the distinguishing features of human conscious awareness has been the ability to size up a situation, and based upon similar, past situations, envision how to act in the future. There is reason to believe that this reflective envisioning and planning capacity has been a highly adaptive, and thus valued and admired aspect of the human condition for a very long time.[62] Historically, and today still, not everyone has had equal access to positions of authority, equal ability to exercise their envisioning capabilities. However, whether inherited or achieved through merit, individuals who exhibit this capability are admired and followed. This is true in business, government, and even within the limited social sphere of families and community groups.

Whether achieved by virtue of brains, brawn, or inheritance, we live in a society where a few individuals "win" big and many others merely get by. Our society has evolved all kinds of ways to recognize those with higher status, the most common being wealth. As the saying goes, attributed to the financial magazine magnate Malcolm Forbes, "He who dies with the most toys wins." And it is true, whether the "toys" be belongings or some other items of cultural value such as the most beautiful mate or the most children, the correlation between high status and greater survivability is well established.[63] In our society, like every other society current and past, we consistently associate these culturally defined examples of high status with greater well-being.

Social status is a product of a social style of life, and humans are quintessentially social animals. Over and above status, social animals value group belonging. Even the lowest status individual craves acceptance and recognition of the group and derives sustenance from association with the group. Modern humans are no exception. Everyone derives feelings of well-being from being loved by others and being recognized as being part of a larger group. As a society, we value those we consider good parents, good team players, and good citizens.

Despite living in modern cities, with all the gizmos and gadgets of the Information/Knowledge Age, all of us still seek out and value things that satisfy our basic biological needs. Although it can sometimes be hard to appreciate the time and attention we pay to these physical needs because of all the layers and layers of cultural trappings in which these needs come wrapped in.

Take for example the basic human desire for sex. There is no reason to believe that present-day humans crave sex any less than did our ancestors, nor is there any reason to believe that people invest less time in pursuit of this need. Whether one approves or not, it has been asserted that the Internet has made it possible for more people to experience the pleasure of sexual materials and hookups than ever before in human history.[64] Also related to our human need for sex is our fascination with and valuing of beauty, particularly physical beauty. Of course, beauty is always "in the eye of the beholder," but the basic norms of beauty are strongly influenced by culture, with every culture having its own definitions and criteria of beauty. However, at its core, research has shown that the perception of attractiveness in others is strongly related to survival, since biologically and culturally, those with the greatest "beauty" are more often than not the healthiest and most fit, and thus the most desirable mates.[65]

Security and safety are always issues of high priority for people, and the individuals who ensure these needs are met for us are regularly accorded high acclaim—soldiers, fire fighters, first responders, and health providers. We value and seek out situations and resources that ensure our safety and security—safe neighborhoods, safe cars, and safe travel destinations. Ironically, despite the fact that modern humans are the safest people to have ever lived, with unprecedentedly safe homes and workplaces, an almost total lack of predatory animals, and widespread availability of advanced medicines designed to fight disease, concerns about safety seem to be as prevalent and as important to people as ever, if not more so.

Finally, we also value those most basic of all physical needs—food, shelter, and clothing. In today's world, where record numbers of people enjoy considerable affluence and plenty, concerns about these basic needs seem less pressing than in the past, but even so, no one is oblivious to these needs. With affluence and plenty has come a shifting of priorities; rather than merely valuing the fulfillment of these needs, now people most value the food, shelter, and clothing that come with the imprimatur of high cultural status attached. For example, we particularly admire and disproportionately value gourmet meals, architect-designed buildings, and "fashionable" clothing.

Collectively, then, we can see that value and well-being derive from each of the seven key domains of well-being-related needs. We find memorable those events that we believe positively enhance our sense of health, safety, and sexual satisfaction, our feelings of social relationship and status, our ability to feel a sense of intellectual understanding of, and control over, events in the world, and experiences that we find exceptional and significantly self-fulfilling. We find each of these different types of well-being-related experiences salient and memorable, but we are particularly drawn to experiences that combine multiple facets of well-being. Most of our stand-out memories are blended well-being-related memories. We remember the great meal we had on our first date with our loved one. We remember the building we were in when we first heard an unforgettable musical performance. We recall the outfit we were wearing, who was in attendance, and what was said on the day we were married. So many events in our life, so few that are truly memorable, but those that are, are almost always complex, multi-dimensional well-being-related memories, memories that we felt somehow or in some way, significantly related to either our short- and/or long-term success in life. And it is all of these understandings about the nature and role of well-being in the human condition, when combined, that lead us to the key insight and premise of this book.

CONNECTING WELL-BEING AND MUSEUM EXPERIENCES

What I have tried to clarify in this chapter is that the human tendency to selectively perceive particular life events as consistent with their personal, intellectual, physical, and social well-being is directly tied to the deep, underlying purpose of well-being, namely the evolutionary correlation between perceived well-being and greater short- and long-term success (i.e., survival).

From this perspective, we can see perception of well-being is not just something nice like feeling happy but rather an ongoing and fundamental necessity of life. That paying attention to what makes one feel whole and satisfied, while avoiding that which makes one feel limited and bad, are essential parts of life. The range of feelings associated with well-being, even if not fully or consciously understood by an individual, provide clues as to how that individual perceives what has value in their life. Feelings of well-being provide a person feedback as to what things they have done that are likely to be of lasting value, things likely to help them and/or their loved ones lead a more successful life, now or in the future.

The extensive evidence that millions of people, all over the globe, consistently report that they find museum experiences both satisfying and highly memorable,[66] combined with what we know about what makes something memorable, suggests the likelihood that there is a strong and direct link between museum experiences and perceived well-being. The only reason so many people would find museums both so satisfying and so indelibly memorable, considering the limitations of conscious awareness in general and linguistically retrievable memory in particular, would be if somehow, someway, these museum experiences were directly connected to people's sense of well-being. In other words, millions of people have had museum experiences, and for most, these experiences were perceived by them as contributing to their and/or their family's health, safety, social bonds or status, their ability to better understand and navigate the world in which they live, their sense of accomplishment, and/or their appreciation of themselves and their place in the world. Consciously, or more likely unconsciously, all these satisfied people must have perceived that their museum experiences in some way contributed to their or their family's long-term survival and success.

It seems clear that this link between museum experiences and enhanced well-being not only exists but is profound. It is profound because an appreciation and exploitation of this connection can be used by museum professionals as a veritable "Rosetta Stone," revealing how to decode the long elusive "language" of the museum experience. Armed with this newly translated "text," museums professionals might finally be able to achieve three fundamentally important, long sought-after goals:

> First, and central to the purpose of this book, this new understanding makes it clear how museums can best make the case for defining and measuring the value of the experiences they offer.
>
> Second, these understandings open the door to figuring out how to make museum experiences even more valuable and successful. It can provide museum professionals with clues as to how to invent a whole new generation of museums practices, practices designed to remain relevant and valuable for a public who themselves are changing and adapting in order to survive within a rapidly changing leisure and educational landscape.
>
> Third, and perhaps just as important as the first two, these understandings can allow museum professionals to expand and diversify who they serve and how. Since the pursuit of enhanced well-being is something *all* people aspire to, these insights should make it possible for museum professional to better understand how they can reach and satisfy the well-being-related needs of a much broader audience, including those who have been historically underserved by museums in the past.

Over the next four chapters, I will attempt to translate the writing that appears on this metaphorical Rosetta Stone. Each chapter will, in turn, feature a series of "best case" examples of the various ways in which people have historically utilized museums to satisfy and enhance their well-being, with each chapter focusing on one particular form of well-being. I will begin with examples of personal well-being, followed in turn by examples of intellectual, social, and physical well-being.

NOTES

1. See https://en.wikiquote.org/wiki/Albert_Einstein. Retrieved June 7, 2020.

2. For example, Cloninger, C. R. (2004). *Feeling Good: The Science of Well-Being.* Oxford: Oxford University Press.

Diener, E., and Biseas-Diener, R. (2008). *Happiness.* Malden, MA: Blackwell Publishing.

Dolan, P. (2014). *Happiness by Design: Finding Pleasure and Purpose in Everyday Life.* London: Penguin.

Eid, M., and Larsen, R. J. (Eds.). (2008).*The Science of Subjective Well-Being.* New York: The Guildford Press.

Ryff, C. D. (1989). "Happiness Is Everything, or Is It? Explorations on the Meaning of Psychological Well-Being." *Journal of Personality and Social Psychology* 57(6), 1069–81.

Ryff, C. D. (2014). "Psychological Well-Being Revisited: Advances in the Science and Practice of Eudaimonia." *Psychotherapy and Psychosomatics* 83(1), 10–28.

3. See Falk, J. H. (2018). *Born to Choose: Evolution, Self and Well-Being.* London: Routledge.

4. Durie, M. (1994). *Whaiora: Māori Health Development.* Auckland: Oxford University Press.

5. Lovern, L. (2008). "Native American Worldview and the Discourse on Disability." *Philosophy of Disability* 9(1). http://pieducators.com/sites/default/files/Native-American-World view-Discourse-on-Disability.pdf. Retrieved July 31, 2020.

6. Daley, B. (2014). "Indigenous Australians Offer a Broader Concept of Wellbeing." *The Conversation*, November 19, 2014. https://theconversation.com/indigenous-australians-offer-a-broader-concept-of-wellbeing-32887. Retrieved July 31, 2020.

7. "Sukha." Wikipedia. https://en.wikipedia.org/wiki/Sukha. Retrieved August 2, 2020.

8. Imafidon, E. (2012). "The Concept of Person in an African Culture and Its Implication for Social Order." *Lumina* 23(2). https://ejournals.ph/article.php?id=7365. August 2, 2020.

9. "Taoism." Wikipedia. https://en.wikipedia.org/wiki/Taoism. Retrieved August 2, 2020.

10. "Doctrine of the Mean." Wikipedia. https://en.wikipedia.org/wiki/Doctrine_of_the_Mean. Retrieved August 2, 2020.

11. Kraut, R. (2015). "Aristotle on Well-Being." In G. Fletcher (ed.), *Routledge Handbook of Philosophy of Well-Being*. London: Routledge.

12. See Ryff, C. D. (1989). "Happiness Is Everything, or Is It? Explorations on the Meaning of Psychological Well-Being." *Journal of Personality and Social Psychology* 57(6): 1069–81.

13. For example, Ryff, C. D. (2014). "Psychological Well-Being Revisited: Advances in the Science and Practice of Eudaimonia." *Psychotherapy and Psychosomatics* 83(1), 10–28.

Cloninger, C. R. (2004). *Feeling Good: The Science of Well-Being*. Oxford: Oxford University Press.

Diener, E., and Biseas-Diener, R. (2008). *Happiness*. Malden, MA: Blackwell Publishing.

Eid, M., and Larsen, R. J. (Eds.). (2008). *The Science of Subjective Well-Being*. New York: The Guildford Press.

14. For example, Ryff, C. D. (2014). "Psychological Well-Being Revisited: Advances in the Science and Practice of Eudaimonia." *Psychotherapy and Psychosomatics*, 83(1), 10–28.

Cloninger, C. R. (2004). *Feeling Good: The Science of Well-Being*. Oxford: Oxford University Press.

Diener, E., and Biseas-Diener, R. (2008). *Happiness*. Malden, MA: Blackwell Publishing.

Dolan, P. (2014). *Happiness by Design: Finding Pleasure and Purpose in Everyday Life*. London: Penguin

Eid, M., and Larsen, R. J. (Eds.). *The Science of Subjective Well-Being*. New York: The Guildford Press.

15. For example, Dodge, R., Daly, A., Huyton, J., and Sanders, L. (2012). "The Challenge of Defining Wellbeing." *International Journal of Wellbeing*, 2(3), 222–35.

16. Sartorius, N. (2006). "The Meaning of Health and Its Promotion." *Croatian Medical Journal* 47, 662–64.

17. Henrich, J., Heine, S. J., and Norenzayan, A. (2010). "The Weirdest People in the World?" *Behavioral and Brain Sciences* 33(2–3), 61–83.

18. Davis, T. (2019). "What Is Well-Being? Definition, Types, and Well-Being Skills." *Psychology Today*, January 2, 2019. https://www.psychologytoday.com/us/blog/click-here-happiness/201901/what-is-well-being-definition-types-and-well-being-skills. Retrieved June 21, 2020.

19. For some intriguing insights on this topic, one long neglected, I suggest some really intriguing recent books: Wohlleben, P. (2016). *The Hidden Life of Trees*. London: William Collins. Wohlleben, P. (2017). *The Inner Life of Animals*. Vancouver, CA: Greystone Books.

Coren, S. (2004). *How Dogs Think*. New York: Atria. Chamovitz, D. (2012). *What a Plant Knows*. New York: Scientific American/Farrar Straus and Giroux.

20. See Ma, W. (2016). "The Essence of Life." *Biology Direct*, 11(1). DOI: 10.1186/s13062-016-0150-5. Retrieved June 28, 2020. See also, Schrodinger E. (1944). *What Is Life?* Cambridge: Cambridge University Press. Watson, J. D. and Berry, A. (2003). *DNA: The Secret of Life*. New York: Knopf Doubleday.

21. For a fuller explanation, see Falk, J. H. (2018). *Born to Choose: Evolution, Self and Well-Being*. London: Routledge.

22. Darwin, C. (1859). *On the Origin of the Species by Means of Natural Selection*. London: John Murray.

23. Falk, J. H. (2018). *Born to Choose: Evolution, Self and Well-Being*. London: Routledge.

24. Kramer, M., and Alim, K. (2021). "Encoding Memory in Tube Diameter Hierarchy of Living Flow Network." *Proceedings of the National Academy of Sciences*. DOI: 10.1073/pnas.2007815118. See also, Technical University of Munich. (2021). "Memory without a Brain. How a Single Cell Slime Mold Makes Smart Decisions." SciTechDaily, February 26, 2021. https://scitechdaily.com/memory-without-a-brain-how-a-single-cell-slime-mold-makes-smart-decisions/. Retrieved February 27, 2021. Sayin, S., De Backer, J.-F., Siju, K. P., Wosniack, M., Lewis, L., Frisch, L.-M., Gansen, B., Schlegel, P., Edmondson-Stait, A., Sharifi, N., Fisher, C., Calle-Schuler, S., Lauritzen, J. S., Bock, D., Costa, M., Jefferis, G., Gjorgjieva, J., and Kadow, I. G. (2019). "A Neural Circuit Arbitrates between Persistence and Withdrawal in Hungry *Drosophila*." *Neuron*. DOI: 10.1016/j.neuron.2019.07.028.

25. Wagner, G. P., and Tomlinson, G. (2020). "Extending the Explanatory Scope of Evolutionary Theory: The Origin of Historical Kinds of Biology and Culture." https://doi.org/10.20944/preprints202004.0025.v1. Retrieved June 24, 2020.

26. For a fuller description, see Falk, J. H. (2018). *Born to Choose: Evolution, Self and Well-Being*. London: Routledge.

27. Martin, W., and Russell, M. J. (2003). "On the Origin of Cells: A Hypothesis for the Evolutionary Transitions from Abiotic Geochemistry to Chemoautotrophic Prokaryotes, and from Prokaryotes to Nucleated Cells." *Philosophical Transactions of the Royal Society of London, B-Biological Sciences* 358(1429), 59–85. Also, Margulis, L., and Sagan, D. (1986). *Microcosmos*. New York: Summit Books.

28. Torday, J. (2016). "The Cell as the First Niche Construction." *Biology* 5, 19–26.

29. Engelhart, A., Adamala, K. and Szostak, J. (2016). "A Simple Physical Mechanism Enables Homeostasis in Cells." *Nature Chemistry* 8(5), 448–53. Also, Torday, J. (2015). "Homeostasis as the Mechanism of Evolution." *Biology* 4, 573–90. Woese, C. (1998). "The Universal Ancestor." *Proceedings of the National Academy of Sciences (USA)* 95(12), 6854–59. And, Yin, Z., Pascual, C. and Klionsky, D. (2016). "Autophagy: Machinery and Regulation." *Microbial Cell* 3(12), 588–96.

30. Woese, C. (1998). "The Universal Ancestor." *Proceedings of the National Academy of Sciences* (USA) 95(12), 6854–59.

Gramling, C. (2016). "Hints of Oldest Life on Earth." *Science*, August 31, 2016. http://www.sciencemag.org/news/2016/08/hints-oldest-fossil-life-found-greenland-rocks. Retrieved August 31, 2016

31. For additional detail, see Falk, J. H. (2018). *Born to Choose: Evolution, Self and Well-Being*. London: Routledge.

32. For more on the process of "exaptation," see Adami, C., Ofria, C., and Collier, T. C. (2000). "Evolution of Biological Complexity." *Proceedings of the National Academy of Sciences* (USA) 97, 4463–68.

33. For more detail, see Falk, J. H. (2018). *Born to Choose: Evolution, Self and Well-Being*. London: Routledge.

34. The terms *individuality* and *continuity* come from Wiggins, D. (2001). *Sameness and Substance Renewed*, second edition. Cambridge, Cambridge University Press.

35. See Brown, S., and Gao, X. (2011). "The Neuroscience of Beauty." *Scientific American*, September 27, 2011. https://www.scientificamerican.com/article/the-neuroscience-of-beauty/. Retrieved June 21, 2020.

36. Adami, C., Ofria, C., and Collier, T. C. (2000). "Evolution of Biological Complexity." *Proceedings of the National Academy of Sciences* (USA) 97, 4463–68. See also, Torday, J. S. (2015). "A Central Theory of Biology." *Medical Hypothese*, 85, 49–57.

37. Maslow, A. (1943). "A Theory of Human Motivation." *Psychological Review* 50(4), 370–96.

38. For example, Devonis, D. C. (2014). *History of Psychology 101*. New York: Springer. See also, Hunt, E., and Collander, D. (2014). *Social Science: An Introduction to the Study of Society*, fifteenth edition. London: Routledge. Wikipedia. (2020). "Maslow's Hierarchy of Needs." https://en.wikipedia.org/wiki/Maslow%27s_hierarchy_of_needs. Retrieved July 5, 2020.

39. Falk, J. H. (2018). *Born to Choose: Evolution, Self and Well-Being*. London: Routledge.

40. For example, Kenrick, D. T., Griskevicius, V., Neuberg, S. L., and Schaller, M. (2010). "Renovating the Pyramid of Needs: Contemporary Extensions Built upon Ancient Foundations." *Perspectives on Psychological Science*, 5, 292–314. See also, Zimmer, C. (2014). "Secrets of the Brain." *National Geographic* 225(2), 28–57. Eagleman, D. (2015). *The Brain: The Story of You*. New York: Pantheon.

41. See Brown, S., and Gao, X. (2011). "The Neuroscience of Beauty." *Scientific American*, September 27, 2011. https://www.scientificamerican.com/article/the-neuroscience-of-beauty/. Retrieved June 21, 2020.

42. The total number of combinations possible if one randomly "mixed" seven different modalities of need together would be about five thousand.

43. The total number of combinations possible if one randomly "mixed" several thousand different types of need together would be a number with more than 250 zeros after it.

44. Torday, J. (2015). "Homeostasis as the Mechanism of Evolution." *Biology* 4, 573–90.

45. For additional detail, see Falk, J. H. (2018). *Born to Choose: Evolution, Self and Well-Being*. London: Routledge.

46. Markowsky, G. (2004). "Information Theory." *Encyclopedia Britannica*. https://www.britannica.com/science/information-theory/Physiology. Retrieved June 26, 2020.

47. "Consciousness." Merriam-Webster. https://www.merriam-webster.com/dictionary/consciousness. Retrieved June 24, 2020.

48. Van Gulick, R. (2004). "Consciousness." *Stanford Encyclopedia of Philosophy*. Palo Alto, CA: Metaphysics Research Lab, Stanford University. Also, Falk, J. H. (2018). *Born to Choose: Evolution, Self and Well-Being*. London: Routledge.

49. Dolan, P. (2014). *Happiness by Design: Finding Pleasure and Purpose in Everyday Life*. London: Penguin.

50. Jaynes, J. (1976). *The Origin of Consciousness in the Breakdown of the Bicameral Mind*. Boston: Houghton Mifflin, 23.

51. Kahneman, D. (2011). *Thinking, Fast and Slow.* New York: Farrar, Straus and Giroux.

52. Jaynes, J. (1976). *The Origin of Consciousness in the Breakdown of the Bicameral Mind.* Boston: Houghton Mifflin. See also, Scaruffi, A. (2013). *The Nature of Consciousness: The Structures of Life and the Meaning of Matter.* https://www.scaruffi.com/nature/preface.html. Retrieved June 27, 2013.

53. Scaruffi, A. (2013). *The Nature of Consciousness: The Structures of Life and the Meaning of Matter.* https://www.scaruffi.com/nature/preface.html. Retrieved June 27, 2013.

54. Edelman, G., and Tononi, G. (2000). "Reentry and the Dynamic Core." In T. Metzinger (ed.), *Neural Correlates of Consciousness: Empirical and Conceptual Questions,* 121–38. Cambridge, MA: MIT Press. See also, Freeman, W. (2000). *How Brains Make Up Their Mind.* New York: Columbia University Press.

55. Wegner, D. M. (2002). *The Illusion of Conscious Will.* Cambridge, MA: MIT Press.

56. Siegel, J. (2005). *The Idea of the Self: Thought and Experience in Western Europe since the Eighteenth Century.* Cambridge: Cambridge University Press.

57. See Peacock, S., and Patel, S. (2008). "Cultural Influences on Pain." *Reviews in Pain* 1(2), 6–9.

58. For example, Ryff, C. D. (2014). "Psychological Well-Being Revisited: Advances in the Science and Practice of Eudaimonia." *Psychotherapy & Psychosomatics,* 83(1), 10–28. See also, Eid, M., and Larsen, R. J. (Eds.). (2008). *The Science of Subjective Well-Being.* New York: The Guildford Press. Diener, E. (Ed.). (2009). *The Science of Well-Being: The Collected Works of Ed Diener.* Dordrecht: Springer. Dolan, P. (2014). *Happiness by Design: Finding Pleasure and Purpose in Everyday Life.* London: Penguin.

59. For more on the cultural bias of Western social scientists, see Henrich, J., Heine, S. J., and Norenzayan, A. (2010). "The Weirdest People in the World?" *Behavioral and Brain Sciences* 33(2–3), 61–83. Accordingly, extreme caution needs to be used when inferring that just because some *weird* person experienced well-being in a particular way, all people experience well-being in this way.

60. Diamond, J. (2012). *The World until Yesterday.* New York: Viking.

61. Hamblin, J. (2014). "Buy Experiences, Not Things." *The Atlantic,* October 7, 2014. https://www.theatlantic.com/business/archive/2014/10/buy-experiences/381132/. Retrieved October 25, 2020.

62. See Donald, M. (2012). "Evolutionary Origins of Autobiographical Memory Systems: A Retrieval Hypothesis." In D. Berntsen and D. C. Rubin (eds.), *Understanding Autobiographical Memory: Theories and Approaches,* 269–89. Cambridge: Cambridge University Press.

63. See Van Vugt, M., and Tybur, J. M. (2015). "The Evolutionary Foundations of Status and Hierarchy: Dominance, Prestige, Power, and Leadership." In D. Buss (ed.), *Handbook of Evolutionary Psychology, second edition,* 788–809. New York: Wiley.

64. Grubbs, J., Wright, P., Braden, A., Wilt, J., and Kraus, S. (2019). "Internet Pornography Use and Sexual Motivation: A Systematic Review and Integration." *Annals of International Communication Association* 43(2), February 20, 2019. https://www.tandfonline.com/doi/abs/10.1080/23808985.2019.1584045?journalCode=rica20. Retrieved July 12, 2020.

65. Perry, S. J. (1998). "A Study of Physical Appearance and Level of Attraction to the Opposite Sex." *Modern Psychological Studies* 6(2), 12–17. See also, Honekopp, J., Rudolph, U., Beier, L., Liebert, A., and Mueller, C. (2007). "Physical Attractiveness of Face and Body as Indicators of Physical Fitness in Men." *Evolution and Human Behavior* 28(2), 106–111.

66. Falk, J. H., and Dierking, L. D. (1995). "Recalling the Museum Experience." *Journal of Museum Education* 20(2), 10–13. See also, Falk, J. H., and Dierking, L. D. (1996).

"Recollections of Elementary School Field Trips." In D. Herrmann and M. Johnson (eds.), *The Third Practical Aspects of Memory Conference*, 512–26. University of Maryland: College Park. Bamberger, Y. (2008). "An Experience for the Lifelong Journey: The Long-Term Effect of a Class Visit to a Science Center." *Visitor Studies* 11(2), 198–212. And, Anderson, D., Storksdieck, M., and Spock, M. (2007). "Understanding the Long-Term Impacts of Museum Experiences." In J. H. Falk, L. Dierking, and S. Foutz (eds.), *In Principle, in Practice: Museums as Learning Institutions*, 197–215. Lanham, MD: AltaMira Press.

II

VALUE ACHIEVED

4

Personal Well-Being

What does not satisfy when we find it was not the thing we were desiring.

—C.S. Lewis[1]

I go to museums all the time, both for work and for pleasure. Despite all these museum visits, one experience particularly stands out even though it occurred nearly thirty years ago. It was Tuesday, December 22, 1992, and I was visiting Amsterdam with my wife and then thirteen-year-old son. On this particular day we decided to visit the Rijksmuseum, which was less than a block from the hotel where we were staying. On this particular day, my visit motivation could best be described as falling within the category I have described as an "explorer,"[2] someone highly interested in general knowledge but with no particular content or object agenda. I was eager to just see what I could see and discover what I could discover.

The Rijksmuseum, for those who have never been there, is a large museum housed in a building that first opened in 1885. My wife, son, and I wandered through the museum individually and at our own pace. Not surprisingly, the Rijksmuseum has a large and impressive collection of Dutch masters' paintings, which was fine with me since I happen to be very fond of this style of art. However, after more than an hour of wandering through darkened room after darkened room, each filled with seventeenth- and eighteenth-century Dutch paintings, even I was growing a bit weary. Then, suddenly and unexpectedly, I saw a painting that made me stop dead in my tracks. Although relatively small, only about 39 × 46 cm (15 × 18 inches), the painting was so striking and so different from all of the other paintings I had just seen that it literally took my breath away. There before me was Johannes Vermeer's *Woman Reading a Letter*.

I of course knew who Vermeer was and had seen images of his work before in art books, but I had never actually seen an original. This was several years before

Vermeer exploded as a cultural icon due to a major blockbuster exhibition of his works that toured the United States in 1995, and nearly a decade before the book *Girl with a Pearl Earring* and then the movie of the same name became best sellers. There was just this painting and a couple of his other works in this room, and nothing else—not even any other people.

I was in awe at the beauty of the painting. The light just radiated from the woman's forehead as she read a letter. The woman in the painting actually shows little emotion as she reads the letter, and of course, we have no idea what the letter is about. Yet, the emotion emanating from the painting is electric. I was so moved by this painting that after several minutes of staring at it I felt compelled to go looking for my wife so she too could share this moment with me. Then, together we stared, we talked, and we stared some more.

Although I remember feeling like I stood in front of this painting forever, it probably was only about fifteen minutes or so. Then my wife and I moved on and found our son. Although I cannot remember the details, I know we continued to talk about this painting later that day, likely over a wonderful meal, as well as after we got home. And now, even though more than a quarter of a century has passed since that day, both the events surrounding my almost accidental discovery of the painting, and the image of this pregnant woman in a blue dress reading a letter, have remained indelibly burned into my memory. I can honestly say that seeing this painting feels like one of the more memorable experiences of my life.

I relay this story not because it is so unique but rather because it is remarkably common. Millions of people have experiences like this every year in museums—obviously not exactly like this and certainly not always related to art, but consistently people have highly emotionally moving, awe-inspiring, and thus memorable experiences. These kinds of experiences are transformative for people and have been shown to result in increased feelings of well-being.[3]

Early in my career, as I was just beginning to try to wrap my mind around the museum experience, I started randomly interviewing anyone who would humor me about their museum memories. For example, in the 1980s I was flying across country and was sitting next to a middle-aged white man. We struck up a conversation. I asked him about his work and he asked about mine. I told him I worked at the Smithsonian Institution and then asked him if he had ever been there. Here is what he said:

A: Oh, it must have been nearly forty years ago since I was at the Smithsonian. I went with my family—my father, mother, and older brother. I was eight or ten years old. We went as part of a family vacation.

Q: Wow, that was a long time ago. What do you remember about the visit?

A: I remember the museum. It was a massive building, full of lots and lots of hallways and so many rooms. We also saw the Washington Monument and the Jefferson Memorial that day; we went to the Smithsonian last.

> I remember being sort of bored. We spent hours there looking at art and butterflies, and all that sort of thing, until late in the afternoon. My mother really wanted us to go, but I didn't want to go. My mother was particularly interested in dresses—First Ladies' dresses, and other period gowns. My father just patiently watched. My brother was bored like I was.
>
> Q: Anything else?
>
> A: Yes, the thing I remember best was seeing the *Spirit of St. Louis.* It was suspended from the ceiling. I had heard about it in school, and I marveled at the history. I was really struck by the way it was designed, the fact that it had no forward [facing] windows. I had never realized that Lindbergh couldn't even see in front of him as he flew, that he was flying blind. I was also impressed by the scalloped effect of the metal. It was such a weird, special type of plane. I remember just how amazed I was by that plane. I was so inspired I went home wanting to be like him.[4]

Although this man primarily remembered being bored from spending hours looking at art and butterflies, and all sorts of other things during that long-ago family vacation to DC, he became quite animated when he described his experience viewing the *Spirit of St. Louis.* When this man was growing up, in the 1920s and early 1930s, Charles Lindbergh was a national hero and celebrity. Virtually every school child would have known about Lindbergh's solo flight across the Atlantic and have read about the *Spirit of St. Louis*. We know that this individual knew about Lindbergh and his plane before arriving at the museum that day because he said, "I had heard about it in school." However, for this man, like it was for me with Vermeer, sort of knowing about something was not the same as actually seeing the real thing. And like my nearly thirty-year-old art museum experience, what stood out in memory for this man after nearly forty years was not only the details of what he saw but the feelings that he had at that moment—"I remember just how amazed I was by that plane." He remembered feeling so inspired, he "went home wanting to be like him." Clearly something very important is going on here.

PEAK PERSONAL EXPERIENCES

These types of "epiphanies" or "peak personal experiences" have, not surprisingly, drawn the attention of a wide assortment of psychologists. As with so many types of human behavior, the pioneering psychologist William James was among the first to call out these experiences and provide an initial description.[5] So too did another pioneer of psychology, Carl Jung.[6] However, the individual most associated with legitimizing the investigation of these types of experiences was Abraham Maslow, who used the term *self-actualization* to describe these types of singularly momentous personal events. According to Maslow, these are moments when the individual is able to bring together and "actualize" his or her full personal potential, as well as moments when a person feels a sense of "wonder, awe, reverence, humility, surrender, and even worship before the greatness of the experience."[7] In my case, it would have been my sense of appreciation for a person achieving a pinnacle of human creativity, of seeing something truly beautiful. While in the case of the man sitting next to me on the plane, it would have been his appreciation for a person accomplishing an amazing feat of skill and determination, and perhaps he too perceived a sense of beauty in the strange craft that was the *Spirit of St. Louis*.[8] Mihaly Csikszentmihalyi, another notable psychologist, has also talked about peak experiences, but he would have described what my seatmate and I experienced as being in a state of *flow*, a mental state in which we were totally immersed in a feeling of energized focus, full involvement, and enjoyment in the process of the activity.[9] Without disagreeing with either Maslow or Csikszentmihalyi, I would call both of these museum experiences examples of heightened well-being.

Over many years, and based upon hundreds of interviews and surveys with individuals from many countries representing individuals engaged in a wide range of activities, psychologists have discovered an amazingly consistent pattern in the ways people describe experiences of peak personal engagement and satisfaction. It did not matter if the person was a museumgoer, an artist, rock climber or chess player, scientist or street sweeper, professional dancer or amateur naturalist, when in a state of peak well-being, individuals describe being completely absorbed in what they are doing. They also feel a great sense of control, as they perceive that everything in the world functionally seems to shrink down to just that thing they are focusing on at that moment. Combining observations from both Maslow[10] and Csikszentmihalyi and his colleague Jeanne Nakamura,[11] typical characteristics of these kinds of experiences include the following:

- A feeling of intense and focused concentration on the present moment
- A sense of spontaneity, with a merging of action and awareness
- A loss of reflective self-consciousness, free of inner conflict or disharmony
- A sense of effortlessness and personal control or agency over the situation or activity
- A distortion of the subjective experience of time, time "flies by"
- A perception of the experience as intrinsically rewarding, and highly satisfying
- A sense of having done something important, memorable

All of these qualities perfectly describe what happens when a person perceives that their well-being-related needs are in positive balance.[12] These are joyful and energizing moments, moments that feel like life is definitely worth living. Adults are not the only ones who experience these types of moments. Children too seem able to get into this positive state of mind; in fact, they may be able to be in this mode more frequently and more readily than do adults! In children, we typically call this highly focused and engaged state "play."[13] Just like adults, when children become deeply engaged in play, they too experience a heightened sense of well-being and pleasure.[14] Examples abound of children having these types of peak, play-related experiences while visiting children's museums, zoos, and science centers.[15]

Because these types of well-being/flow/peak/play experiences are so energizing and pleasurable, individuals experiencing them will strive to keep them going for as long as possible. Sustaining these experiences for very long, though, turns out to be difficult. People do not live in a bubble where they can forever keep the vicissitudes of the world at bay. Whether it is the dehydration of cells creating an overpowering thirst or someone's companion indicating that it is time to move on, eventually some other need impinges on the person, making it impossible to remain single-mindedly focused on satisfying this one particular, well-being-related need, no matter how good it feels. For this reason, peak personal experiences are always transient. Despite their relative brevity, these types of experiences elicit strong positive emotions and create deep feelings of well-being, and because of this, people find them extremely memorable and attach a high degree of meaningfulness to such experiences. For all these reasons, in general people are also highly motivated to want to try, if possible, to have these kinds of experiences repeatedly, all in the hope of replicating these powerful feelings again.[16]

What is going on the brain turns out to be very interesting and very revealing. Although "peak" experiences such as my "discovery" of Vermeer, my seatmate's encounter with the *Spirit of St. Louis,* or the sheer joy exhibited by a child playing at a water table in a children's museum all seem like examples of some kind of very special, very unique type of human experience, neuroscientists have discovered that neurologically, these experiences appear to be not as unique as most people, including most psychologists, have historically imagined them to be. It turns out that the mental processes that undergird these "peak" events are virtually indistinguishable from mental processing events that happen all the time. When such "events" happen, each is perceived in the moment as important, each commands the immediate and focused attention of the individual, but only a few enjoy the "cultural privileging" that the above examples have received.

Recent brain studies have discovered that neurologically, museum experiences such as those described above, are totally indistinguishable from other, more common positive experiences like the joy of biting into a perfectly ripe peach or the attention-grabbing experience of seeing a really beautiful person walking past you on the street. For hundreds of thousands or perhaps even millions of years, our ancestors came to associate such pleasurable emotions as wonder, amazement, beauty, delight, and awe with evolutionary success.[17] All of these "peak personal experiences" activate similar regions of the brain[18] and all create similar cascades of pleasure-inducing neurotransmitters and hormones, including dopamine, oxytocin, serotonin, endorphins, and adrenaline.[19] From an evolutionary perspective, all of these time-stopping, emotion-laden, memorable experiences serve a similar biological function. They all are experiences that strongly correlate with the realities and circumstances we culturally and biologically have evolved to associate with increased fitness and survivability.

What is interesting is that many in our current society would consider the ability to discriminate and appreciate a fine piece of art as a higher more refined capacity than the ability to discriminate and appreciate a fine piece of fruit. Certainly, there are and have been many cultures where the opposite would be true. From an evolutionary perspective, what is important is the ability to discriminate and appreciate those things that will result in enhanced survivability. Brain research suggests that for modern humans living in the West, appreciation of both fine art and fine fruit seem to qualify.

Cultural biases aside, memorability here is the key. Not only did we evolve to have and appreciate these experiences in the moment, but we also evolved to remember these experiences so that we can hang onto, and to the degree possible, repeat them again in the future. Since, after all, any experience that allows one to achieve well-being is an experience worth replicating. Over evolutionary time, humans evolved increasingly sophisticated conscious awareness, memory, and retrieval skills. These cognitive tools in turn enabled humans to become ever better at recognizing and, when possible, replicating these well-being-related experiences.

Add language and social arrangements into this formula and the value of these personal well-being experiences becomes even further magnified. Not only does discovering an exquisite piece of art or a one-of-a-kind societal icon create a sense of awe, wonder, and personal pleasure, but also if someone can share that moment with someone else, it also has the potential to allow the benefits of that experience to be extended beyond the moment. Sharing the experience affords the experiencer a way to relive that experience, and it also provides a mechanism for helping to reinforce and maintain a memory of that experience.[20] This is why only rarely does an individual experience a moment of peak personal well-being and opt to keep that moment totally to him- or herself. This seems particularly true of peak personal experiences we associate with spirituality and creativity.

This propensity to want to "hang onto" and reinforce the value of these well-being-associated experiences turns out not to be limited to just "peak" personal experiences. Clearly only a relatively small number of moments in a person's life can truly be said to qualify as a "peak" experience, but everyone has a variety of other experiences—let's call them "mini-peak" personal experiences that are also highly memorable and sharable. These "mini-peak" personal moments tend to be associated with feelings of pleasure and satisfaction, and these experiences are worth taking notice of and being appreciated for what they are—personal well-being-related experiences.

THE SATISFACTION OF THINGS

The following is an excerpt from an interview I recently conducted with a dear friend, a white woman in her mid-sixties who I will call Linden. I asked Linden to tell me about an experience she had related to a museum visit, one that stood out for her as really memorable. This is what she said:

> We were in Wisconsin to see my family. We also were there to attend the wedding of the son of dear friends of ours. We had an extra day and went to Taliesin 1, Frank Lloyd

> Wright's house. Frank Lloyd Wright is a really important person to me. My husband and I have visited several of his houses, including Falling Waters, visited an exhibition of someone who was similar to him in Glasgow, and his work influenced the design of two of our homes. Anyway, I could go on.
>
> I've also read several books about him. In particular, I'm really interested in how he dealt with the women in his life, and I believe I bought a book related to that during this particular visit, but I'm not sure. In fact, I can't even remember many details of the house, but what really stands out for me as special about that visit was that we went into the gift shop. I always like to get something at the gift shop, but for some reason, I was not very inspired. I may have bought a book, the one I mentioned about Wright's wife, but what I do remember as special was that my husband bought me a beautiful Frank Lloyd Wright–design scarf. It's all black silk, and it has panels of sheer silk intermixed with opaque patterns of simple, geometric shapes, and I keep it in my place for special scarves. It's the only thing that my husband has ever bought me related to Frank Lloyd Wright—so it is very special to me. It is also special to me because of how important that weekend was.
>
> It was around our anniversary. We went out to dinner and I wore that scarf—that is part of the scarf's story. Now, whenever I wear it, I think of my husband, my visit to Taliesin, that whole day, that week—my time with my sister, the wedding of our friends' son who we saw grow up—all those memories. For me, that scarf is not just a scarf, it is a way for me to remember an important time in my life.

As the above interview suggests, Linden, like most people, did not have any problem thinking of a particularly memorable museum-related experience. Also like most people I have talked to, her story revolved around a particular thing she saw or did—an exhibition, object, or event. However, what was different about Linden's story was the nature of the object that was memorable for her. It is far from unusual for people to remember, often fondly, objects and things they bought in the gift shop, though most feel a little guilty about sharing those memories with me—culturally, we know the gift shop is not supposed to be the focus of our museum experiences. Fortunately, Linden was sufficiently uninhibited to share this memory. The memory she shared was quite genuine and important for it revealed one of the important but often little-discussed ways present-day museums support users' personal well-being.

Possessions are one of the things that define us as a species. Even hunting-gathering peoples manage to collect and treasure possessions, albeit by necessity they have fewer possessions than more sedentary people. By contrast, our closest living relatives, the great apes, possess nothing. Chimpanzees, for example, employ crude tools and build sleeping nests but abandon them after one use. At some point along our evolutionary trajectory, human-like creatures began not only making stuff but hoarding stuff as well. Evidence of "stuff" first appears in the archaeological record some 2.5 million years ago in the form of stone tools; but of course people likely collected and carried around a variety of objects—gourds or bladders for carrying water, clubs for protection and predation—not prone to surviving the ravages of time. However, early in human history, even these objects were likely considered expendable.[21]

As humans continued to evolve, particularly culturally, humans started investing more time and effort in the creation of objects with the result that these objects became increasingly valuable. According to University of Connecticut in Storrs archaeologist Sally McBrearty, the concept of ownership took off with the advent of the spear and arrow heads, which first appeared in Africa at least three hundred thousand years ago. "They are made to specific designs that vary from group to group," she says. "The spears and arrows took time and effort to make and were probably the property of a single hunter."[22] Hunters would have retrieved these weapons from kills and used them repeatedly. Another key early possession was probably fire. Some contemporary hunter-gatherer groups carry embers around with them, and thus in this way "possess" fire. Our ancestors likely did the same thing. The earliest convincing evidence of controlled use of fire dates to around eight hundred thousand years ago.[23] All of these possessions would have been valued because they directly enhanced survival and arguably would have become forever associated with well-being.

The rise of increasingly complex, sedentary human cultures also drove the creation and hoarding of things. Gary Feinman, of the University of Illinois in Chicago, argues that our human urge to accumulate stuff is based on a desire to minimize risk. "When people settled down, they became more susceptible to environmental disaster," he says.[24] A way to insure against this was to domesticate and store surplus food—a process that created the need for possessions, not only of food stuffs directly but also the tools required for gathering and hoarding both plant and animal types of food. Another insurance policy was to develop relationships with neighboring groups through the exchange of goods. Eventually objects became valued not only for their utility but also as prestige goods to advertise the skill or social status of their owner. Certain objects became valued for these reasons alone, for example, jewelry and fine clothing such as scarves. In fact, some archaeologists, such as Ian Hodder of Stanford University, argue that societies could not have become complex and hierarchical without an associated "material culture."[25]

Fast forward to today, all modern people own and value a wide variety of objects, arguably more than needed. Value judgments aside, clearly these objects, like the example of Linden's scarf above, have the ability to bring people great satisfaction and often represent an important aspect of both an individual's personal as well as collective identity.[26] The fact that people like Linden use museums as vehicles for building their identity in this way is non-trivial and worthy of notice and note. The value giftshop sales create transcends the revenues generated. As the example above highlights, the true value these museum stores generate might actually be the enhanced personal well-being they deliver to countless users.

Of course, the vast majority of stuff museums offer up to the public is not on sale in the gift shop but preserved on display within exhibitions. However, in a very real sense, these items too are available for "acquisition" just not in the same way as the scarf that was gifted to Linden.

With greater affluence and education, more and more people are buying not just things but experiences.[27] The ability to seek out and savor quality experiences can end up providing much the same satisfaction as those associated with actually owning something; particularly if the experiences are associated with things that are directly relevant and meaningful to the individual.[28] Interestingly, recent research has shown that people who spent money on experiences rather than material items were on average happier and felt their money was better spent.[29] As more than two decades of research has documented, typically the thrill of purchasing something fades quickly, but the joy and memories of experiences, whether derived from the thrill of seeing the *Spirit of St. Louis* for the first time or receiving a gift of a Frank Lloyd Wright scarf, can last a lifetime.[30] This is because ultimately the real value to a person of an object or an experience depends upon how that object or experience supports and builds that person's sense of self.[31]

Thus, beyond merely providing objects to visitors so that they can "learn" or "appreciate" better, museums also appear to support well-being by creating opportunities for people, either through experiences or purchases, to build their sense of self. As suggested by Jay Rounds,[32] and made clear by my earlier work, people regularly utilize museums as ways to support and build their sense of personal identity. People find these identity-building experiences, including and particularly within museum contexts, emotionally reinforcing and ultimately very satisfying.[33] Not surprisingly, there is also strong evidence to support the contention that humans evolved to believe that experiences that elicited these kinds of feelings of self-reinforcement and satisfaction, these "mini-peak" personal experiences, were experiences worth remembering and repeating.[34] Subliminally, we understand that these types of personal well-being-related experiences correlate with enhanced survival and fitness.

SPIRITUALITY AND CREATIVITY

The following is an excerpt from an extended interview with an individual who, for the sake of anonymity, I will call Portia.[35] Portia is Jamaican American, who at the time of this interview, was in her early thirties, and taught mathematics at the college level.

Q: Do you remember your last visit to an art museum?

A: Yes, it was about a year ago at least, to this very museum [National Gallery of Art].

Q: Do you remember if it was a weekday or a weekend?

A: It was the Sabbath. It was Saturday.

Q: With whom did you go to the museum?

A: My boyfriend at the time; now he's my husband.

Q: Whose decision was it to come?

A: We stumbled upon it; we were just wandering around. We were looking for the [Smithsonian's] Natural History Museum—and we still haven't found it—we were going there [Natural History Museum] and ended up at the art museum.

Q: So it was okay for you to visit an art museum?

A: On Saturday it is the Sabbath. So God said take pleasure in my creation on the Sabbath. So it didn't really matter whether it was a natural history museum or an art museum.

Q: So your purpose in visiting was spiritual?

A: Yes, to cherish God's creation, to take a part and take notice. But also to find out more for ourselves, to enrich ourselves in the process.

Q: What did you think was the most memorable thing you saw at the museum?

A: The most memorable thing was that it was interesting. That is why we came back today.

Q: Any specific exhibition stand out in memory?

A: The whole thing.

Q: What about particular works of art?

A: Yes, there was a beautiful painting that was quite abstract but reminded me of a sunrise. It had amazing shades of reds, pinks, and oranges; all seeming to emanate from one source. It reminded me of the times I've sat and watched sunrises and thought about the glory of God and how much I have to be grateful for each and every day.

Below is a blog written by Mark Champkins, a celebrated British inventor and industrial designer who for two years was "Inventor in Residence" at the Science Museum in London.

There are a couple of items in *Making the Modern World* that have directly inspired new products. One of the first glass cases that you encounter in the gallery contains what looks like a whisk with an accompanying pot. In fact it is the apparatus, made by James Prescott Joule, that defines the standard unit of energy, or "Joule." Filling the pot with water, a "Joule" of energy is defined as the energy required to whisk the water until it has raised the temperature of the water by one degree.

This device got me thinking about how SI units are defined, and of measurement in general, and led to the creation of the *Word Count Pencil*, a pencil that has a scale printed along its length, to estimate the number of words you have written as the pencil wears out.[36]

Like the previous examples in this chapter, both Portia and Mr. Champkins had memorable museum experiences; both had experiences they described as inspiring. For Portia, the inspiration she derived from her museum experience was very expansive and spiritual. She describes how her experience helped her make a connection between the beauty of art and the beauty of nature, which in turn helped her appreciate why she should "be grateful for each and every day." By contrast, Mark Champkins describes how seeing a particular object and thinking about its use helped him make the creative leap to applying a similar idea to an entirely different kind of object. Why would I combine these two stories here? Spirituality and creativity seem like such very different human attributes. Actually, they are not.

Humans, like all living things, are constantly faced with challenges and uncertainty, and like all creatures, humans have evolved various strategies for resolving these. However, unlike other living creatures, humans evolved the ability to harness conscious awareness to the task of answering questions and solving problems. This ability, inherent in both creativity and spirituality, has allowed humans to project their thoughts forward and backward in time, to infer cause and effect, generate abstract ideas, and through this process arrive at novel explanations and solutions. Although some people are certainly more spiritual and/or creative than others, spirituality and creativity are not rarified capacities that only a few exceptional people possess—quite the contrary.

The capacity for spirituality and creativity are a defining characteristic of our entire species. All humans seem to innately have the ability and desire to explain, and through explanation, they exercise a degree of control over the events in their world. Creativity and spirituality appear to have evolved as a mechanism for helping fulfill this need. Although not always accurate, both creative and spiritual approaches to solving problems have proven sufficiently successful, enough of the time to have become highly selected for within the human behavioral repertoire.

That most readers of this book buy into the Eurasian intellectual tradition of viewing creative acts like art, science, and religion as totally unique and discrete human endeavors should not blind us to the fact that for most of human history, and even still today, most people would find such distinctions strange.[37] Based upon compelling anthropological and archaeological evidence, it appears that for the vast majority of human history, spirituality and creativity were tightly intertwined. I have argued that it is highly likely that they co-evolved.[38] Even today, across thousands of indigenous cultural groups, it is nearly impossible to discern any real boundaries between the practice of art, music, dance, technology, and spirituality.

Whether separate or distinct, though, what is important to understand is that both capabilities, historically and still in modern humans, enhance human survival and well-being. For example, there is considerable evidence that creative acts like singing, doing art, or dancing reduce stress,[39] so too does spirituality. For example, studies of modern urban dwellers find that individuals invoke their religion most when they experience difficult and trying circumstances.[40] Studies of hunter-gatherers show similar results; individuals use religion to help them deal with trying circumstances, such as a string of unsuccessful hunts or the fears associated with voyaging in a small boat during times of bad weather.[41] Researchers have also found that individual as well as group prayer reduces blood pressure, high blood pressure being a reliable index of psychological stress and a precursor to a range of illnesses.[42]

The interview with Portia and the blog by Mark Champkins suggests that "aha"-inducing museum experiences can result in spiritual/creative inspirations that facilitate enhanced satisfaction and well-being. Such experiences may be relatively rare, but clearly they happen. Perhaps the most celebrated example of the inspirational value of museum experiences is the case of Pablo Picasso's encounter in 1907 with African masks while visiting an African Art exhibition at the Ethnographic Museum in Paris. This museum experience is credited with helping Picasso to free himself from the long-practiced conventions of traditional European art and directly resulted in his painting *Les Demoiselles d'Avignon*, a work considered by many to be a seminal landmark in the development of modern art.[43]

It is highly unlikely that the museum professionals who mounted the exhibitions at the National Gallery of Art in Washington, Science Museum in London, or the Ethnographic Museum in Paris, visited respectively by Portia, Mark Champkins, and Pablo Picasso, designed them in order to achieve the outcomes they did or even could have imagined them achieving any of these three outcomes. Yet, the exhibitions did achieve those outcomes because ultimately people use museum experiences to satisfy their needs, as opposed to the museum's needs.

It is notable that all of the examples of "peak" museum experiences featured in this chapter were highly personal and quite unpredictable, almost serendipitous in quality. These outcomes stand in stark contrast to the very reasoned and calculated outcomes many in the museum community today seem to be striving for. Most present-day museums invest considerable time and effort crafting experiences designed to yield very specific, often learning-focused outcomes. In fact, education, broadly defined, is the stated goal of most of today's museum experiences. Although the desire to learn is certainly not the sole reason the public values and engages in museum experiences, this manifestation of intellectual well-being is certainly a key motivator for many museum users. Although knowing exactly what aspect of a museum experience any particular user will find personally relevant and educationally beneficial is hard to predict, museums hope that every user will be able to find at least something in the experience of interest, something that will engage them intellectually, and ideally, many things that spark the user's curiosity.

NOTES

1. Lewis, C. S. (1933). *The Pilgrim's Regress*, Book 7. Grand Rapids, MI: Eerdmans, p. 128.

2. See Falk, J. H. (2009). *Identity and Museum Visitor Experience*. Walnut Creek, CA: Left Coast Press.

3 Cameron, K. S. (2012). *Positive Leadership: Strategies for Extraordinary Performance*. San Francisco: Beret-Koehler Publishers.

Rudd, M., Vohs, K. and Aaker, J. (2012). "Awe Expands People's Perception of Time, Alters Decision Making, and Enhances Well-Being." *Psychological Science*, 23(10), 1130–36.

4. Falk, J. H., and Dierking, L. D. (1992). *The Museum Experience*. Washington, DC: Whalesback Books.

5. James, W. (1902/1985). *The Varieties of Religious Experience*. Cambridge, MA: Harvard University Press.

6. Jung, C. G. (1992). *Psychological Types*. Collected Works. Princeton, NJ: Princeton University Press.

7. Maslow, A. H. (1964). *Religions, Values, and Peak Experiences*. London: Penguin Books Limited.

8. Maslow, A. H. (1943). "A Theory of Human Motivation." *Psychological Review* 50, 370–396.

9. Csikszentmihalyi, M. (1990). *Flow: The Psychology of Optimal Experience*. New York: Harper Perennial.

10. Maslow, A. H. (1962). *Toward a Psychology of Being*. Princeton, NJ: Van Nostrand-Reinhold.

11. Maslow, A. H. (1943). "A Theory of Human Motivation." *Psychological Review* 50(4), 370–96. *Handbook of Positive Psychology*, 195–206. Oxford: Oxford University Press.

12. Falk, J. H. (2018). *Born to Choose: Evolution, Self and Well-Being*. London: Routledge.

13. Gray, P. (2008). "The Value of Play 1: The Definition of Play Gives Insights." *Psychology Today*, November 19, 2008. https://www.psychologytoday.com/us/blog/freedom-learn/200811/the-value-play-i-the-definition-play-gives-insights. Retrieved September 27, 2020.

14. Dergisi, E. (2017). "Play and Flow: Children's Culture and Adult's Role." *Journal of Early Childhood Studies* 1(2), 247–61.

15. Luke, J., Letourneau, S., Rivera, N., Brahms, L., and May S. (2017). "Play and Children's Museums: A Path Forward or a Point of Tension?" *Curator* 60(1), 37–46.

16. Csikszentmihalyi, M. (1990). *Flow: The Psychology of Optimal Experience*. New York: Harper Perennial.

17. Prum, R. O. (2017). *The Evolution of Beauty: How Darwin's Forgotten Theory of Mate Choice Shapes the Animal World—and Us*. New York: Doubleday.

18. Brown, S., and Gao, X. (2011). "The Neuroscience of Beauty." *Scientific American*, September 27, 2011. https://www.scientificamerican.com/article/the-neuroscience-of-beauty/. Retrieved June 21, 2020.

19. Kirshenbaum, S. (2011). *The Science of Kissing*. New York: Grand Central Publishing. Keeler, J., Roth, E., Neuser, B., Spitsbergen, Waters, D., and Vianney, J.-M. (2015). "The Neurochemistry and Social Flow of Singing: Bonding and Oxytocin." *Frontiers of Human Neuroscience* 9, 518–25. https://www.ncbi.nlm.nih.gov/pmc/articles/PMC4585277/. Retrieved December 31, 2016.

20. Donald, M. (2012). "Evolutionary Origins of Autobiographical Memory Systems: A Retrieval Hypothesis." In D. Berntsen and D. C. Rubin (eds.), *Understanding Autobiographical Memory: Theories and Approaches*, 269–89. Cambridge: Cambridge University Press.

21. Lawton, G. (2014). "Stuff: The First Things Humans Owned." *New Scientist*, March 26, 2014. http://www.newscientist.com/gallery/first-possessions/2. Retrieved June 21, 2020.

22. As quoted in George, A. (2014). "Hunters and Gatherers." *New Scientist*, 221 (2962), p. 38. https://www.newscientist.com/article/mg22129620-700-stuff-humans-as-hunters-and-mega-gatherers/#ixzz6Q1SwlPCU. Retrieved June 21, 2020.

23. George, A. (2014). "Stuff: Humans as Hunters and Mega-Gatherers." *New Scientist*, March 26, 2014. https://www.newscientist.com/article/mg22129620-700-stuff-humans-as-hunters-and-mega-gatherers/#ixzz6Q1SwlPCU. Retrieved June 21, 2020.

24. As quoted in George, A. (2014). "Hunters and gatherers." *New Scientist*, 221 (2962), p. 38. https://www.newscientist.com/article/mg22129620-700-stuff-humans-as-hunters-and-mega-gatherers/#ixzz6Q1SwlPCU. Retrieved June 21, 2020.

25. As quoted in George, A. (2014). "Hunters and gatherers." *New Scientist*, 221 (2962), p. 38. https://www.newscientist.com/article/mg22129620-700-stuff-humans-as-hunters-and-mega-gatherers/#ixzz6Q1SwlPCU. Retrieved June 21, 2020.

26. Belk, R. W. (1988). "Possessions and the Extended Self." *Journal of Consumer Research* 15, 139–69.

27. Bradberry, T. (2016). "Why You Should Spend Your Money on Experiences, Not Things." *Forbes*, August 9, 2016. https://www.forbes.com/sites/travisbradberry/2016/08/09/why-you-should-spend-your-money-on-experiences-not-things/#70ab29366520. Retrieved June 21, 2020.

28. Kim, J., Seto, E., Christy, A., and Hicks, J. (2016). "Investing in the Real Me: Preference for Experiential to Material Purchases Driven by the Motivation to Search for True Self-Knowledge." *Self and Identity* 15(6), 727–47.

29. Pchelin, P., and Howell, R. (2014). "The Hidden Cost of Value-Seeking: People Do Not Accurately Forecast the Economic Benefits of Experiential Purchases." *The Journal of Positive Psychology* 9(4), 322–34.

30. Compare, Bradberry, T. (2016). "Why You Should Spend Your Money on Experiences, Not Things." *Forbes*, August 9, 2016. https://www.forbes.com/sites/travisbradberry/2016/08/09/why-you-should-spend-your-money-on-experiences-not-things/#70ab29366520. Retrieved June 21, 2020.

31. Jarrett, C. (2013). "The Psychology of Stuff and Things." *The Psychologist* 26, 560–65.

32. Rounds, J. (2006). "Doing Identity Work in Museums." *Curator* 49(2), 133–50.

33. Falk, J. H. (2009). *Identity and Museum Visitor Experience*. Walnut Creek, CA: Left Coast Press.

Anderson, D. and Shuichi, Y. (2020). "My Identity in the Garden—Self Reflections of Expatriates' Garden Visits." *Journal of Museum Education*, 45(2), 176–86.

34. Buss, D. (2016). *Evolutionary Biology: The New Science of the Mind*, fifth edition. London: Routledge.

35. Falk, J. H. (2008). "Identity and the Art Museum Visitor." *Journal of Art Education* 34(2), 25–34.

36. Champkins, M. (2013). "Generating Ideas: Drawing Inspiration from the Science Museum." London: Science Museum, July 22, 2013. https://blog.sciencemuseum.org.uk/generating-ideas-drawing-inspiration-from-the-science-museum/. Retrieved November 8, 2020.

37. See Henrich, J., Heine, S. J. and Norenzayan, A. (2010). "The Weirdest People in the World?" *Behavioral and Brain Sciences* 33(2–3), 61–83.

38. Falk, J. H. (2018). *Born to Choose: Evolution, Self and Well-Being*. London: Routledge.

39. For example, Stuckey, H. L., and Nobel, J. (2010). "The Connection between Art, Healing, and Public Health: A Review of Current Literature." *American Journal of Public Health* 100(2), 254–63. See also, Kaimal, G., Ray K., and Muniz, J. (2016). "Reduction of Cortisol Levels and Participants' Responses Following Art Making." *Art Therapy* 33(2), 74–80. Fukui, H., and Toyoshima, K. (2008). "Music Facilitates the Neurogenesis, Regeneration and Repair of Neurons." *Medical Hypotheses* 71(5), 765–69. Yamamoto, M., Naga, S., and Jun Shimizu, J. (2007). "Positive Musical Effects on Two Types of Negative Stressful Conditions." *Psychology of Music* 35(2), 249–75.

40. Barber, N. (2012). "Why Did Religion Evolve?" *Psychology Today*, June 13, 2012. https://www.psychologytoday.com/blog/the-human-beast/201206/why-did-religion-evolve. Retrieved January 15, 2017.

41. Barber, N. (2012). "Why Atheism Will Replace Religion: The Triumph of Earthly Pleasures over Pie in the Sky." E-book, available at http://www.amazon.com/Atheism-Will-Replace-Religion-ebook/dp/B00886ZSJ6/.

42. Paul-Labrador, M. D., Polk, J. H., Dwyer, I., Velasquez, S., Nidich, S., Rainforth, M., Schneider, R., and Merz, C. N. (2006). "Effects of a Randomized Controlled Trial of Transcendental Meditation on Components of the Metabolic Syndrome in Subjects with Coronary Heart Disease." *Archives of Internal Medicine* 166(11), 1218–24.

43. Hunter, S., and Jacobus, J. (1977). *Modern Art*. New York: Prentice-Hall. See also, Green, C. (Ed.). (2001). *Picasso's Les Demoiselles d'Avignon*, Cambridge, UK: Cambridge University Press.

5

Intellectual Well-Being

Knowledge which is acquired under compulsion obtains no hold on the mind.

—Plato[1]

Part of the treasure trove of interviews my colleague Martin Storksdieck and I collected roughly twenty years ago was this gem from a thirty- to forty-year-old white woman who I will call Sara.[2]

Q: When you went [to the science center] the purpose of the visit was what?

A: Well, to see what I could learn. Now that my daughter, she's in the sixth grade, and she's transitioned to junior high; so they have a lot more things going in those grade levels, and I didn't want to be an ignorant parent with questions she'd ask. Not that I'm the most intelligent person, but you know science is always updating and finding new things, and so I said okay, we'll go, and we'll learn together.

Q: What do you remember most; what was most memorable?

A: I remember saying to you when I came out [referring to the post-visit interview immediately following the visit] about the babies in the jars. That was very interesting to me.

Q: Why?

A: Because I was really able to see the different stages of the pregnancy, real bodies. That really caught my attention.

Q: Was it a positive experience?

A: You could say that it was, as bad as that may sound, only because it was interesting to me, and because I myself have three children. It was interesting to see the process and at the same time kind of, well it kind of was and it kind of wasn't, only because the children in there were no longer alive, but that really stood out in my mind.

Q: Did you see similar things in books?

A: Yes, I had when I was in high school in biology. And then I went to junior college, LA Community College and took psychology, so yeah, they introduced us to pictures like that. Not in reality but in pictures.

Q: But the difference between the picture and the jar?

A: It's realistic when you see them in a jar. In a book, you could see anything in a book, you know, but for me it was more fascinating to see the actual things.

Q: What you saw there, did you think about these experiences afterwards?

A: Absolutely, because I mean, I myself have had three children so it was interesting to me the stages that they went through being during my pregnancy. I also read up and took up a lot of that. That was just something that was interesting to me.

Q: Did you ever compare what you saw, your mental notes, to what you read in your book?

A: Absolutely, and I think that I unconsciously maybe did that not realizing all the information and the data that I took from when I did all that reading. It kind of made sense [to me] when I saw the actual babies there.

Q: So you actually read about this beforehand?

A: Oh absolutely.

Q: And then you went there and the effect was . . . ?

A: It made a lot more sense.

Q: Did you continue to read about this afterwards?

A: No, but I probably will. I still have my children's questions, my daughter when she brings home projects, or now that she's growing to be a young adult, she'll ask me questions. We have better answers for her, or at least I'll know what I'm talking about when I try to describe something to her. I know that what I'm trying to say to her makes sense. It might not make sense to her until she's older. She didn't like going through that [exhibit] because there were dead children, and she's too small to comprehend the stages. Being a mother myself, I think it just made a lot more sense, and it's much easier for me to explain the different cycles. . . . But this was the most fascinating for me.

Q: The reproduction.

A: The reproduction and the genetics.

Q: Would you say it was interesting [to you] because of your daughter's interest or are you interested yourself?

A: I'm interested myself. I now have three children; before I had my three children, I lost two children at nine months—they died at birth. So I took up a lot of reading before my very first child. Usually the very first time a woman is pregnant, you want to soak yourself with information. After what had happened to me, I wanted to know more. And it happened a second time, so by the time my third daughter, which is my oldest now, by the time she was born I really soaked myself with information. So this made it even more interesting to me.

Q: I hate to ask, but you had two stillborn pregnancies?

A: Yes, two stillborns.

Q: Wow, that's tough.

A: That is very tough. Now I'm over that, because I went through a lot of grieving and I went through a lot of counseling, but I guess I was just trying to get so much information, being that the doctors weren't able to give me a lot of detailed information that I wanted. They were just, "Well, things happen," and I wanted to know the details, which is probably pretty difficult for them to explain to me. I don't know; I'm not a doctor. After going through something so traumatic you want to know all there is to know about what you're going through and what you have to deal with. So maybe that's the reason why this part for me was so important and attracted my attention.

Q: That would certainly explain quite a bit.

A: And being a woman, I think anybody who has either had an abortion or a miscarriage or a stillbirth, this is probably very attractive to a woman who has gone through that to want to know all that there is about that.

Sara's interview reveals a characteristic of virtually all museum experiences, including virtually all examples of learning from museums, her reasons for spending time at this particular exhibit as well as the things she perceived she learned were quite personal. Although, as indicated at the end of the last chapter, the designers of museum experiences typically have specific educational outcomes they hope to achieve, the actual things learned are often quite person-specific and unique. Research has shown that the topics people are most attracted to while engaged in museum experiences, and thus the topics they disproportionately actually learn the most about, are those that they already know at least a little something about before the experience began.[3] Although people also find new things and topics of interest, reality is not, as presumed (and hoped for) by most museum professionals. Learning about "new" topics is relatively limited, with most learning gains, as determined by self-reports of visitor learning, coming in areas people claimed to have already had some knowledge.[4] As was the case for Sara, her desire to learn about human development was fueled by her prior knowledge and interest in this topic, which in turn was a function of her particular lived experiences.[5] Despite already having considerable knowledge about prenatal development, Sara expressed the belief that her science center experience significantly enhanced her knowledge and understanding of this topic. Significantly, she reported she perceived that she appreciated the opportunity to learn more about a topic she found both personally relevant and important to her.

Ultimately, though, the importance of relevance here is not about whether it enhances people's ability to learn from their museum experiences—it does[6]—but how it factors into why people choose to engage in learning experiences at museums in the first place and why these experiences are so memorable. Whether consciously or unconsciously, people understand that increased understanding about topics of interest and perceived importance to them enhances their well-being; learning positively enhances fitness.

LEARNING AND FITNESS

Learned behaviors, abilities, and skills are essential for survival.[7] Most biologists agree, that learning evolved as a highly adaptive mechanism for allowing individuals to effectively respond to a changeable environment, a mechanism for behaviorally dealing with life challenges that occurred over time frames too short to depend upon genetically programmed strategies.[8] All living things are capable of learning, including bacteria, fungi, plants, and of course animals. However, high intelligence and a heightened ability to learn appears to be relatively rare, having independently evolved just three times on earth, first in the group of mollusks called cephalopods and then again in vertebrates, first within the dinosaurs and their successors the birds and again in the mammals. I say independently evolved because these three groups last shared a common, worm-like ancestor some 600 million years ago, with cephalopods first appearing on earth some million years later at around 530 million years ago. Clearly birds and mammals are more closely related to each other than either are to cephalopods, but they too diverged a long time ago, with their last shared common ancestor living some 200+ million years ago. Among living creatures, the brainiest cephalopods are octopi and squid,[9] while among vertebrates, the most intelligent birds appear to be parrots and ravens and the most intelligent mammals being dolphins, whales, and the great apes. In this latter group is arguably the smartest species of them all, humans.

Somewhere between 5 million and 8 million years ago, a relatively modest-sized population of forest-living, chimpanzee-like primates moved out of their ancestral habitat and adapted to the challenges of living in more open, savanna-like environments. This new environment was a challenging place for these apes to live, being comprised of largely unfamiliar, and often marginal food resources, not to mention a whole suite of novel, fast, and aggressive predators like lions, wild dogs, cheetahs, and hyenas. Forced by climate change to abandon their ancestral rain forest homes, these pioneering, highly vulnerable apes somehow managed to scratch out a living. However, the fossil record suggests that these creatures did more than just scrape by in this new environment. Over just a few short millions of years, humanity's early ancestors—collectively known as *hominins*—changed from creatures equally at home in a tree or on the ground, to ones that almost exclusively lived on the ground. They morphed from lumbering, knuckle walkers, like modern-day gorillas and chimpanzees, into numerous species of upright, two-legged striders with opposable thumbs. Along the way, hominins also evolved from a line of intelligent, social apes who individually foraged for plants within a fairly restricted ecological niche into a line of very smart, highly social apes who collectively foraged for both plants and meat, capable of exploiting resources across a wide array of settings and situations.[10] Although, there are many theories as to what might have propelled these profound evolutionary changes, all seem to agree that heightened abilities to learn played a critical role.[11]

Learning is at the heart of what it means to be a successful human. Seemingly, that was true millions of years ago, and it certainly is true today as we find ourselves in the midst of the Knowledge Age, a time when learning and the ability to flexibly and creatively apply that learning to new situations are critical survival skills. Although I found it surprising to discover just how little research has actually been done on the relationship between learning and well-being, particularly related to non-school-related learning, what evidence there is leaves no doubt that individuals who engage in regular, lifelong learning have higher levels of well-being than those who do not.[12]

Underlying the ability to learn are three distinct processes.[13] The first of the three is of course intelligence, the mental capacity to take in and process numerous bits of information. Complex environments by their nature create a welter of signals, which can cognitively overload a lesser mind. Humans are capable of inputting and processing inordinately rich information loads. The second key aspect of learning is the desire to learn, the drive to constantly seek new, additional information and understanding. Psychologists generically refer to this "drive" as curiosity.[14] All young mammals are curious, particularly all primates, but humans are not just curious when young; they remain curious throughout life, and that lifelong curiosity has played a particularly important role in human success down the ages. The final capability is all about what one does with all that learned information, what these days is usually referred to as critical thinking and defined as the ability to actively and skillfully conceptualize, analyze, synthesize, evaluate, and ultimately apply what has been observed and learned into action.[15] All three of these capabilities are important and all are inter-related and highly correlated, but they are not the same. Not all intelligent people are curious, nor are the most intelligent people always the best critical thinkers. In fact, it has been widely observed that the smartest people are often neither the wisest nor necessarily the best decision makers.[16] Facing a problem, having encyclopedic knowledge about the situation can be useful, but that knowledge alone is no guarantee that a person will make good choices.

As for how museum experiences support learning, and thus well-being, they, in and of themselves, do not have much impact on intelligence. At least half or more of the factors that determine intelligence are genetic, and thus innate, with the other half determined by environmental factors.[17] However, despite the ability of lived experience to influence intelligence, the relatively short and ephemeral nature of most museum experiences generally mean they make only the tiniest dent in most people's intellectual capabilities. That is probably okay in the context of understanding the impact of museum experiences, since research has shown that despite the importance of intelligence, intelligence alone contributes virtually nothing to well-being.[18] The major well-being payoff, it turns out, is delivered through curiosity and critical thinking. Museum experiences regularly support and facilitate the exercise of curiosity; and though not as commonly, museum experiences have also been shown to foster better critical thinking.

CURIOSITY

Like the vast majority of people who engage in museum experiences, Sara described herself as fundamentally a curious and interested person.

> Q: How did you decide between what you wanted to see and what [your children] wanted to see?
>
> A: If it was pretty interesting, I would just stick it out and just tell my children you guys can go in front of me or meet me in the corner and walk real slow and I'd catch up. I just tried to catch on to as much as I could and my children, they pretty much weren't interested in too much. I love to find out about things and always try to stretch my understanding of how stuff works and why things are the way they are.

Sara speaks for many people who experience museums; the museum represents a space for generalized exploration and discovery rather than a place for satisfying a specific outcome. Citing statistics showing that most people in museums only stop at a small percentage of exhibits within an exhibition/museum, Jay Rounds argues that rather than seeing this selectivity as some kind of deficiency on the part of visitors, it should instead be seen as an intelligent and effective strategy for piquing and satisfying curiosity.[19] Building off of ideas derived from "optimal foraging theory" in ecology, Rounds hypothesized that curiosity-driven visitors would seek to maximize what he called the "Total Interest Value" of their museum visit, finding and focusing attention only on those exhibit elements they deem to combine high interest value and low search costs. According to Rounds, this "selective use of exhibit elements results in greater achievement of their own goals than would be gained by using the exhibition comprehensively."[20] It is the employment of this curiosity-optimizing approach that makes the museum experience only generally, but never specifically, predictable. What exhibits people decide to stop at and spend time investigating in depth ultimately depends upon what a visitor encounters that resonates with his or her various needs and interests. Therefore, despite there being considerable uniformity in the general pathways people traverse through a museum—with most visitors starting at the "beginning" of the museum and working their way through to the "end," often following deliberately designed tracks, there is considerably less uniformity in what people say they actually learned from their experiences. Specific learnings are quite variable and nearly always highly idiosyncratic.[21]

Extensive research now exists showing that it is curiosity, about art, history, nature, or science, rather than learning per se, that is the primary motivator for a large percentage of museum users.[22] A third or more of the public describe their reasons for engaging in museum experiences using phrases like these:

> I am not an expert but I like to learn about things.
>
> Going to places like museums are more inspiring than going to the mall or a movie.
>
> These are kinds of places that people like me go to.
>
> I am a curious person, and places like this satisfy my curiosity.

Being curious and engaging in learning during one's leisure-time has been shown to boost self-confidence and self-esteem, helping individuals build a sense of purpose and fostering connections with others. People who have engaged in this type of learning report feeling better about themselves and feeling a greater ability to cope with stress, as well as feeling more self-confident and engaged.[23] This is particularly true for those who most deeply and persistently engage in these kinds of experiences. Although even short-term experiences, as exemplified by Sara's, can have long-term beneficial consequences, longer-term, more deeply engaging experiences can quantitatively benefit an individual's long-term health, self-esteem, and sense of purpose in life.[24] Through repeated visits or volunteering, millions of people each year achieve these kinds of deeper, longer lasting well-being benefits. The following interview excerpt is illustrative of these kinds of longer-term experiences.

> Q: Do you ever visit places like museums?
>
> A: Yes, I go to the [L.A. County] Natural History Museum a lot. I volunteer in the paleontology department there and clean fossils.
>
> Q: What makes you volunteer there?
>
> A: I just suddenly took an interest in paleontology. We went on a fossil dig with the museum and my son and I went camping at the Redrock. I just got hooked. I met nice people there, and they told me about volunteer opportunities. And I went on the Internet and looked around and there was something available. So, I volunteered, and we also have continued to go on fossil digs since then.
>
> Q: Has this been good? Do you feel like you've benefited from this?
>
> A: Absolutely. Not only do I feel that I'm being useful to the Natural History Museum, I feel like I'm doing something worthwhile with my time, making a difference, helping advance the world's knowledge and all of that.[25] (thirty-five-year-old Japanese American female)

Although not all museum experiences result in life-changing choices, some do; and when they do, they can be particularly profound. In the case above, one museum experience led to another, ultimately resulting in a significant life choice. Taken together, these museum experiences appear to have not only yielded considerable short-term well-being, but they have helped give long-term meaning to this individual's life.

CRITICAL THINKING

The main evolutionary pay-off of learning comes when it results in the making of better, more informed decisions. To understand why this is so, and in particular why this is so important for humans, it helps to once again go back in time and space to that period in the story of human evolution, when hominins first emerged. That time was roughly 5 million to 8 million years ago, defined by scientists as the end of the geological period known as the Miocene, and the beginning of the geological era known as the Pliocene. This, as it turns out, was not really a great time to be living in the eastern parts of Africa if you were a rain-forest-dwelling creature, as our ancestors were.

The world at the beginning of the Pliocene era has some striking parallels to our present world. Worldwide, climate was changing dramatically and becoming much more erratic. On the African continent, both average temperatures and average rainfall declined precipitously, which in turn led to significant shrinkage of the vast rain forests that had up to that time, covered much of the continent. Vast stretches of semi-arid savanna replaced these rapidly disappearing rain forests. This was the place, the time, and the situation in which humanity's hominin ancestors diverged from their forest-living relatives the chimpanzees and first began to evolve human-like qualities. It is fair to presume that it was not just curiosity and a sense of adventure that pushed these early hominins out onto the savannas, but rather a desperate need to survive in a rapidly changing world.

Although the odds were clearly stacked against these earliest proto-hominins, as suggested earlier, this progenitor population managed to flourish and give rise to as many as a dozen or more species.[26] For this burst of evolution to have occurred, this new form of savanna-dwelling creature must have possessed a skill set that enabled it to be more than just marginally successful in this new environment; it needed to possess some capabilities that allowed it to be highly successful. My preferred explanation involves the adaptive advantages that conscious learning afforded to these pioneering apes, a capability they already possessed but repurposed. I have argued that the key to hominin success was the ability to voluntarily retrieve information and make "informed" choices in the service of perceived well-being.[27] If true, all of the various other anatomical, neural, and social adaptations that gave rise to the genus *Homo* were pulled along over time in response to the opportunities afforded by this one fundamental neural adaptation.

Historically, most theories about how and why early human-like creatures achieved their dramatic success assumed that it was because of the superior intelligence and increased brain size of hominins. However, the fossil evidence has not supported this theory. Over the past quarter century, a wealth of new hominin fossils has shown that increases in brain size only came relatively late in the development of the hominin line, trailing long after many of the most distinctive hominin attributes such as upright posture and an opposable thumb.[28] The best available evidence seems to suggest that early hominins had almost exactly the same size and same shaped brains as their chimpanzee relatives; in other words, these early hominins were likely no more and no less intelligent than today's chimps. This level of brain size / intelligence apparently persisted throughout the first couple of million years of hominin evolution. Thus, we must conclude that whatever it was that made the hominin lifestyle so ecologically successful at this time that it resulted in the evolution of multiple species, it was not gross intelligence.[29] I believe the data suggests that the key to early hominin success on the savanna was not a dramatic *increase* in intelligence, but rather a dramatic *repurposing* of existing intelligence, the repurposing of conscious learning from primarily social well-being purposes to increasingly physical well-being purposes.

Almost certainly, since the cognitive abilities associated with self-initiated recall of memory are common to both chimpanzees and humans,[30] it is reasonable to conclude that these capabilities developed prior to the hominin line diverging from the chimpanzee line some 5 million to 8 million years ago. The ability to consciously recall memory thus likely existed in this common ancestor, a creature that lived some 10 million or more years ago.[31] The gist of this capability was the ability to focus one's attention outside of one's self, either on another creature or some event in the environment, and infer, based upon observation of similar experiences in the past, what was likely to happen in the future. In other words, combining past learnings with conscious analysis, synthesis, and evaluation, these apes possessed an innate ability to infer likely future scenarios.

As is the case today for chimpanzees, and likely was equally the case for the common ancestors of chimpanzees and humans, rain forest food sources are relatively predictable and easy to find, so the evolution of this heightened cognitive capacity for critical thinking was primarily utilized for managing and gaming the challenges and complexities of ape social society.[32] However, once the ancestors of modern humans ventured into the great unknown of the savanna, these innate critical-thinking capacities became, by necessity, applied to other, nonsocial challenges. Despite being physically maladapted for life on the savanna, these unique cognitive skills, this ability to learn and consciously apply what was learned to new situations and settings, proved to be the necessary preadaptation that enabled these early hominins to survive.

One can imagine these early hominins consciously learning to make associations between things in their environment and specific survival-related outcomes; for example, trees the look like this often grow where there is water, while grasses that look like this often harbor lions. Or, if you see flowers that look like Y growing in a place like Z, it is highly likely that you will also find other plants at this time growing there, plants without flowers that are thus easy to miss but which are important nonetheless because they have edible, underground tubers. During the Pliocene, it was likely that all these survival-related "signs" could, and likely did, change from month to month and even year to year. The individuals who, by virtue of the right blend of intelligence, curiosity, and critical-thinking skills, were best able to learn to read these signs in this way would have been favored by natural (and cultural) selection.

Looking backward, it is easy for us now to see how and why, over time, adept learners would have become increasingly common and important to the evolutionary success of hominins. First, these adaptations propelled hominins into becoming successful savanna dwellers. Then, the same suite of learning skills—intelligence, curiosity, and critical thinking—allowed these hunting and gathering ancestors to be so sufficiently flexible and resourceful that they could move beyond the savanna and successfully colonize other environments occurring in every corner of the world. Learning also proved critical to success in the Agrarian Age, catalyzing major advances in plant and animal husbandry that allowed ever-larger populations of humans to congregate and innovate. The resulting learning that allowed the development of science and technology then fueled first the Industrialist age and now the Knowledge Age, with the value and importance of learning increasing every step of the way. Although far from a straight line, in general and over time, the individuals with the greatest capacity and motivation for learning, and particularly those with best ability to apply that learning to better life choices, have achieved higher social status and greater reproductive success. This is why enhanced intellectual well-being is so highly valued, and of course, why museum experiences that support not just learning but critical thinking are highly valued.

In a study I conducted with colleagues in Australia some fifteen years ago, as we talked to visitors weeks after their museum experiences, time and again individuals described examples of how what they saw and did at the museum resulted in their reflections on their life and behavior.[33] Here are some examples:

> It was surprising and mind-blowing and opened my mind to what is really happening; we thought we were doing well [related to environmental conservation] until [we] realized there is much more to be done. [After seeing an exhibition that allowed one to calculate his or her "environmental footprint"]

> I now feel very conscious of speed and danger. [After using an exhibit on driving tired]

> I realized that my five-year-old was not [intellectually] ready for [solving a problem like this]. [Referring to a tangrams exhibit]

However, beyond these selected examples, a major study conducted by researchers at the University of Arkansas about the outcomes of one-time school field trip experiences at the Crystal Bridges Museum of American Art found that among a range of statistically significant outcomes was an increase in critical thinking.[34] This, of course, was one of the intellectual well-being-related outcomes the designers of these field trip experiences would have said they hoped for, but museum experience designers are not the only ones who have expectations for achieving intellectual well-being-related outcomes, so too do the users themselves.

WELL-BEING BY DESIGN

The following is an excerpt from an interview with, Shawn,[35] a twenty-six-year-old white male, conducted soon after he exited the Smithsonian Institution's National Museum of Natural History.

> Q: So tell me about your visit to the Natural History Museum. Did you have a good time?
>
> A: Yes, it was great. My girlfriend and I got to see all the things we were hoping to see.
>
> Q: That's great. What were you hoping to see?
>
> A: Oh, you know, the usual. We wanted to see the Hope Diamond, the dinosaurs, all the usual stuff.
>
> Q: So these things, the Hope Diamond and the dinosaurs, were these things you knew about before you visited or were they things you found out about once you got here?
>
> A: Oh, definitely knew about before we got here. We'd read the guides and talked to friends and been thinking about and planning for this trip to DC for nearly a year. All our friends were giving us advice on what to see and do; this museum was a must-see. We needed to see the Hope Diamond, the dinosaurs, we also need to see the big flag and Wizard of Oz stuff over at the History Museum and all the air and space stuff like the space capsule and moon rock over at the Air and Space Museum.
>
> [Later in the interview]
>
> Q: So how would you rate your overall visit, from a one not satisfied at all, to a seven, totally satisfied?
>
> A: Oh, definitely a seven; yea, definitely a seven. This was really great. We got to see what we came to see and we had a blast. And it's only our second day in DC! We're really stoked now to see the rest of DC.[36]

Shawn is a wonderful example of a museum user having what I have called an "experience seeking" visit motivation.[37] Not only was he a tourist in Washington, DC, he was a man on a mission! As Shawn told me, he and his girlfriend had been planning this visit for months, and between the guides and his friends the two of them had accumulated a visitor's "shopping-list" of sights to see and experiences they aspired to "collect." High on their list were the various Smithsonian museums, and they were happily ticking them off, one by one. Shawn came to see the Hope Diamond and the dinosaurs, and he was not disappointed as that was exactly what he and his girlfriend did.

The satisfaction of this expectation directly contributed to satisfaction with his museum experience. Although later in the interview Shawn was able to share with me tidbits of the exhibition-related "knowledge" he had acquired as a consequence of his visit, this did not seem to be all that important to Shawn. As he made abundantly clear to me, the reason he rated his satisfaction with his experience a seven out of a possible seven was that he and his girlfriend had accomplished exactly what they had hoped and planned to accomplish. They had set a goal to see these rare, awe-inspiring national treasures, and by god, they had accomplished that goal. This was a "once-in-a-lifetime" trip. They had built up their expectations and then done the things they needed to do to fulfill those expectations. Shawn was very satisfied.

Like Shawn, the vast majority of the people who partake in museum experiences find their experiences to be satisfying. I would, and have, argued that this overwhelming satisfaction arises in large part from the fact that users have found their experiences to be exactly what they expected them to be.[38] For example, experience seekers like Shawn go to places like the Smithsonian Museums, the Louvre Museum, or British Museum with the expectation that they will see specific rare and valuable, one-of-a-kind, important, and irreplaceable cultural artifacts, things that they can see nowhere else in the world, and likely only once in their lives. Even less internationally famous institutions, though, can and do fulfill these kinds of expectations, as each in their own way, typically affords users an opportunity to have novel, out-of-the-ordinary experiences—the small museum with the jacket worn by a famous, local citizen or the small natural history museum with the only example of a two-headed sheep anyone has ever seen. The wonder of it all is that despite these experiences being novel and out of the ordinary for individual users, they are collectively neither novel nor unusual. Across museums worldwide, every day, large numbers of museum users regularly have these kinds of extra-ordinary experiences, doing things they have never done before and seeing things they have never seen before. These wonderous experiences are so predictable, in fact, that people like Shawn can actually plan on having this kind of once-in-a-lifetime experience—plan for it, and then fulfill it.

What a great formula, and what a perfect recipe for enhancing one's sense of intellectual well-being—set out to discover things you have always wanted to do and see, and then do and see those things. Considerable research on leisure satisfaction has demonstrated that this formula is actually the norm rather than the exception. In study after study, people report that their perceived satisfaction with a leisure experience is always determined by a combination of two key factors—the expectations they had for an experience before engaging in it and the realities of the experience that they actually had. Surprisingly, it turns out that prior expectations are overwhelmingly the more important of these two sets of variables.[39] Research has shown that this non-intuitive finding is true; the public's post-experience ratings of leisure satisfaction are predominantly driven by people's hopes and desires for the experience.[40] In other words, expectations really matter.

One other important, and again non-intuitive result emerging from this line of leisure and tourism research on satisfaction has been that not only do most people's satisfactions derive from their entering expectations but that these expectations are frequently manipulated by visitors to ensure that they fit. For example, research by Spanish tourism researchers Ignacio Rodrıguez del Bosque and Hector San Martin found that tourists consistently adjusted their post-experience judgments of events to conform to their pre-experience beliefs about how those events would transpire, all in an effort to minimize cognitive dissonance.[41] The theory of cognitive dissonance holds that inconsistency among beliefs or behaviors will cause an uncomfortable psychological tension. This perceived psychological tension can cause people to change their beliefs so they better fit their actual behaviors, but the opposite can happen—and seemingly, in the case of leisure experiences, is more likely to happen.[42] Del Bosque and Martin's research showed that in the case of leisure and tourism, people routinely seemed to place a really high level of importance on satisfying their preconceived expectations for their experiences. Thus, even when occasionally something in their experience did not quite measure up to their expectations, they still tended to excuse away these problems as relatively insignificant in the grand scheme of things. For example, Shawn indicated during his interview that his girlfriend and he had found it challenging to locate the exhibition that contained the Hope Diamond, and even when they found the exhibition, they still had difficulty actually finding the Hope Diamond. Although frustrating, this difficulty made nary a dent in Shawn's enthusiasm for having seen this iconic stone. Who knows, perhaps this little bit of adversity might have actually even heightened the sweetness of his accomplishment.

Museum experiences are now so common and popular that virtually all users have a reasonable idea of what to expect from such experiences. This was not the case when I first started studying museums nearly fifty years ago, but it is today. As a consequence, for the vast majority of museum users, museum experiences support a form of self-fulfilling prophecy—they are situations where it becomes possible to achieve a specific outcome in large part because one has the ability to predict and control events in ways that almost guarantee one will achieve that outcome.

First proposed more than fifty years ago by the sociologist Robert Merton,[43] the effects and impact of self-fulfilling prophecies have been documented across an amazingly large number of contexts and situations, ranging from teacher effects on student learning, to selling decisions in real estate, to research scientists reporting of results, to the impact of mothers on children's underage drinking behaviors.[44] The reason self-fulfilling prophecies occur is because personal expectations are subjective; therefore, the influence of expectations undermines building an objective knowledge base. A self-fulfilling prophecy is simply a cause-and-effect scenario, with assumptions about what will happen in the future, typically based on the outcomes of similar events that have happened, often repeatedly, in the past. So, for example, in the past when my friend went to the Smithsonian and saw the Hope Diamond, he said he was amazed by its size and beauty. Thus, there is every reason to believe that I too will have the same reaction when I see the Hope Diamond. Most importantly, even if it turns out that I am not totally "blown away" by the Hope Diamond, I am inclined to believe the problem was caused by some personal flaw in me rather than in the diamond. After all, I know that everyone else who has ever seen this diamond was impressed, so that is the reaction I am supposed to have.

This kind of "well-being on demand" is not limited to experience seekers like Shawn. Museums are also notable for being able to predictably satisfy explorers who can arrive, knowing in advance that they will find something interesting that tickles their curiosity. Professionals and hobbyists arrive at museums knowing that they will be able find a specific object or accomplish a specific objective. Rechargers arrive fully expecting that they will find exactly the kind of quiet respite they are seeking. And facilitators confidently enter into the experience convinced that this will be just to place to go in order to satisfy someone else's interests and desires. Here, by way of example, is another excerpt from Martin Storksdieck's and my long-term recollections study,[45] this time with a thirty-something, Asian American woman:

> Q: So you came to [the science center] to have quality time with your daughter. What do you mean by "quality time"?
>
> A: I understand quality time as a time when I am in my highest level of parent role; I am mommy to the tenth extreme. All of [my daughter's] questions are answered; all of [my daughter's] dreams come true. I'm in a position where I am behaving so that she is able to mold herself after me.
>
> Q. Did you have specific learning goals for [daughter] on the day you visited [the science center]?
>
> A: Well, she's in first grade so everything that she's been doing up until now is stuff that I've been directing her to do.

CHOICE AND CONTROL

Of course, it is important to note that the ability of the public to use museum experience in this way is no accident. Museum experiences are highly curated. A vast array of individuals, at considerable cost, have worked to ensure that these types of user-anticipated affordances are present. Although highly curated, the best museum experiences are ones that afford users a smorgasbord of such affordances; and like a smorgasbord, the users get to exercise an amazing degree of choice and control over which bits to "consume" on any given visit. In fact, I, and others, have come to believe that this free-choice aspect of museums is what makes them so unusually satisfying and memorable for so many people.[46]

Humans, and other organisms, actively seek out choices and the ability to control the events in their lives.[47] In general, living things have evolved to equate choice and control with enhanced survival.[48] Thus, again typically unconsciously, people gravitate toward situations that allow greater choice and control. This, according to leisure expert John Kelly, is why people so highly value leisure time—it's often the only time in one's life where one can exercise considerable choice and control over what one does.[49] Museums afford users an unprecedented level of choice and control, something that is missing from much of most people's lives. Museum users like Shawn and the mother above not only have the ability to actively choose whether or not to visit a museum, but they equally get to choose which parts of the museum to visit, and even within those parts, which particular bits to attend to. It is this latter part of museum-supported choice and control that particularly makes museums such powerful settings for learning. Some 2,500 years ago, Plato observed, "knowledge which is acquired under compulsion obtains no hold on the mind."[50] An observation now fully substantiated by extensive research.[51]

One of the few museum-based studies on the importance of choice and control was conducted by museum visitor researcher Deborah Perry as part of her doctoral work at Indiana University. Perry found that the confidence that came along with free-choice learning, coupled with the motivation to control one's environment, were among the most important variables determining successful learning from a children's museum exhibit.[52] Perry discovered that children actively sought out opportunities to feel in control and confident about their environment, and when they achieved that, significant learning occurred. Perhaps one of the reasons so little attention has been focused on choice and control in museum learning has been because it has been perceived as almost too obvious. Since these variables tend to be intrinsic to the museum experience, it is perhaps all too easy to overlook how important a contribution they make to most museum-based experiences. Investigations by Finnish museum researcher Hannu Salmi confirmed that the motivating effects of freedom and control over the environment can be used by museums to enhance student learning.[53] In fact, these motivational attributes of museums have been observed by a wide range of investigators, and they are frequently cited as justification for why schools should take children on field trips to museums.[54]

However, perhaps the best evidence for how central choice and control is to the museum experience comes from the handful of studies that have attempted to understand what happens when free choice is denied to museum visitors. In what amounts to a natural experiment, researchers have been able to compare the learning that happens when children participate in both an overly structured school field trip and what happens on less-structured, more self-directed field trips.

Australian museum researcher Janette Griffin investigated matched groups of school children in museums under these two conditions. The first condition was an organized, traditional, teacher-directed school field trip situation. The second condition involved a group of students who were freed from the typical constraints and structures imposed by teachers and were allowed to freely define their own pathway and agenda in the museum. The second condition was not only perceived by the students as more enjoyable, but learning, though not required, was actually facilitated when children were not "forced" to learn.[55] Interestingly, students in this second condition were observed to behave and learn in ways similar to children in family groups.[56] Griffin identified three variables important to students in these learning situations: choice, purpose, and ownership. Given ownership of learning, learning and enjoyment became intertwined, and according to Griffin ultimately inseparable in the minds of the children.

Although it was certainly not always true, due to the exponential rise in popularity of museums over the last half century, today many people in the developed world possess sufficient museum savvy to be able to predict what a museum experience will entail. People have learned roughly how long a visit should last, generally how the content of the museum will be displayed, and roughly what kinds of experiences they and their loved ones can expect to have (e.g., they can view exhibitions, programs, films, etc.). They also have a reasonably good idea of what additional amenities a museum experience will afford (e.g., food services and gift shops). It is not that museums deliver *total* certainty of experience, but rather that they deliver *optimal* certainty. A little bit of novelty and uncertainty are good. For most users, most of the time, museum experiences deliver just the right balance of certainty and uncertainty, a balance that yields a high degree of satisfaction to nearly 100 percent of users, nearly 100 percent of the time.

The desire for choice and control is hardwired into our species,[57] but opportunities for real choice and control in life are often few and far between. The fact that museums make it possible for millions of people to actively achieve a high degree of choice and control over meaningful aspects of their lives unquestionably figures prominently into why so many people rate museum experiences as so satisfying. It is even possible, that this heightened sense of choice and control, over and above any "learning" that might occur, represents the most significant, intellectual well-being-related "benefit" people derive from their museum experience.

NOTES

1. Plato. (375 BC). *The Republic*. http://www.literaturepage.com/read.php?titleid=therepublic&abspage=284&bookmark=1. Retrieved October 30, 2020.
2. Falk, J. H., and Storksdieck, M. (2004). *Investigating the Long-Term Impact of a Science Center on Its Community*. Final Report to National Science Foundation. Annapolis, MD: Institute for Learning Innovation.
3. Falk, J. H., and Dierking, L. D. (2019). *Learning from Museums*, second edition. Lanham, MD: Rowman & Littlefield.
4. Falk, J. H., and Needham, M. (2011). "Measuring the impact of a science center on its community." *Journal of Research in Science Teaching* 48(1), 1–12.
5. See, Falk, J. H., and Dierking, L. D. (2019). *Learning from Museums*, second edition. Lanham, MD: Rowman & Littlefield.
6. For a review of current evidence, see Falk, J. H., and Dierking, L. D. (2019). *Learning from Museums*, second edition. Lanham, MD: Rowman & Littlefield.
7. Anderson, R. W. (1995). "Learning and Evolution: A Quantitative Genetics Approach." *Journal of Theoretical Biology* 175, 89–101.
8. Brown, R. L. (2013). "Learning, Evolvability and Exploratory Behavior: Extending the Evolutionary Reach of Learning." *Biological Philosophy* 28, 933955. See also, Jablonka, E., and Lamb, M. J. (2014). *Evolution in Four Dimensions*. Cambridge, MA: MIT Press.
9. To learn more about cephalopod intelligence, see Godrey-Smith, P. (2016). *Other Minds: The Octopus, the Sea, and the Deep Origins of Consciousness*. New York: Farrar Straus and Giroux.
10. Lieberman, D. E. (2013). *The Story of the Human Body*. New York: Pantheon.

11. "Brains." Smithsonian National Museum of Natural History. http://humanorigins.si.edu/human-characteristics/brains. Retrieved August 9, 2013. In 2000, Martin Pickford and Brigitte Senut discovered in the Tugen Hills of Kenya a 6-million-year-old bipedal hominin that they named *Orrorin tugenensis*. And in 2001, a team led by Michel Brunet discovered the skull of *Sahelanthropus tchadensis*, which was dated as 7.2 million years ago and which Brunet argued was a bipedal and therefore a hominin.

12. For examples, see the following: Desjardins, R. (2004). *Learning for Well-Being*. Stockholm: Stockholm University Institute for International Education.

Feinstein, L., Hammond, C., Woods, L., Preston, J., and Bynner, J. (2003). *The Contribution of Adult Learning to Health and Social Capital*, Research Report 8. London: Centre for Research on the Wider Benefits of Learning.

Field, J. (2009) "Good for Your Soul? Adult Learning and Mental Well-Being." *International Journal of Lifelong Education* 28(2), 175–91.

Jenkins, A., and Mostafa, T. (2013). "The Effects of Learning on Wellbeing for Older Adults in England." *Ageing and Society* 35(10), 1–18.

Leung, D. S. Y., and Liu, B. C.-P. (2011). "Lifelong Education, Quality of Life and Self-Efficacy of Chinese Older Adults." *Educational Gerontology* 37(11), 967–81.

Narushima, M., Liu, J., and Diestelkamp, N. (2016). "Lifelong Learning in Active Ageing Discourse: Its Conserving Effect on Wellbeing, Health and Vulnerability." *Ageing and Society* 38(4), 1–25.

Schuller, T., Preston, J., Hammond, C., Bassett-Grundy, A., and Bynner, J. (2004). *The Benefits of Learning: The Impacts of Formal and Informal Education on Social Capital, Health and Family Life*. London: Routledge.

13. Macphail, E. M. (1995). "Cognitive Function in Mammals: The Evolutionary Perspective." *Cognitive Brain Research* 3, 279–90.

14. Grand, S. (1998). "Curiosity Created the Cat [the Relationship between Curiosity and Intelligence]." *IEEE Intelligent Systems and Their Applications* 13(3), 2–4.

15. Glaser, E. (2019). "Defining Critical Thinking." The International Center for the Assessment of Higher Order Thinking (ICAT, US)/Critical Thinking Community. https://www.criticalthinking.org/pages/defining-critical-thinking/766. Retrieved November 1, 2020.

16. Butler, H. (2020). "Why Do Smart People Do Foolish Things?" *Scientific American*, October 3, 2017. https://www.scientificamerican.com/article/why-do-smart-people-do-foolish-things/. Retrieved October 31, 2020.

17. Deary, I. J. (2013). Intelligence. *Current Biology* 23(16), R673–76. See also, Plomin, R. and Deary, I. J. (2015). "Genetics and Intelligence Differences: Five Special Findings." *Molecular Psychiatry* 20(1), 98–108. Sternberg, R. J. (2012). "Intelligence." *Dialogues in Clinical Neuroscience* 14(1), 19–27.

18. Butler, H. (2020). "Why Do Smart People Do Foolish Things?" *Scientific American*, October 3, 2017. https://www.scientificamerican.com/article/why-do-smart-people-do-foolish-things/. Retrieved October 31, 2020.

19. Rounds, J. (2004). "Strategies for the Curiosity-Driven Museum Visitor." *Curator* 47(4), 389–412.

20. Rounds (2004). "Strategies for the Curiosity-Driven Museum Visitor." *Curator* 47(4), 389.

21. Falk, J. H., and Dierking, L. D. (2014). *The Museum Experience Revisited*. Walnut Creek, CA: Left Coast Press.

22. See review of the research in Falk, J. H., and Dierking, L. D. (2019). *Learning from Museums*, second edition. Lanham, MD: Rowman & Littlefield.

23. Field, J. (2009). "Good for Your Soul? Adult Learning and Mental Well-Being." *International Journal of Lifelong Education* 28(2), 175–91. See also, Gallagher, M. W., and Lopez, S. J. (2007). "Curiosity and Well-Being." *The Journal of Positive Psychology* 2(4), 236–48. Reio, T. G., and Sanders-Reio, J. (2020). "Curiosity and Well-Being in Emerging Adulthood." *New Horizons in Adult Education and Human Resource Development* 32(1), 17–27. Schuller, T., Preston, J., Hammond, C., Bassett-Grundy, A., and Bynner, J. (2004). *The Benefits of Learning: The Impacts of Formal and Informal Education on Social Capital, Health and Family Life*. London: Routledge.

24. Feinstein, L., Hammond, C., Woods, L., Preston, J., and Bynner, J. (2003). *The Contribution of Adult Learning to Health and Social Capital*, Research Report 8. London: Centre for Research on the Wider Benefits of Learning. See also, Jenkins, A., and Mostafa, T. (2013). "The Effects of Learning on Wellbeing for Older Adults in England." *Ageing and Society* 35(10), 1–18. Narushima, M., Liu, J., and Diestelkamp, N. (2016). "Lifelong Learning in Active Ageing Discourse: Its Conserving Effect on Wellbeing, Health and Vulnerability." *Ageing and Society* 38(4), 1–25.

25. Falk, J. H., and Storksdieck, M. (2004). *Investigating the Long-Term Impact of a Science Center on Its Community*. Final Report to National Science Foundation. Annapolis, MD: Institute for Learning Innovation.

26. Stringer, C. (2011). *The Origin of Our Species*. London: Allen Lane.

27. Falk, J. H. (2018). *Born to Choose: Evolution, Self and Well-Being*. London: Routledge.

28. "Brains." Smithsonian National Museum of Natural History. http://humanorigins.si.edu/human-characteristics/brains. Retrieved August 9, 2013.

29. "Brains." Smithsonian National Museum of Natural History. http://humanorigins.si.edu/human-characteristics/brains. Retrieved August 9, 2013.

30. For further details and explanation, see Falk, J. H. (2018). *Born to Choose: Evolution, Self and Well-Being*. London: Routledge.

31. For further details and explanation, see Falk, J. H. (2018). *Born to Choose: Evolution, Self and Well-Being*. London: Routledge.

32. For further details and explanation, see Falk, J. H. (2018). *Born to Choose: Evolution, Self and Well-Being*. London: Routledge.

33. Falk, J. H., Dierking, L. D., Rennie, L., and Scott, C. (2005). "In Praise of 'Both-And' Rather Than 'Either-Or' Thinking: A Reply to 'Interacting with Interactives.'" *Curator* 48(4), 475–77.

34. For example, Greene, J. P., Kisida, B., and Bowen, D. H. (2014). "The Educational Value of Field Trips." *Education Next* 14(1), 78–86.

35. Shawn is a pseudonym.

36. Falk, J. H. (2009). *Identity and Museum Visitor Experience*. Walnut Creek, CA: Left Coast Press.

37. See Falk, J. H. (2009). *Identity and Museum Visitor Experience*. Walnut Creek, CA: Left Coast Press.

38. See, Falk, J. H. (2009). *Identity and Museum Visitor Experience*. Walnut Creek, CA: Left Coast Press.

39. Lee, B. K. and Shafer, C. S. (2002). "The Dynamic Nature of Leisure Experience: An Application of Affect Control Theory." *Journal of Leisure Research* 34(2), 290–310. Also, Lee, B. K., Shafer, C. S. and Kang, I. (2005). "Examining Relationships among Perceptions of

Self, Episode-Specific Evaluations, and Overall Satisfaction with a Leisure Activity." *Leisure Sciences* 27, 93–109.

Mannell, R., and Iso-Ahola, S. E. (1987). "Psychological Nature of Leisure and Tourism Experience." *Annals of Tourism Research* 14, 314–31.

Stewart, W. P. (1998). "Leisure as Multiphase Experiences: Challenging Traditions." *Journal of Leisure Research* 30(4), 391–400.

Stewart, W. P., and Hull IV, B. R. (1992). "Satisfaction of What? Post Hoc versus Real-Time Construct Validity." *Leisure Sciences* 14, 195–209.

40. For example, Graefe, A. R., and Fedler, A. J. (1986). "Situational and Subjective Determinants of Satisfaction in Marine Recreational Fishing." *Leisure Sciences* 8, 275–95. See also, Lapa, T. Y. (2018). "Life Satisfaction, Leisure Satisfaction and Perceived Freedom of Park Recreation Participants." *Procedia—Social and Behavioral Sciences* 93, 1985–93. Schroeder, S. A., Cornicelli, L., Fulton, D., and Merchant, S. (2019). "The Influence of Motivation versus Experience on Recreation Satisfaction." *Journal of Leisure Research* 50(2), 107–31. Whisman, S. A., and Hollenhorst, S. J. (1998). "A Path Model of Whiteriver Boating Satisfaction on the Cheat River of West Virginia." *Environmental Management* 22(1), 109–17.

41. del Bosque, I. R., and Martin, H. S. (2008). "Tourist Satisfaction: A Cognitive-Affective Model." *Annals of Tourism Research* 35 (2), 551–73.

42. Harmon-Jones, E., and Mills, J. 1999. *Cognitive Dissonance: Progress on a Pivotal Theory in Social Psychology*. American Psychological Association, Washington, DC.

43. Merton, R. K. (1957). *Social Theory and Social Structure*, revised edition. New York: Free Press.

44. For example, Finn, P. (2006). "Bias and Blinding: Self-Fulfilling Prophecies and Intentional Ignorance." *The ASHA Leader* 11(8), 16–17, 22. See also, Jussim, L., and Harber, K.D. (2005). "Teacher Expectations and Self-Fulfilling Prophecies: Knowns and Unknowns, Resolved and Unresolved Controversies." *Personality and Social Psychology Review* 9, 131–55. Madon, S., Guyll, M., Spoth, R. L., Cross, S. E., and Hilbert, S. J. (2003). The self-fulfilling influence of mother expectations on children's underage drinking. *Journal of Personality and Social Psychology* 84, 1188–205. And, Wong, J. T., and Hui, E. C. M. (2006). "Power of Expectations." *Property Management* 24, 496–506.

45. Falk, J. H., and Storksdieck, M. (2004). *Investigating the Long-Term Impact of a Science Center on Its Community*. Final Report to National Science Foundation. Annapolis, MD: Institute for Learning Innovation.

46. Falk, J. H., and Dierking, L. D. (2014). *The Museum Experience Revisited*. Walnut Creek, CA: Left Coast Press. Also, Packer, J. (2006). "Learning for Fun: The Unique Contribution of Educational Leisure Experiences." *Curator: The Museum Journal* 49(3), 329–44.

47. Lyengar, S. (2010). *The Art of Choosing*. New York: Hachette Book Group.

48. Weinschenk, S., and Wise, B. (2013). "Why Having Choices Makes Us Feel Powerful." *Psychology Today*, January 24, 2013. https://www.psychologytoday.com/us/blog/brain-wise/201301/why-having-choices-makes-us-feel-powerful. Retrieved July 22, 2020.

49. Kelly, J. (1996). *Leisure*, third edition. Boston: Allyn and Bacon.

50. Plato. (375 BC). *The Republic*. http://www.literaturepage.com/read.php?titleid=therepublic&abspage=284&bookmark=1. Retrieved October 30, 2020.

51. See, Falk, J. H., and Dierking, L. D. (2019). *Learning from Museums*, second edition. Lanham, MD: Rowman & Littlefield.

52. Perry, D. (1989). *The Creation and Verification of a Developmental Model for the Design of a Museum Exhibit*. Unpublished doctoral dissertation. Indiana University.

53. Salmi, H. (1998). "Motivation and Meaningful Science Learning in Informal Settings." Paper presented at the annual meeting of the National Association for Research in Science Teaching, April, San Diego, CA.

54. Rennie, L. J., and McClafferty, T. P. (1995). "Using Visits to Interactive Science and Technology Centers, Museums, Aquaria, and Zoos to Promote Learning in Science." *Journal of Science Teacher Education* 6(4), 175–85.

55. Griffin, J. (1998). *School-Museum Integrated Learning Experiences in Science: A Learning Journey*. Unpublished doctoral dissertation. University of Technology, Sydney.

56. Griffin, J. (1998). *School-Museum Integrated Learning Experiences in Science: A Learning Journey*. Unpublished doctoral dissertation. University of Technology, Sydney.

57. Siegel, D. (2008). *Mindsight*. Oxford: Oneworld.

6

Social Well-Being

> Let us be grateful to people who make us happy, they are the charming gardeners who make our souls blossom.
>
> —Marcel Proust[1]

People are quintessential social creatures and as a range of humanists and social scientists of all stripes have observed, to understand humans requires an understanding of relationships. People are born into relationships and then spend the rest of their lives making relationship-related choices, virtually all of which are designed to support their well-being. Take for example this excerpt of an interview I did with Elizabeth,[2] a retired, white woman in her late sixties who I interviewed a few years ago while visiting Portland, Oregon.

Q: Do you remember your last visit to a museum?

A: Sure, that's easy. The last museum I visited was the Portland Art Museum. I was there just a few days ago.

Q: Tell me about your visit? Did you go by yourself?

A: Oh, I never go by myself. My good friend Margaret and I meet there for coffee every Wednesday.

Q: That's very interesting, why do you go to the museum for coffee? There's no shortage of great places to get coffee in Portland.

A: Well, I would have to say it's primarily just because it's such a comfortable place and Margaret really likes it. So I primarily go because Margaret and I find it nice.

[Later in the interview]

Q: So what started you and Margaret going to the art museum for coffee? Do you enjoy art?

A: Sure, I enjoy art, but that's not mainly why I go. I go to be with my friend. Margaret is the one who really enjoys art. She introduced me to the place. So I go to be with Margaret. These days we hardly ever actually walk around the museum. We just drink coffee and catch up. You know, old lady talk. Sometimes if they have a new exhibit we look, and I enjoy it, but mostly I just go there because it is a nice place to spend time with my friend.

For many people, the primary and in some cases, such as above, the only reason people go to museums is to support social relationships. This social aspect of museums has long been appreciated and countless studies have been done on the role and value of museums for supporting social encounters,[3] as well as more broadly, fostering community social cohesion.[4] In fact, many people, particularly parents, use museums as a tool for facilitating and supporting the experiences of others. Take for example, the comments of a parent interviewed by university administrator Jennifer Bachman as part of her doctoral research on homeschooling.[5]

Q: Tell me about a recent [home schooling] trip you took with your son.

A: We visited Fort Stevens—my son is studying U.S. history and loves military history especially. We also visited Fort Clatsop, Fort Worden, and the Firefighters Museum in Astoria. . . .

Q: Why did you visit these museums?

A: As a homeschooling parent, I supplement our curricula with additional reading and flexible experiences to accommodate my son's interests. These experiences help him build his knowledge of military history and extend his library research. My son and I enjoy lengthy discussions (which he often initiates), and we take trips to supplement his science and history learning. In this specific case, we wanted to see a piece of the history of the Northwest and also get an idea of the conditions personnel lived in at the fort during the various wars.

As was the case of this particular mother, the motivation of many parents for going to museums with their children is education related. Like Frank in chapter 1 and the woman described at the end of chapter 4, parents perceive museums as settings that allow them to positively fulfill their social role as parents; in fact, they perceive that museums enable them to excel at this role. For example, a Utah parent described her experience at Thanksgiving Point Museums as follows:

Absolutely [the visit inspired inquiry, curiosity and wonder]! We thought about new ideas and had great family discussions about the things we saw and even what the children might become when they grow up in relation to our experiences at Thanksgiving Point.[6]

Here is another, slightly longer set of excerpts from a set of interviews with a forty-year-old white female, who I'll call Susan, which like Frank's from chapter 1, came from research at the California Science Center. I've included three time points in

Susan's museum experience—a brief section of an interview conducted prior to her entering the science center, a field note–based distillation of her in-museum behavior, and an excerpt from an interview conducted with Susan eighteen months after her visit. The first of these interviews was conducted with Susan on a weekday in the summer of 2001. There were a total of six individuals in the group. There was Susan and her three children and her two elderly parents. As we soon discovered, Susan was not from Los Angeles but was in town visiting her parents.

THREE MUSEUM TIME POINTS

Outside the Museum

> Q: Tell me about why you decided to visit the science center today? Whose idea was it to visit today?
>
> A: I [decided]. My parents like to do things with the family, so we were spending the week with them; so we sort of decided this week to go [to the science center]. My kids are out of school and we are spending the week with [my parents] and my husband is traveling, so we thought it would be a good time to go.
>
> Q: Why the California Science Center? Have you been here before?
>
> A: Yes, I've taken my kids before and they loved it.
>
> Q: What about your parents?
>
> A: They haven't been in a long time, and I thought it would be fun for them to see it and they showed interest in going.
>
> Q: Since you have been here before and it was your idea to come today, what are you hoping will happen? What's your goal for the visit?
>
> A: Well, I guess I just want to have fun with my kids and parents, but I also want them to learn something.
>
> Q: Sure, that makes sense. But tell me more about what would be fun for you and what kinds of things do you think you want your children to learn.
>
> A: What will be fun for me is if my children enjoy themselves and enjoy being with their grandparents. I also want the kids to learn something, that they'll see some things that will help them in school and generally in their life.

Inside the Museum

Susan's in-museum behavior follows the pattern of many parents with a facilitator motivation. Her pathway through the exhibition is by and large child-driven, and thus might appear to an outside observer, as if it is somewhat random. Far more of Susan's time is devoted to social interaction than in looking at and interacting with exhibitions. Since Susan had two groups she was trying to facilitate, her children and her parents, she divided her time between them.

Susan's social interactions are mostly directed toward her parents rather than her children. However, at a few exhibits she becomes quite engaged with her children and enters into significant learning-focused social interactions. And in one case, the *Surgery Theater*, her engagement with the exhibit appears to be at least equally motivated by her own personal curiosity.

There does not appear to be any particular exhibit that Susan stopped at specifically because of her parents. Her parents, every once in a while, also looked at the exhibits that the children showed interest in, but by and large they hung back and seemed content to just watch the children, and now and then talk with Susan.

Overall, Susan appeared quite amenable to allowing her children to enjoy the museum on their own terms. Occasionally, Susan imposed her own learning agenda on the group, but mostly she allowed the children to select what they wanted to see and do.

Eighteen Months Later (Interview Conducted by Phone)

Q: Do you remember why you went to the California Science Center?

A: Absolutely. I remember that my kids were out of school, and we were visiting my parents while my husband was away. It was my idea to go. We went to the science center because we thought it would be a good time to go. My parents live not too far from the science center, and we all agreed that it would be fun and educational.

Q: Now having gone there, you said your children loved it and your parents hadn't been in a while and might like it. Going there, did that have anything to do with the fact that it was a science center, that it presented science, or was it just that it was a place to go and do stuff as a family.

A: The fact that it was a science center was good. The fact that it was educational and interactive was really important.

[Later in the interview]

Q: What I was trying to get at is how does that make you feel doing that with your children and your parents?

A: Oh, it's fun. You look for things to do that are memorable and sort of different; and that's a great day, a great thing to do. The science center or Sea World. You feel like you're getting it all in one. You're getting education, you get a fun outing, you get together as a family. The kids have a day they remember specifically as opposed to just another day at the park or something. It's very interactive, the kids can get involved; the interactive characteristic of it helps them remember, recall.

Several things stand out in this recollection. The first is that Susan clearly recalled this visit and in particular remembered that everyone enjoyed themselves. She makes it clear that she thought this was an important experience for her children and it helped them in their intellectual development. She also indicated that her parents enjoyed the experience and made the projection that they too learned from the experience. In this way she reveals the strength of her entering motivations for the day—the goal of doing something that simultaneously supported the interests and needs of both her children and her parents. However, if we can take her comments at face value, her strongest goal was helping her children grow and become healthier and happier. She made a point of stating that this was not like just taking your children to the park; this kind of experience had greater value.

In other parts of the interview, Susan talked at length about what her children did that day and what kinds of things they might have learned. For example, she went into great depth about her children's interactions with several of the health-related exhibits, explaining how her children developed a greater appreciation for the dangers of smoking and the importance of hand washing. When pressed, she indicates that she too enjoyed picking up a few things, but she's quick to point out that this was not really the purpose of the visit. As suggested by her actual behavior in the exhibition, the one exhibit that stood out for her in this latter regard was the surgery exhibit. Other than that, she dwells on the exhibits that she particularly wanted the children to see and learn from; most were exhibits that she entered the museum already knowing about and had wanted her children to see and learn from. By contrast with the depth of her social memories, Susan has precious few memories of the actual physical museum and its exhibitions itself. She is hard pressed to remember any details of what she specifically saw and did that day at the museum. Also absent from her recollections are any negative memories such as the noisiness and crowdedness of the science center on that day; these memories have seemingly been swept away by her overarching facilitator narrative. Again, her interest and needs entering, while in the museum, and then again after the visit were focused primarily on her children and secondarily on her parents. Because of her facilitator agenda, Susan was only minimally concerned with her own personal curiosity and interests or even comfort.

Her entering facilitator identity-related motivations created the framework for both her actual visit experiences and her memories of those experiences, and thus formed an overall trajectory for her visit. Susan had a working model of what the science center would afford her and her family—an enjoyable, educational experience—and then used the science museum to accomplish these goals. Ultimately, she felt very positive about this whole experience. Both in the short- and long-term, her family gave her feedback suggesting that her goal was achieved. On the day of the visit, everyone—children and parents—did indeed seem to have an enjoyable time, and over the ensuing weeks, her children gave evidence of having learned some of the things she had hoped they would.

THE WELL-BEING BENEFITS OF SOCIAL RELATIONSHIPS

Whether the goal is supporting one's children, sustaining a positive relationship with one's parents, or nourishing a relationship with a good friend, countless studies have shown a strong positive correlation between positive social relationships and perceptions of well-being (as traditionally measured), as well as between social relationships and evolutionary fitness.[7]

Arguably, one of the most persuasive pieces of evidence comes from the longest study of human development ever conducted, the Harvard University "Grant Study."[8] Beginning in 1938, the Grant Study set out to follow the lives of a group of Harvard University students—among them President John F. Kennedy and former *Washington Post* editor Ben Bradlee—and it has been tracking every aspect of these individuals' lives ever since. In the 1970s, the study began collaborating with a similar longitudinal study of young men from the tenements of inner-city Boston; that study had been going on since the 1940s. The result of these combined studies is an unprecedented compendium of long-term data of individuals (though it is important to note that all study participants are white males) of varying social status and upbringing. At regular intervals, all of the men's physical and psychological health was assessed, including the addition in recent years of genetic testing. Robert Waldinger, a Harvard psychiatrist, assumed the project's leadership in 2003. Although there is a wealth of data and many conclusions that have been gleaned from monitoring these many lives from young adulthood through old age, Waldinger believes that there is but one clear takeaway: The happiest and healthiest participants in both groups were the ones who made the decision that maintaining close, intimate relationships was their highest priority.

Many in both study groups, but particularly the men from Harvard, were very success-oriented and chose to invest their time and energy in building careers and wealth. In no small measure due to the social advantages they began life with, many did achieve significant fame and amass great fortunes. However, the process of acquiring fame and wealth often resulted in these same individuals becoming quite socially isolated. According to Waldinger, "people who are more isolated than they want to be from others find that they are less happy, their health declines earlier in midlife, their brain functioning declines sooner and they live shorter lives than people who are not lonely. . . . [G]ood, close relationships seem to buffer us from some of the slings and arrows of getting old."[9] According to Waldinger, wealth, fame, and career success, long assumed to be vital to a person's sense of well-being, did not correlate with long-term health or happiness; what did correlate with long-term health and happiness was having close connections with other human beings.

Corroborating evidence for this conclusion comes from situations where an individual feels lonely,[10] or where social bonds break down and individuals feel socially adrift, for example, when an individual decides to leave a social group in which she or he has been a long-time member[11] or when someone decides to change jobs.[12] These disruptions to social relationships have been shown to precipitate a range of negative effects, including decreased blood flow and breathing, negative moods such as fatigue and depression, and weakening of the immune system.[13]

The bottom line is that the people have a fundamental need to have relationships and feel like they belong to a group.[14] An incredibly large percentage of a person's daily thoughts, actions, and feelings are motivated by these needs. In this respect, humans are quite similar to a whole host of other social species, including most mammals and birds. Biologists have defined three critical ways that sociality supports enhanced survival: (1) by banding together, each individual reduces his or her personal risk of predation; (2) by cooperating, each individual increases his or her capabilities and resources beyond that which would be possible if he or she acted alone; and (3) by exercising altruistic behaviors, where individuals are able to significantly increase the survival of others in their group by acting in ways that might be detrimental to themselves.[15] All human societies exhibit all three of these key hallmarks of sociality, and people have evolved hundreds of thousands of culturally unique ways for encouraging members to act in these kinds of prosocial ways. These social adaptations have significantly benefited human survival.[16]

Not surprisingly, given the survival benefits of sociality, a range of physiological feedback mechanisms have evolved to support and encourage social interactions. One of the best understood of these is oxytocin, a hormone secreted by the posterior lobe of the pituitary gland, a pea-sized structure at the base of the brain. Oxytocin has sometimes been called the "cuddle hormone" or "love hormone" because it is released when people snuggle up or bond socially. A wide range of both animal (oxytocin-like substances are found in all vertebrates) and human studies have shown that increased oxytocin levels play a role in a broad range of social interactions, ranging from mother-infant bonding, romantic connection and sex, to group-related attitudes and prejudice.[17] In general, the greater the oxytocin level, the greater the perceived level of social intimacy a person feels.[18] Importantly, the effects of elevated oxytocin levels are not just short-term; elevated oxytocin has also been shown to facilitate memory formation.[19] Thus, when someone like Susan has a museum experience that elicits heightened positive social feelings, it likely resulted in a rise in oxytocin levels in her bloodstream, which, in turn, likely resulted in making that experience, as well as all of the events and associations that surrounded that experience, highly memorable.

SOCIAL STATUS

However, what sets humans apart from nearly all other species is the ability to mentally ponder their social relationships and consciously and strategically attempt to align their actions with those of others. Humans not only continuously act in ways that support the greater well-being of the group, they also spend an inordinate amount of time actively attempting to position themselves in ways that promote their own status and success relative to the group.

One of the interesting by-products of sociality is the development of social awareness and the desire to achieve social status within one's group. The nature of sociality is that invariably some individuals emerge as having greater relative status than others.[20] Although not all human societies are totally hierarchical, all contain social hierarchies.[21] Individuals with higher status invariably enjoy greater power, wealth, and access to interested mates.[22] Because of the inherent, fitness-related benefits associated with higher status, all people are innately driven to seek higher status, and the emotions, traits, and behaviors that facilitate that drive are part of the human condition.[23] All humans continuously act in ways designed to build their self-esteem, and to the degree possible, enhance their social status.[24]

It would have been too difficult for our ancestors to have had to consciously figure out the relative benefits of each and every social behavior so it is believed that humans evolved a variety of built-in psychological mechanisms that helped them automatically calculate the relative costs and benefits of employing a given strategy, with feedback on success provided in the form of emotions.[25] One of the most powerful emotions tied to social status is pride. What researchers refer to as "authentic pride" (as opposed to the self-aggrandizing, narcissistic pride some people exhibit).[26] Authentic pride "is fueled by the emotional rush of accomplishment, confidence, and success. Authentic pride is associated with prosocial and achievement-oriented behaviors, extraversion, agreeableness, conscientiousness, satisfying interpersonal relationships, and positive mental health."[27] In general, people who are confident, agreeable, hard-working, energetic, kind, empathic, non-dogmatic, and high in genuine self-esteem are noticed and emulated by others, and afforded significant social status.[28]

The need for esteem, for pride, is an important motivator of human behavior. All humans have a need to feel respected and valued by others, to be appreciated as someone who is making a contribution.[29] Fortunately, there are myriad positive ways an individual in our modern society can build and sustain self-efficacy as well as gain recognition. The most typical way for many is through their work, though for many others, personal hobbies represent a major, alternative vehicle for achieving esteem, as are public performances such as sports or the arts. Of course, many seek to achieve esteem through displays of wealth, often exhibited through conspicuous forms of consumption.[30] In addition, as exemplified by all the interviews cited earlier in this chapter, people also derive significant feelings of self-esteem and recognition through their social relationships, by being perceived as a good parent or a loyal friend. In all of these situations, feelings of self-esteem as well as feelings of pride associated with the respect and appreciation of others support a sense of social well-being.[31]

Esteem is primarily regulated by positive, rather than a negative feedback mechanisms.[32] The more one does things that garner esteem, the greater the sense of pleasure one feels and the more one wants to keep doing those things. For example, studies have shown that individuals who perceive that others respect them for exercising, increase their levels of exercise.[33] Similarly, if people perceive that being healthy garners respect, then research has shown that these people report feeling less depressed and having fewer aches and pains.[34] Over all, individuals who perceive that they have high esteem self-report that they are happier, have more cheerful memories and generally higher levels of life-satisfaction than do individuals who perceive they have low esteem.[35] As exemplified in the interviews with individuals like Frank in an earlier chapter and Elizabeth and Susan in this chapter, museums are places many people believe support their sense of self-worth as a parent, a child, or a friend. Because these experiences are so positive, people regularly and willingly share these memories with others. By sharing these tangible examples of good parenting and/or friendship with others, the person receives acknowledgment and reinforcement for the value of the experience, which in turn fosters a sense of pride and a heightened perception of self-esteem. Collectively, all of this serves to reinforce for these people the perception that museums and museum-going are something of great value.

MUSEUMS AND STATUS

There is no escaping the reality that most people perceive museums as being places of "high" culture, certainly as compared with most other types of leisure destinations such as movie houses, shopping malls, or theme parks. In fact, museums in general, and art museums in particular, have long been considered by many as elitist organizations. Although many in the museum profession have found this situation problematic, since it has created a barrier to the kind of broad, equalitarian usage a majority of museum professionals aspire to support, the air of social cache associated with museums has also been a significant attractor for some users; notably many donors, trustees, and docents.

For as long as there has been civilization, both the production as well as the display of art has been associated with and dependent upon wealth. This was as true for the Medicis during the Renaissance as it was for the Fricks and Morgans in the United States during the Gilded Age of the late nineteenth century. Most art museums, as well as many other types of museums, largely depend upon wealthy board members and their friends to help ensure their economic survival. For example, a recent story in the *New York Times* highlighted that roughly 90 percent of the Museum of Modern Art's trustees work in finance, the corporate world, real estate or law, or are the heirs or spouses of the superrich. Accordingly, membership on the board comes with the clear expectation that they will give millions of dollars to the institution.[36] And of course these individuals join the board willingly, with a waiting list of others equally willing and able to follow in their footsteps. The reason is of course clear: membership on a museum board brings significant benefits, including an increase in social status, access to powerful people, and an enhancement of one's image within one's social circles—all benefits that would not exist if the museum itself was not considered prestigious.[37]

Similar benefits accrue to all who associate with such museums, including volunteers and users. Although exact data on how this works and in what measure is hard to come by since people do not like to talk about this aspect of their museum experience, presumably because it is not considered socially acceptable to admit that you volunteer or visit a museum largely, or even in part, because of the social status it affords. However, there is evidence that this type of motivation exists. For example, in a study of docents at a California environmental visitor center, all of the docents interviewed overwhelmingly agreed with statements like "I volunteered . . . because it feels good that I make a contribution to the [p]ark." and "I volunteered because it makes me feel good about myself."[38] While in another study, this one involving docents at three different types of museums, researchers found that some docents were considered higher status than others in large part due to their history with, and knowledge of, the institution.[39]

As for museum users, explicit statements of status are difficult to come by, but the idea that there are status-related benefits associated with museum use can be inferred from statements like this snippet from an interview with Rosa,[40] a Latina woman in her late thirties describing a conversation she had with her friend about her recent visit to a local marine science center with her two children:

> Q: So you talked with your friend about your visit [to the children's museum]?
>
> A: Yes, we were at a party and chatting about fun things to do with our kids. I told her I took my children to the marine science center in Newport. I said we had a great time. She was very impressed.
>
> Q: Why, what made you think she was impressed?
>
> A: Well, she's never taken her kids to any place like that, and she gave me this kind of look, like, well aren't you "big stuff."
>
> Q: So you thought that meant she was impressed?
>
> A: Oh, I know it did. In fact, I found out a couple of weeks later that she took her kids there.

Of course, no matter how much status some behavior might yield, if it doesn't feel comfortable or safe, people won't do it.

NOTES

1. "Marcel Proust Quotes." BrainyQuote. https://www.brainyquote.com/quotes/marcel_proust_105251. Retrieved July 22, 2020.
2. Elizabeth is a pseudonym.
3. For review, see Falk, J. H., and Dierking, L. D. (2014). *The Museum Experience Revisited.* London: Routledge. Also, Falk, J. H. (2009). *Identity and Museum Visitor Experience.* Walnut Creek, CA: Left Coast Press.
4. For example, McKinley, K. (2017). "What Is Our Museum's Social Impact?" Medium.com, July 10, 2017. https://medium.com/new-faces-new-spaces/what-is-our-museums-social-impact-62525fe88d16. Retrieved July 23, 2020. See also, Jones, J. (2020).

"Quantifying Our Museum's Social Impact." Medium.com, May 14, 2020. https://medium.com/new-faces-new-spaces/quantifying-our-museums-social-impact-e99bff3ef30e. Retrieved July 26, 2020. Dafoe, T. (2020). "Attendance Has Always Been a Narrow Way to Define Success. That's Why This Museum Is Using Data Science to Measure Its Social Impact." Artnet News, February 19, 2020. https://news.artnet.com/art-world/oakland-museum-social-impact-1780698#.XlEnYoZUia0.twitter. Retrieved February 23, 2020. And, Korn, R. (2018). *Intentional Practice for Museums*. Lanham, MD: Rowman & Littlefield.

5. Bachman, J. (2011). *STEM Learning Activity among Home-Educating Families*. Unpublished doctoral thesis. Corvallis: Oregon State University.

6. Ashton, S., Johnson, E., Ross Nelson, K., Ortiz, J., and Wicai, D. (in prep.). "Social Impact at Thanksgiving Point." *Curator*.

7. See review by Falk, J. H. (2018). *Born to Choose: Evolution, Self and Well-Being*. London: Routledge.

8. Itkowitz, C. (2016). "Harvard Researchers Discovered the One Thing Everyone Needs for Happier, Healthier Lives." *The Independent*, March 2, 2016. http://www.independent.co.uk/life-style/harvard-researchers-discover-the-one-thing-everyone-needs-for-happier-and-healthier-lives-a6907901.html. Retrieved March 2, 2016.

9. Waldinger, R. (2015). "What Makes a Good Life? Lessons from the Longest Study on Happiness." https://www.ted.com/talks/robert_waldinger_what_makes_a_good_life_lessons_from_the_longest_study_on_happiness?language=en. Retrieved March 2, 2016.

10. Hawkley, L. C., and Cacioppo, J. T. (2007). "Aging and Loneliness: Downhill Quickly?" *Current Directions in Psychological Science* 16(4), 187–91. See also, Hawkley, L. C., Thisted, R. A., Masi, C. M., and Cacioppo, J. T. (2010). "Loneliness Predicts Increased Blood Pressure: Five-Year Cross-Lagged Analyses in Middle-Aged and Older Adults." *Psychol Aging* 25(1): 132–41. And, Jaremka, L. M., Fagundes, C. P., Glaser, R., Bennett, J. M., Malarkey, W. B., and Kiecolt-Glaser, J. K. (2012). "Loneliness Predicts Pain, Depression, and Fatigue: Understanding the Role of Immune Dysregulation." *Psychoneuroendocrinology* 38(8), 1310–17. doi: 10.1016/j.psyneuen.2012.11.016.

11. For example, Harris, K. J. (2015). Edith Cowan University. *Leaving Ideological Social Groups Behind: A Grounded Theory of Psychological Disengagement*. Retrieved from http://ro.ecu.edu.au/theses/1587. Retrieved March 13, 2016.

12. For example, Faragher, E. B., Cass, M., and Cooper, C. L. (2005). "The Relationship between Job Satisfaction and Health: A Meta-Analysis." *Occupational and Environmental Medicine* 62(2),105–12.

13. Goleman, D. (2006). *Social Intelligence: The New Science of Human Relationships*. New York: Bantam Books.

14. Baumeister, R., and Leary, M. (1995). "The Need to Belong: Desire for Interpersonal Attachment as a Fundamental Human Motivation." *Psychological Bulletin*, 117(3), 497–529.

15. Wilson, E. O. (1975). *Sociobiology: The New Synthesis*. Cambridge, MA: The Belknap Press, 38.

16. Henrich, J., and Gil-White, F. J. (2001). "The Evolution of Prestige: Freely Conferred Deference as a Mechanism for Enhancing the Benefits of Cultural Transmission." *Evolution and Human Behavior* 22(3), 165–96.

17. "Oxytocin." (2020). Wikipedia. https://en.wikipedia.org/wiki/Oxytocin. Retrieved November 15, 2020.

18. Kirsch, P. (2015). "Oxytocin in the Socioemotional Brain." *Dialogues in Clinical Neuroscience* 17(4), 463–76.

19. Guastella, A., Mitchell, P., and Mathews, F. (2008). *Biological Psychiatry* 64(3), 256–58.

20. Wilson, E. O. (1975). *Sociobiology: The New Synthesis*. Cambridge, MA: The Belknap Press, 38.

21. Fried, M. H. (1967). *The Evolution of Political Society: An Essay in Political Anthropology*. New York: Random House.

22. Koski, J., Xie, H., and Olson, I. (2015). "Understanding Social Hierarchies: The Neural and Psychological Foundations of Status Perception." *Social Neuroscience* 10(5), 527–50.

23. Kaufman, S. B. (2010). "Two Routes to Social Status." *Psychology Today*, August 6, 2010. https://www.psychologytoday.com/us/blog/beautiful-minds/201008/two-routes-social-status#:~:text=The%20bulk%20of%20the%20evidence%20suggests%20that%20pride,each%20form%20may%20have%20evolved%20along%20different%20paths. Retrieved July 26, 2020.

24. Koski, J., Xie, H., and Olson, I. (2015)." Understanding Social Hierarchies: The Neural and Psychological Foundations of Status Perception." *Social Neuroscience* 10(5), 527–50.

25. Kaufman, S. B. (2010). "Two Routes to Social Status." *Psychology Today*, August 6, 2010. https://www.psychologytoday.com/us/blog/beautiful-minds/201008/two-routes-social-status#:~:text=The%20bulk%20of%20the%20evidence%20suggests%20that%20pride,each%20form%20may%20have%20evolved%20along%20different%20paths. Retrieved July 26, 2020.

26. Bonnellan, M. B., Trzesniewski, K. H., Robins, R. W., Moffitt, T. E., and Caspi, A. (2005). "Low Self-Esteem Is Related to Aggression, Antisocial Behavior, and Delinquency." *Psychological Sciences* 16(4), 328–35.

27. Kaufman, S. B. (2010). "Two Routes to Social Status." Psychology Today, August 6, 2010. https://www.psychologytoday.com/us/blog/beautiful-minds/201008/two-routes-social-status#:~:text=The%20bulk%20of%20the%20evidence%20suggests%20that%20pride,each%20form%20may%20have%20evolved%20along%20different%20paths. Retrieved July 26, 2020.

28. Cheng, J. T., Tracy, J. L., and Henrich, J. (2010). "Pride, Personality, and the Evolutionary Foundations of Human Social Status." *Evolution and Human Behavior* 31(5), 334–47.

29. Lester D. (1990). "Maslow's Hierarchy of Needs and Personality." *Personality and Individual Differences* 11(11), 1187–88.

30. Bandura, A. (1977). "Self-Efficacy: Toward a Unifying Theory of Behavioral Change." *Psychological Review* 84(2), 191–215.

31. Bollo, H., Bothe, B., Toth-Kiraly, I., and Orosz, G. (2018). "Pride and Social Status." *Frontiers of Psychology*, October 25, 2018. https://doi.org/10.3389/fpsyg.2018.01979.

32. Zahn, R., Moll, J., Paiva, M., Garrido, G., Krueger, F., Huey E., and Grafman, J. (2009). "The Neural Basis of Human Social Values: Evidence from Functional MRI." *Cerebral Cortex* 19(2), 276–83.

33. Sapolski, R. M. (2004). "Social Status and Health in Humans and Other Animals." *Annual Review of Anthropology* 33(1), 393–418.

34. Sapolski, R. M. (2004). "Social Status and Health in Humans and Other Animals." *Annual Review of Anthropology* 33(1), 393–418.

35. Diener, E., and Biswas-Diener, R. (2008). *Happiness: Unlocking the Mysteries of Psychological Wealth*. Malden, MA: Blackwell.

36. Massing, M. (2019). "How the Superrich Took over the Museum World." *New York Times*, December 14, 2019. https://www.nytimes.com/2019/12/14/opinion/sunday/modern-art-museum.html. Retrieved July 26, 2020.

37. Ostrower, F. (2003). "Trustees of Culture: Power, Wealth, and Status of Elite Arts Boards." *Contemporary Sociology* 32(6), 711–12.

38. Ford, M. R. (2016). *"Sharing Joy": Volunteers' Motivations at California's Crystal Cove State Park.* Unpublished Masters Capstone. Corvallis, OR: Oregon State University.

39. Abu-Schumays, M., and Leinhardt, G. (2000, October). "Two Docents in Three Museums: A Study of Central and Peripheral Participation." *Museum Learning Collaborative Technical Report #MLC-02*, p. 6. http://www.lrdc.pitt.edu/mlc/documents/mlc-02.pdf. Retrieved July 26, 2020.

40. Rosa is a pseudonym. The interview was conducted for me in 2007 by a colleague.

7

Physical Well-Being

Better a thousand times careful than once dead.

—Proverb [1]

To read most social science research you would think you were reading about a race of humans living in the science fiction world of ten thousand or a hundred thousand years from now, a time when people had evolved to the point where they are nothing but a large brain suspended in a bubbling vat of nutrient solution. Rarely do most social science studies ever mention or give credence to the fact that their subjects possess physical bodies with biological needs, living within real-world environments. Presumably, none of the subjects in any of these studies ever needed to eat or urinate or put on a sweater because they were cold during the course of the study, and no doubt none of these issues ever impacted results. For that matter, also rarely if ever considered as an issue is the fact that much of the published psychological research has been conducted in small, claustrophobic offices in the basement of some psychology building, spaces that most subjects are experiencing for the first, and most hope, for the last time in their lives. However, real people do have bodies and do live in the actual world. All people are directly influenced by the qualities of their surroundings and all have unignorable biological needs. The seemingly trivial aspects of day-to-day life such as eating, sleeping, warmth (but not too much warmth), staying dry, and the need to eliminate bodily wastes through urination and defecation are not incidental to existence, they are fundamental. So too is awareness of one's physical surroundings; when the surrounding world is not familiar or comforting, people experience real anxiety and even fear.[2] All of these physical dimensions of life have real impacts on the ways people act, think, derive satisfaction, and achieve well-being.[3]

Unlike today, historically people would have spent virtually their entire waking hours in search of food or working the fields in order to generate food. Also, historically, staying warm in the winter, cool in the summer, and dry during rainstorms were major, life-critical tasks. Today, most of us live within climate-controlled environments and can satisfy our energetic needs through a vast food supply infrastructure. Despite these conveniences and a societal blind spot with regard to the importance of these basic needs, each of us still spends more than half of every day attending to bodily needs such as eating, sleeping, and eliminating waste.[4] These needs equally demand our attention at home, at work, and during our leisure time—particularly during leisure time, since often we are in unfamiliar environments and thus have to worry about both access to, and the quality of, these fundamental aspects of life.

In her important doctoral research on the reasons people utilize museums, Theano Moussouri found that among her sample of eighty-six families visiting three different UK museums, a surprisingly high percentage indicated that a major motivation for their visit was physical comfort—a place to get out of the rain or keep cool during a hot spell.[5] Washington, DC museum lavatories have long served as a respite for both the homeless and for individuals engaged in protest marches in this capital city. Acknowledgment of, and heightened attention to, users' biological needs represents one of the most significant changes in museum practice of the past thirty years, and arguably is at least partially responsible for significant increases in use of museums during this time period. The addition of quality, clean, readily accessible bathrooms, as well as the addition of seating, better lighting, and greater cleanliness in exhibition halls, as well as the expansion of food services, have all significantly contributed to the growing public perception of museums as premium leisure attractions. As one museum visitor in Australia was quoted as saying,

> It's welcoming, it's clean. . . . I remember taking the kids there a zillion years ago, so probably the old-style museum sticks in my brain. So I was probably pleasantly surprised—it's more up-to-date, it's clean, it's modern.[6]

Perhaps the most notable of the museum experience enhancements has been in the area of improved food services; as attested to, for example, by the following paid advertisement about food services at the St. Louis City Museum:

> Samwiches in the City Museum is the place to go to when you are hungry. After all that climbing, sliding, running, playing, and stomping, well you are going to get hungry.[7]

In fact, at some museums, the food has become as much an attraction as the exhibitions. Here is the lead for a 2017 article in a fine dining magazine:

> Your mouth may not start to water in front of Andy Warhol's famous *Campbell* soup but how would it be if your visit to the museum were followed up by a fantastic gourmet experience on a par with the exhibition itself?

> This is exactly what has been happening for some time now in various museums around the world where the concept of a quick snack during or after the visit has now become old hat. This is because the meal consumed at the museum receives the same care as an authentic work of art. In fact, it is a work of art.[8]

An equally rarified but definitely gastronomically inspired example was the Museum of Modern Art in New York's 2013 "Edible Magritte," a dinner party series held in conjunction with their special exhibition of the Belgian artist's challenging, surreal art pieces. Local artist Elaine Tin Nyo partnered with MoMA Cafe 2 chef Lynn Bound to create a hands-on meal that transformed Margitte's art work into edible concoctions. According to a contemporary description,

> Patrons ate the first surrealist meal last week, which included blue cocktails and pink cheese puffs, evoking "Pink Bells, Tattered Skies" and prosciutto with a large black olive that echoed the eerie dinner scene in "The Portrait." Il Flottant, a classic French dessert, was reimagined to resemble puffy clouds floating across an azure sky. Diners also feasted on a large chocolate bird filled with raspberries and syrup, a nod to macabre "The Pleasure," which depicts a young woman gnawing on a bloodied bird.[9]

As the above examples suggest, an increasing number of people are attracted to museums for physical well-being reasons that transcend the personal, intellectual, or even social well-being aspects of museums, though the food examples above likely apply to only a relatively small subset of the population. If a person is really hungry and desperately in need of food, or freezing to death and in need of shelter, it is unlikely he or she would immediately look to museums for support. Disproportionately, the people who benefit from the experiences offered by most museums do not suffer from significant physical privation. That has not historically been the niche museums have filled, nor is it likely to be the niche most aspire to play in the future. However, the needs represented by what I have described as the needs of "continuity"—things like food, shelter, clothing—are not to be taken lightly.

As an increasing number of museums have discovered, user satisfaction increases markedly when users can get a good cup of coffee and a reasonable meal at an affordable price in a comfortable environment. Satisfaction also increases when people do not feel lost or overwhelmed within the space, when there are ample places to sit and rest and the ambient temperature is not too hot or too cold. Gone are the days that people willingly put up with cold, dusty, and physically unpleasant, inhospitable settings and experiences. Clearly, this is an area where many museums still have a long way to go, but collectively the community has made great strides in becoming more comfortable settings.

However, these most basic of physical well-being attributes are not the only important dimensions of physical well-being. There are, comparably important dimensions of physical well-being that museums actually do fulfill admirably well. The physical well-being dimensions of safety and security are of particular importance. A large majority of the public say this is an aspect of museums that they particularly find attractive and, at least historically, proactively utilized museums because they perceived them as particularly safe and secure environments.

SAFETY AND SECURITY

Few aspects of well-being are more visceral, more emotion-laden than the need to feel safe and secure. Although the earliest evolving well-being systems, with their origins dating to about 3.7 billion years ago, were those dedicated to the needs of physiological continuity, things like the taking in and processing of nutrients and elimination of wastes, not far behind was the evolution of systems associated with the well-being dimension I have labeled individuality.[10] The earliest living things were not around long before they faced severe selection pressure to protect themselves from a host of external dangers, some of them abiotic, but many others very much biotic. On the early earth, as is still the case today, there existed a whole host of organisms, large and small, eager to use other living things as their food supply.[11] In response to these serious threats, life has evolved a range of strategies for recognizing and combating attacks by both pathogens and predators. As suggested by the epigram at the beginning of this chapter, life has evolved to appreciate the wisdom of "better a thousand times careful than once dead."

The well-being systems that originally evolved as mechanisms for insuring safety from microscopic invaders such as bacteria and viruses ultimately evolved into well-being systems capable of detecting and responding to the self-destroying effects of a succession of increasingly large and complex predators. The result has been the evolution of a series of physical well-being/survival-related strategies at successively higher and more complex levels of organization—the tissue, organ, the individual, and even beyond the single individual, including well-being systems aimed at regulating life at the social, family, community, and some even argue the ecosystem level.[12] At each level, maintaining physical well-being involves multiple steps, but it always begins with awareness. Living things invest considerable energy in early warning systems, some genetic and some neural, designed to alert them to attack. After all, life is fragile, and even the largest, toughest, and fiercest organisms have vulnerabilities. Vigilance is key, for any breach in the integrity of the organism's "individuality" nearly always results in diminished fitness, which in turn results in reduced chances of survival.[13] As a consequence, all living things, including people, actively seek to place themselves in situations where the threat of disease and or attack are minimized.

Compared to our ancestors, modern humans are lucky. Modern humans no longer need to be constantly on the lookout for large predators like lions, tigers, and bears, or stealth predators such as venomous snakes and leopards. The "predators" most modern people now fear the most are other people. Although the actual risk of being attacked by another person these days is relatively low, fear of such attacks remains high.[14] As one user described:

> One of the things I really like about taking my children [to the children's museum] is I don't have to worry about their safety. I can just sit and let them roam around and not have to worry about them getting lost or anything like that.[15]

Historically, museums were consistently considered one of the safest public places; places where someone could go, even with children, without fear of adverse consequences.[16] Not only is this sense of security valuable in and of itself, it is also an essential ingredient for all other forms of well-being. As suggested earlier, Abraham Maslow is justifiably celebrated for his pioneering efforts related to self-actualization, but arguably his more enduring legacy was his clear-eyed appreciation that without a basic feeling of security and safety, most humans would find it near impossible to partake in other forms of well-being, including socialization, intellectual pursuits, and of course, personal actualization.[17] In recent years, many museums have strived to push the boundaries of the content they present, hosting exhibitions and forums on controversial or challenging topics, such as slavery, death, or sex,[18] or creating programs to facilitate deep reflection and psychic healing on topics such as racism, colonialism, and spousal abuse.[19] These efforts would be impossible to achieve if the public felt that the physical setting in which they were encountering these ideas were in any way physically threatening. People are only willing to take intellectual risks, or for that matter personal or social risks, when they feel physically safe and secure.[20]

This reality has become painfully apparent as I write this book during a world-wide pandemic. The classic lyrics by Joni Mitchell, "You don't know what you've got until it's gone,"[21] seem particularly apt at the moment, as fear of contagion precipitated the closing of nearly all museums worldwide. As museums make the transition to reopening, many organizations are looking for ways to ensure the safety of their staff and users, and how to facilitate public trust in these measures. All museums, including art and history museums, children's museums, science centers, aquariums, zoos, botanical gardens, and nature centers have been affected by both public policies and guidelines and the public's perceptions of the health and safety of returning to these settings. As institutions begin to reopen, all have attempted to variously ensure safety, including having staff wear personal protective equipment (such as facemasks), installation of protective panels in places where staff and users regularly interact (such as at ticket booths and information stations), and of course enforcing safe distance requirements between staff and users at all times. Common is the installation of hand-sanitizing stations throughout the museum. Unfortunately, none of these measures guarantee that the public will uniformly deem these settings safe for use. The best guess is that over time, with the implementation of wide-spread vaccination, things will return to some semblance of normal, but whether the new normal will truly equate with the old normal is anyone's guess.

Ironically, it was only in the past decade or so that museum professionals began to fully appreciate that museum experiences could, and did, play an important role in physical well-being. Not just museum professionals, but the public as well, were becoming increasingly aware of the significant mental and physical health benefits afforded by a museum visit.

HEALING ENVIRONMENTS

Modern humans suffer from a health issue that the vast majority of our ancestors rarely encountered—stress. In fact, so alarming has been the increase in stress that the World Health Organization identified stress as potentially the single greatest health epidemic of the twenty-first century.[22] The effect of stress on emotional and physical well-being can be devastating. In a recent United States study, over 50 percent of individuals felt that stress negatively affected their work productivity, with estimates suggesting that the financial cost to businesses was in excess of $300 billion a year.[23] Between 1983 and 2009, stress levels in the United States increased by 10 percent to 30 percent among all demographic groups, with studies showing that anywhere between 75 percent and 90 percent of all visits to primary care physicians are for stress-related problems.[24] Thus, although seemingly little appreciated, and even less valued, it is highly important that a surprisingly large number of people seek out museums specifically for their rejuvenating or restorative benefits.[25]

Building on the ideas of environmental psychology researchers Rachael and Steve Kaplan,[26] Australian museum researcher Jan Packer has shown that museums provide a setting where people can measurably decompress from the daily grind of modern life. In one study, she interviewed sixty visitors to the Queensland Museum and roughly three-quarters reported restorative benefits, including the ability to focus, relax, reflect, and/or find peace and tranquility.[27]

> You get absorbed in what you're looking at and you do tend to forget about your immediate circumstances and where you've come from. They are very absorbing places. I guess because there's just so much around you that takes your attention. . . . you're concentrating on it, so you're not really thinking about anything else . . . I think if it was hard work and taxing, I wouldn't come.
>
> You can shut off all the noise around you and just concentrate on what you read, what you're looking at. I can do that with most things if I'm enjoying what I'm doing.
>
> You're getting away from the stresses and hassles of life in general to somewhere where you can just relax and look and enjoy.
>
> It's kind of closed off from the rest of the traffic and outside city. It's a bit of a sanctuary from the city outside. . . . you're just focusing on other worlds, rather than the outside reality.
>
> It's almost a little bit of escapism in some ways. . . . I suppose you just realize there's more out there than just worrying about the fortnightly wage and the mortgage and jobs and all the rest of that junk that you think about every day. And just have a think about the environment and people, history and everything that's in a museum. It just takes your mind off all that type of thing.

In a follow-up, confirmatory study, Packer and fellow researcher Nigel Bond surveyed nearly six hundred visitors to a history museum, art museum, aquarium, and botanic garden and found, as predicted, that the vast majority of these museum visitors self-reported finding their experiences restorative and recharging.[28]

A concrete example of this phenomena emerged in an interview I did with Francis,[29] a woman in her late fifties of Japanese American extraction. At the time of the interview, she was working as a bookkeeper and office manager for a San Francisco Bay Area trucking company.

Q: Do you remember your last visit to a museum of some kind?

A: Do you consider a botanical garden a museum?

Q: Yes, have you been to a botanical garden recently?

A: Well, I go to the Berkeley garden almost every week. I was there just about a week ago.

Q: Tell me about your visit? Did you go by yourself?

A: I usually go by myself; I was by myself last Wednesday.

Q: That's very interesting; why do you go to the garden so frequently by yourself?

A: I guess I just really enjoy being there [chuckles]; I don't suppose I'd go so often if I didn't.

Q: I'm sorry, of course you enjoy yourself. Let me rephrase my question. People go to museum-like places for a wide range of reasons. Sometimes it's for social reasons, sometimes it's to find out more about a particular topic, and for others it is just the joy of being in a nice place. I guess I was trying to better understand what specific things might motivate you to visit a place like the Berkeley Gardens so frequently.

A: Well, I would have to say it's primarily just because it's such a beautiful place and I find that going there helps me unwind. It's not that my job is so terribly more stressful than anyone else's, but life today, you know, is quite stressful. So I find going to the Garden quite relaxing.

Q: That makes great sense. I'm actually familiar with Berkeley Botanical Gardens; I used to work there many years ago. I'm curious where you go in the garden in particular. Do you just wander around or is there a special place you like to go?

A: Well, on different days I do go to different places, depending upon what's in bloom. But my favorite place to go, and where I went on Wednesday, if that's what you want to know, is Rhododendron Dell. It's so beautiful and mystical there. The creek runs through the space and there are these nice little benches tucked away where you can sit amongst the ferns and the rhodis and just decompress.

[Later in the interview]

Q: Anything specific stand out in your memory from last Wednesday's visit?

A: The whole thing.

Q: Okay, tell me more.

A: Mainly, just a feeling of calm I had. It was a hot day, by Berkeley standards anyway, and it was so cool and tranquil in the [Rhododendron] Dell. I remember listening to the creek gurgling over the rocks, seeing the sunlight falling in little spots through the leaves of the trees and just soaking in the silence. As usual, it was after work. Fortunately I get off work early because the gardens closes so early. But since it was the end of the day there was virtually no one there. I probably wasn't actually there for more than about fifteen or twenty minutes, but it was enough to do the job.

Q: And the job was?

A: To rejuvenate me, making me feel less stressed, more calm. To allow me to connect with my inner spirit.

Francis could, and occasionally did visit the Berkeley Botanical Garden to see the plants and learn more about horticulture and the like, but primarily she used the garden as her own personal refuge, a place where she could recharge and rejuvenate. Critical to this benefit was the physical setting of the garden—its sights and sounds. The beauty, the sense of peace and security afforded by the garden were like "well-being medicine" for Francis, and she took this "medicine" regularly, by her own account, almost every week.

This healing, almost medicinal benefit of museums has now been explicitly capitalized on by a range of institutions. For example, in a recent review of findings from hundreds of museum projects, reports, publications, and other evidence, Helen Chatterjee and Guy Noble found consistent evidence of museums supporting the mental and physical health of users.[30] Similar results were also presented in a preliminary report from the National Alliance for Museums, Health and Wellbeing.[31] The largest number of efforts have involved work with older populations focused on supporting cognitive improvement and reminiscence work with individuals suffering from dementia. These programs range from largescale and on-going efforts to one-time, smaller scale projects.

For example, with funding from the European Union, five open-air museums and three universities worked together to develop ways to improve the capabilities of people with dementia.[32] Particularly notable was the work at the Danish museum Den Gamle By, where the museum brought Alzheimer patients to a perfectly reproduced typical 1950s home; a home filled with not only with faithfully reproduced furniture and objects, but also the smells and sounds of the era. Research showed that this kind of recreated environment dramatically improved patients' abilities to reconstruct memories; in many cases memories previously erased by their illness.[33] In another highly structured study at Den Gamle By, the memories and behaviors of a group of elderly patients diagnosed with Alzheimer's disease were studied both prior to and after visiting Den Gamle By's House of Memory on repeated occasions. The findings clearly showed a greater degree of memory after a visit, with the memories evoked in more detail. The project also included a control group of Alzheimer-suffering individuals who did not visit the museum. The control group did not show the same striking increases in memories or related behaviors.[34]

Other programs have targeted individuals with other types of mental and physical infirmities. For example, the various botanical garden programs are aimed at supporting plants and gardening as therapies for issues such as post-traumatic stress or anxiety.[35] Particularly notable have been the many efforts focused on youth with various degrees of autism.[36] In recent years, museums have begun using technology as a way to ensure that physical disabilities are not a limitation for participation in museum experiences. For example, when the Smithsonian's Hirschhorn Museum and Sculpture Garden hosted a major exhibition of Japanese painter Yayoi Kusama's "Infinity" rooms, it created a virtual-reality simulation of the three mirrored chambers for wheelchair users who could not physically enter because of the installations' narrow platforms. Similarly, the New Museum in New York created an experiential video for visitors who could not walk through the psychedelic maze of rooms that made up Marta Minujín's exhibition "Menesunda Reloaded." Consistently, museums are creating touch objects and Braille labeling that allow visitors with visual disabilities and enhanced audio materials for individuals with hearing disabilities to ensure that these historically marginalized populations can now equally benefit from the types of physical well-being-related opportunities long unavailable to them. As one wheelchair-bound individual commented about the decision made by staff at London's Kew Gardens to set the pieces off from the pathways so visitors of all types could easily see them,

> I was able to experience it in precisely the same way everybody else [could]. For someone who has spent his lifetime going around the side, the exhibition's design—simple as it might have been—made all the difference.[37]

Although individuals with disabilities are acutely aware of their surroundings, most "normal" people today seem remarkably oblivious of their physical environments. Likely this is because, as stated at the top of this chapter, so much of modern life is lived within virtually identical, highly sanitized, climate-controlled boxes. Most museums, though, are not your typical, everyday box.

Almost by definition, most museums are built to be physical settings unlike those most people normally inhabit. Despite their novelty, in fact because of their modest novelty,[38] people find museum environments compelling settings. The positive effects museums' physical environments have on people are of course not accidental. They are the products of skilled architects and designers who have expertly manipulated space,[39] light,[40] color,[41] sound,[42] and even the smell of the environment to facilitate positive experiences.[43] Not all users consciously appreciate this fact, but when interviewed, there are always a few people able to articulate how important these setting characteristics are to their experience. Here are some examples, the first from a study conducted at a Canadian botanical garden and the second from a study conducted at an Australian natural history museum.[44]

> Initially, I didn't think that a visit to the garden could make me feel any different. However, when I visited the garden, I felt like I was in a different space. It was calm. It was as if I am in a different world. I felt calm.

> They've made it interesting by the texture of the wall and the blocks coming out and you sort of feel like some are a bit more hidden, and then some are sort of really obvious. . . .
> OK, well, I think my immediate thought was it's all very blue . . . and it's definitely the sea. . . . [Y]eah that was a nice feeling in that [Opal Fossils] display area. . . . Well, it felt more open, less enclosed, you didn't—you didn't feel you were in a cave; you felt you were in an area where—you didn't feel so constricted.

Even when museum spaces are dark and claustrophobic, most visitors venture in unafraid. That is because for decades, museums have earned a reputation as "safe" places, places where one's welfare is secure. This reputation for safety is well earned and non-trivial. Being a place viewed by the public as safe turns out to be really important.

One area where museums have increasingly played a role in supporting the public's physical well-being, one which I am willing to bet quickly returns to pre-pandemic levels, is in facilitating mating-related social relationships. Exactly when these activities can again safely resume is of course like everything else uncertain, but that they will resume I have no doubt. The biological imperatives surrounding mating behaviors are just too great to keep them indefinitely suppressed, and museums have come to increasingly play an active role in supporting them. Some may be surprised that I bring up mating behavior as an area of physical well-being-value museums support, as this is not a particularly common way for museums to tout their public value. However, before the disruptions created by the COVID-19 pandemic, the bringing together of young, eligible singles was rapidly becoming one of the signature activities of the museum community.

SEX AND THE MUSEUM

In a study I conducted at the National Museum of Natural History in Washington, DC, my colleagues and I specifically attempted to estimate how much time people spent "checking out" others.[45] Unfortunately, we humans are so unbelievably adept at doing this very common activity that my colleagues and I could not accurately capture this behavior. We certainly noticed that people were stealing glances at others, but even though these behaviors were actually quite common, they were executed so discreetly and fleetingly, that we found it challenging to accurately record either incidence or duration of these behaviors. It seems that we humans have evolved the ability to almost instantaneously make judgments about the qualities of others. In fact, research has shown that these judgments occur constantly and typically last only fractions of a second.[46] So quickly are these judgments made that the only way it is possible to get an accurate sense of just how much time and effort is spent on this behavior is to use highly specialized equipment within a controlled, laboratory setting. Still, we know that people regularly engage in this type of behavior when in museums. We also know that over the years, some people have used museums as not only settings for watching others, but even occasionally as good places for finding and connecting with a potential mate.

Take, for example, the following anecdote relayed by museum researcher Jeffery Smith. One day, while walking through the galleries of the Metropolitan Museum of Art, where he worked for many years, Smith became curious about the behavior of one elderly female visitor, who, as Smith relates it, "had taken up a position" in front of a particular piece of Byzantine art. When he queried her about what she found so engrossing, she said,

> Well it's all beautiful, I've been to Siena several times, but it is this particular piece that is special to me. It was brought here from Siena for the exhibition, you know. But I first saw it in the city of Siena. Fifty years ago, my husband proposed to me in front of this painting. This is the first time I've seen it since then. He was a wonderful man.[47]

However, in the past these events were likely relatively uncommon, driven almost entirely by the inventiveness and individual proclivities of the users. Today, museums are proactively fostering this "mating" role as evidenced by the explosion in the number of institutions hosting evening social hours and events in an effort to attract young, single adults to their institutions. Often unabashedly appealing to the "mating instinct" of young adults, these affairs support an additional, infrequently discussed dimension of museum-enhanced physical well-being—sexual satisfaction.

Pre-COVID, the Perot Museum of Nature and Science in Dallas would stay open late into the night several times a year for an event they called "Social Science." These late-into-the-night events would be adult-only parties featuring signature cocktails, DJs, photo booths, and talks and activities focused around topics deemed to be of interest to young adults. Similar events were held in a wide array of other museums. The Discovery museum in Wells, Nevada, also hosted a similar kind of event, which they also called "Social Science." The California Academy of Science in San Francisco called their event "NightLife," while the Dallas Art Museum promoted its "Late Nights" programs by emphasizing that they are a "fun date night or evening out with your friends." Each "Late Night" offers a "variety of experiences with performances, concerts, artist demos, film screenings, tours, and more!" Similar programs and descriptions have long flourished in Europe and elsewhere.[48] Although these and countless other such programs at museums across the globe are supposedly aimed at attracting young adults to the museum, ostensibly to experience science, art, or history, there is no escaping the fact that the primary appeal these programs afford is the opportunity for young singles, particularly affluent professionals, to meet in a safe, "highbrow" setting. As an Australian dating magazine suggests,

> Melbourne is the cultural capital of Australia, so it's no surprise that . . . that nearly one in four single men visit a museum or art exhibit approximately once a month. Visiting the National Gallery of Victoria, Melbourne Museum or ACMI is ideal for introverts as it gives you an external focus while allowing you to place yourself in a space with

> like-minded people. It's also not unusual for people to visit art galleries and museums by themselves and it's a lot less intimidating to approach one person than it is a group.[49]

Despite the proliferation of dating apps and websites, the task of meeting someone who might share one's interests and sensibilities remains challenging for most. These museum programs afford a particular segment of the youngish population, those with intellectual and aesthetic interests, a safe venue for meeting up and sharing a "good" time with potentially like-minded mates. Perhaps the most famous example is Michelle and Barack Obama's first date being at the Chicago Institute of Art,[50] but the Obamas are far from the only people who have gone this route. As the following testimonials attest, museums can and seemingly do support the mating of the species.

> Thank you so much for the Museum's involvement in my first date, my engagement, and my wedding ceremony. . . . I can't express enough my gratitude . . . from the engagement to the wedding.[51]

> The Hornet is a great tour for both families and individuals. It is well maintained and has good guides and plenty of parking. I met my wife there at a Saint Patrick's Day dance in 2001.[52]

Even when one does meet someone online initially, setting up a first date at a museum affords a safe way to assess whether that person is really the right person for you. Such was the case for one woman who recently wrote on Trip Advisor,

> I agreed to meet a date at the Currier [Museum of Art] because I figured it would be a safe place to meet an on-line acquaintance. A place to judge his taste in art . . . the Currier has an amazing collection of beautiful art, more than you would expect from a small gallery. The paperweight collection (sounds boring, but is NOT) is beautiful. Wonderful place to sit and talk to someone you end up marrying for life.[53]

In summary, although neither museum professionals nor the visiting public often speak about it, museums have long supported multiple dimensions of the public's physical well-being, albeit often in subconscious ways.

NOTES

1. "Safe Quotes." https://www.brainyquote.com/topics/safe-quotes_11. Retrieved July 31, 2020.
2. See Falk, J. H., and Balling, J. D. (1982). "The Field Trip Milieu: Learning and Behavior as a Function of Contextual Events." *Journal of Educational Research* 76(1), 22–28.
3. See Gifford, R. (2014). *Environmental Psychology: Principles and Practice*, fifth ed. Colville, WA: Optimal Books.

4. Bureau of Labor Statistics. (2020). *American Time Use Survey Summary, 2019*. Washington, DC: United States Department of Labor. https://www.bls.gov/news.release/pdf/atus.pdf. Retrieved August 9, 2020.

5. Moussouri, T. (1997). *Family Agendas and Family Learning in Hands-On Museums*. Unpublished doctoral dissertation. University of Leiscester, Leicester, England.

6. Packer, J. (2008). "Beyond Learning: Exploring Visitors' Perceptions of the Value and Benefits of Museum Experiences." *Curator: The Museum Journal* 51(1), 33–54.

7. Samwiches. http://samwiches.com/. Retrieved August 9, 2020.

8. Perasso, E. (2017). "Eating at the Museum: When Food Is a Work of Art." *Fine Dining Lovers*, February 1, 2017, https://www.finedininglovers.com/article/eating-museum-when-food-work-art. Retrieved August 9, 2020.

9. Casey, N. (2013). "Art Made Edible at Magritte-Inspired Dinner Series at MoMA." Food: Gothamist.com, November 5, 2013. https://gothamist.com/food/art-made-edible-at-magritte-inspired-dinner-series-at-moma. Retrieved March 12, 2021.

10. See Falk, J. H. (2018). *Born to Choose: Evolution, Self and Well-Being*. London: Routledge.

11. Falk, J. H. (2018). *Born to Choose: Evolution, Self and Well-Being*. London: Routledge.

12. See Lovelock, J. E. (1972). "Gaia as Seen through the Atmosphere." *Atmospheric Environment* 6(8), 579–80.

13. For additional information, see Falk, J. H. (2018). *Born to Choose: Evolution, Self and Well-Being*. London: Routledge.

14. For example, Shepherdson, P. (2014). "Perceptions of Safety and Fear of Crime Research Report." http://saiwa.asn.au/wp-content/uploads/2016/05/Fear-of-Crime-Perceptions-of-Safety-Research-Report-2014-Patrick-She.pdf. Retrieved August 16, 2020.

15. Falk, J. H. Unpublished data.

16. For example, California Association of Museums. (n.d.). "Foresight Research Report: Museums as Third Places." https://art.ucsc.edu/sites/default/files/CAMLF_Third_Place_Baseline_Final.pdf. Retrieved August 16, 2020.

Farver, J. A. M., Ghosh, C., Garcia, C. (2000). "Children's Perceptions of Their Neighborhoods." *Journal of Applied Developmental Psychology* 21, 139–63.

Spilsbury, J. C., Korbin, J. E., Coulton, C. E. (2012). "'Subjective' and 'Objective' Views of Neighborhood Danger and Well-Being: The Importance of Multiple Perspectives and Mixed Methods." *Child Indicators Research* 5, 469–82.

17. Maslow, A. (1943). "A Theory of Human Motivation." *Psychological Review* 50(4), 370–96.

18. For example, Pedretti, E., and Navas Iannini, A. M. (2020). *Controversy in Science Museums: Re-Imagining Exhibition Spaces and Practices*. London: Routledge.

19. For example, Sykes, C. (2020). "Art Therapy at the Manchester Museum." Art Museum Teaching: A Forum for Reflecting on Practice, July 3, 2020. https://artmuseumteaching.com/tag/reflection/. Retrieved February 21, 2021.

20. See Falk, J. H. (2018). *Born to Choose: Evolution, Self and Well-Being*. London: Routledge.

21. Mitchell, J. (1970). "Big Yellow Taxi." Crazy Crow Music / Siquomb Music Publishing.

22. Fink, G. (2016). "Stress: The Health Epidemic of the 21st Century." Elsevier SciTech Connect, April 26, 2016. http://scitechconnect.elsevier.com/stress-health-epidemic-21st-century/#:~:text=Stress%3A%20The%20Health%20Epidemic%20of%20the%2021st%20

Century.,our%20emotional%20and%20physical%20health%20can%20be%20devastating. Retrieved September 27, 2020.

23. Fink, G. (2016). “Stress: The Health Epidemic of the 21st Century.” Elsevier SciTech Connect, April 26, 2016. http://scitechconnect.elsevier.com/stress-health-epidemic-21st-century/#:~:text=Stress%3A%20The%20Health%20Epidemic%20of%20the%2021st%20Century.,our%20emotional%20and%20physical%20health%20can%20be%20devastating. Retrieved September 27, 2020. Retrieved September 27, 2020.

24. Nerurkar, A., Bitton, A., Davis, R. B., Phillips, R. S., and Yeh, G. (2013). “When Physicians Counsel about Stress: Results of a National Study.” *JAMA Internal Medicine* 173(1), 76–77.

25. Falk, J. H. (2009). *Identity and the Museum Visitor Experience*. Walnut Creek, CA: Left Coast Press.

Packer, J., and Bond, N. (2010). *Museums as Restorative Environments. Curator: The Museum Journal* 53 (4), 421–56. See also, Packer, J. (2014). “Visitors’ Restorative Experiences in Museum and Botanic Gardens Environments.” In S. Filep and P. Pearce (eds.), *Tourist Experience and Fulfilment: Insights from Positive Psychology*, 202–22. London: Routledge.

26. Kaplan, R., and Kaplan, S. (1989). *The Experience of Nature: A Psychological Perspective*. Cambridge University Press.

27. Packer, J. (2008). “Beyond Learning: Exploring Visitors’ Perceptions of the Value and Benefits of Museum Experiences.” *Curator: The Museum Journal* 51(1), 33–54.

28. Packer, J., and Bond, N. (2010). “Museums as Restorative Environments.” *Curator: The Museum Journal* 53(4), 421–56.

29. Francis is a pseudonym. Interview originally published in Falk, J. H. (2009). *Identity and the Museum Visitor Experience*. Walnut Creek, CA: Left Coast Press.

30. Chatterjee, H., and Noble, G. (2016). *Museums, Health and Well-Being*. London: Routledge.

31. Lackoi, K., Patsou, M., and Chatterjee, H. J. (2016). *Museums for Health and Wellbeing. A Preliminary Report*. London. National Alliance for Museums, Health and Wellbeing. Available at https://museumsandwellbeingalliance.wordpress.com.

32. Hanson, A. (Ed.). (2017). *Reminiscence in Open Air Museums*. Ostersumn, Sweden: Jamtli Forlag.

33. Djupdræt, M. B., Fog, L., Kofod, L., Lindberg, H., Mathiassen, T. E., and Rasmussen, A. (2017). “Evaluation.” In A. Hanson (ed.), *Reminiscence in Open Air Museums*, 47–49. Ostersumn, Sweden: Jamtli Forlag. See also, Djupdræt, M. B., and Lindberg, H. (2018). Forskning viser, at erindringsformidling virker, Den Gamle By [Yearbook]. Annual Report 2018, 83–87.

34. Kirk, M., Rasmussen, K. W., Overgaard, S. B., and Berntsen, D. (2019). “Five Weeks of Immersive Reminiscence Therapy Improves Autobiographical Memory in Alzheimer’s Disease.” *Memory* 27(4), 441–54.

35. Steinwald, M., Harding, M., and Piacentini (2014). “Multisensory Engagement with Real Nature Relevant to Real Life.” In N. Levent and A. Pascual-Leone (eds.), *The Multisensory Museum*, 45–60. Lanham, MD: Rowman & Littlefield.

36. Madge, C. (2019). *Autism in Museums: A Revolution in the Making*. Center for the Future of Museums. American Alliance of Museums, July 16, 2019. https://www.aam-us.org/2019/07/16/autism-in-museums-a-revolution-in-the-making/. Retrieved August 9, 2020. See also, “Autism in Museums: Welcoming Families and Young People” (2020). *Kids in*

Museums. Beckenham: UK. https://kidsinmuseums.org.uk/resources/how-can-your-museum-better-welcome-families-and-young-people-with-autism/. Retrieved August 9, 2020.

37. In Voon, C. (2019). "Museums Are Finally Taking Accessibility for Visitors with Disabilities Seriously." Artsy.net, October 14, 2019. https://www.artsy.net/article/artsy-editorial-museums-finally-accessibility-visitors-disabilities-seriously. Retrieved August 9, 2020.

38. Falk, J. H. (1985). "The Impact of Novelty on Learning and Behavior in Museums and Other Informal Settings." In S. M. Nair (ed.), *Proceedings of the Centenary Meeting of the Bombay Natural History Society*. Bombay, India.

39. Schorch, P. (2013). "The Experience of a Museum Space." *Museum Management and Curatorship* 28(2), 193–208.

McLean, K. (1993). *Planning for People in Museum Exhibitions*. Washington, DC: Association of Science Technology Centers.

40. For example, Hunt, E. G. (2009). *Study of Museum Lighting and Design*. Unpublished honors thesis. Texas State University. San Marcos, Texas.

41. Belcher, M. (1991). *Exhibitions in Museums*. Washington, DC: Smithsonian Institution Press.

42. For example, Beliveau, J. (2015). "Audio Elements: Understanding Current Uses of Sound in Museum Exhibits." Unpublished master's thesis. University of Washington, Seattle, Washington. See also the following: Chen, C.-L., and Tsai, C.-G. (2015). "The Influence of Background Music on the Visitor Museum Experience: A Case Study of the Laiho Memorial Museum, Taiwan." *Visitor Studies* 18(2), 183–95. Jakubowski, R. D. (2011). "Museum Soundscapes and Their Impact on Visitor Outcomes." Unpublished doctoral dissertation. University of Washington, Seattle, Washington. Webb, R. C. (1996). "Music, Mood, and Museums: A Review of Consumer Literature on Background Music." *Visitor Studies* 8(2), 15–29.

43. For example, Nieuwhof, A. (2017). "Olfactory Experiences in Museums of Modern and Contemporary Art." Unpublished master's thesis. Leiden University, Leiden, Netherlands.

44. Forrest, R. (2014). *Design Factors in the Museum Visitor Experience*. Unpublished doctoral dissertation. University of Queensland, Brisbane, Australia.

Anderson, D. and Shuichi, Y. (2020). "My Identity in the Garden—Self Reflections of Expatriates' Garden Visits." *Journal of Museum Education*, 45(2), 176–86 (p. 180).

45. Falk, J. H. (1991). "Analysis of Family Visitors in Natural History Museums: The National Museum of Natural History, Washington, D.C." *Curator* 34(1), 44–50.

46. Rule, N., and Ambady, N. (2008). "Brief Exposures: Male Sexual Orientation Is Accurately Perceived at 50 ms." *Journal of Experimental Social Psychology* 44(4), 1100–1105.

Boutin, C. (2006). "Snap Judgments Decide a Face's Character, Psychologist Finds." *Princeton University Education News*, August 22, 2006. https://www.princeton.edu/news/2006/08/22/snap-judgments-decide-faces-character-psychologist-finds. Retrieved September 27, 2020.

47. Smith, J. K. (2014). *The Museum Effect*. Lanham, MD: Rowman & Littlefield, 18.

48. Compare Black, G. (2018). "Meeting the Audience Challenge in the 'Age of Participation.'" *Museum Management and Curatorshi,* 33(4), 302–19.

Culture24. (2018). "Three-Part Study on the Role and Impact of Museum Lates: *A Culture of Lates; An International Culture of Lates; Late Like a Local*." London: Culture24. Museums at Night, February 2, 2018. http://museumsatnight.org.uk/festival-resources/news/our-research-reports-on-museum-lates-are-here/#.Wp5_eufLjIU. Retrieved November 20, 2020.

49. La Terra, M. (2017). "A Single's Guide to Dating in Melbourne." Culture Trip, August 29, 2017. https://theculturetrip.com/pacific/australia/articles/a-singles-guide-to-dating-in-melbourne/.

50. https://www.today.com/news/barak-michelle-obama-s-first-date-story-t156753.

51. Fulkerson IV, R. (2020). "Houston Museum of Natural Sciences." http://www.hmns.org/visit/rent-the-museum/testimonials/. Retrieved August 9, 2020.

52. Reyn, L. (2014). "Review of U.S.S. Hornet Museum." https://www.tripadvisor.com/ShowUserReviews-g29073-d270549-r201218615-USS_Hornet_Museum-Alameda_California.html. Retrieved August 9, 2020.

53. Millie K. (2019). "I Met My Love There." Review of Currier Museum of Art. https://www.tripadvisor.com/ShowUserReviews-g46152-d264427-r716453159-Currier_Museum_of_Art-Manchester_New_Hampshire.html. Retrieved August 9, 2020.

III

VALUE APPLIED

8

Measuring Value

Price is what you pay. Value is what you get.

—Warren Buffett[1]

In the winter of 2021, three dozen education professionals informally interviewed nearly two hundred adults from across America. These mini-surveys were a "homework assignment" conducted as part of a year-long, U.S. National Science Foundation-funded workshop on the future of museums.[2] The assignment was designed to learn more about the intersection between museums and "regular" people's personal well-being-related goals and aspirations. At least initially, people were not asked to frame their answers with reference to museums, people were to just describe their own personal well-being hopes and desires. Hundreds of responses were given. Most people's responses, when asked about their well-being goals, were very personal, though a few framed their responses more outwardly, talking about their goals for society; most gave not one answer but multiple answers. Some examples included the following:

> I would like to have good health and good friends.
>
> I would like everyone to be able to experience what I feel like when I'm in my garden.
>
> I want to always be able to remain curious about the world and those around me.
>
> That people can be nice to each other (empathetic)—at all levels as individuals, as friends as neighbors through to our political systems—let's try to be constructive and work together for the good of everyone rather than point scoring and political posturing.

> I guess what I really wish I had was the time and space to include more physical activity and mindfulness into my life . . . without feeling like I was neglecting other aspects of my life, like work and family.

> I want to feel the self-motivation every day so that I can enhance my daily physical activity, good diet, and [get] ample sleep. I would like to try to get all of those things done every day.

> To live a life that balances my health (mental and physical) with professional learning and growth and relationships with family, friends and my community.

Although people were not asked to define their well-being goals by category, the responses could be easily classified into the four key dimensions of well-being previously discussed. When responses were organized in this way, collectively about a third of the responses represented *personal* well-being-related desires and needs such as emotional health, work-life balance, and the wish by many people to try and be a more positive person in the future. *Intellectual* well-being-related goals such as learning and the need for more evidence-based decision making were also among the aspirations mentioned, but only by about 7 percent of the public. *Social* and *physical* well-being, too, were well represented among the public's aspirations and goals. More than a third of people talked about their social well-being-related desires, including wanting to build and live within more equitable, civil, and inclusive communities. Equally important to many adults was the well-being of their loved ones, including and particularly their children. For many parents, their own well-being was directly tied to being able to help their off-spring live better, more successful lives. And finally, more than a quarter of the public focused on their *physical* well-being, expressing a desire to be free of want and sickness, to live a healthier life, and, if possible, spend more time out in nature.

There were two important takeaways from this exercise. The first was that the public could readily talk about ways in which they hoped to achieve greater well-being in their lives, that having enhanced well-being was something of value to them. Second, although the public does not normally use terms like personal, intellectual, social, and physical well-being when describing their aspirations for a quality life, they readily defined their aspirations and desires in ways totally consistent with this framing.

These turn out to be important and non-trivial findings. Although there was not a total, one-to-one match between the well-being-related outcomes the public aspired to achieve and the specific types of well-being-related benefits museums support, there was considerable overlap. This area of overlap in the needs the broader public desires and the specific outcomes museum experiences deliver, represents a critical sweet spot; this is the place where the value of museum experiences resides. Being able to clearly define the benefit that museum experiences deliver, a benefit specifically desired by the public, opens up unlimited opportunities for those concerned with promoting, facilitating, developing, and supporting museums and the experiences they create, now and in the future.

My goal in this book is to provide an accounting of the value of museum experiences. The first two sections of this book focused on the first of the two meanings of accounting as I attempted to establish a compelling narrative describing the multiple and powerful ways museum experiences deliver enhanced well-being to the public. I now turn my attention to the second, equally important aspect of accounting—measurement. In this chapter I will provide an explanation of how to measure the specific areas of enhanced well-being that the public desires and that museum experiences deliver. Specifically, I will describe the approach I have used to not only measure but assign a specific dollar value to these essential museum experience outcomes.

MEASURING VALUE

Typically categorized as an intangible value, things like well-being are internal to the user, often ephemeral, and not physically viewable. For all of these reasons, intangible value has been notoriously difficult to discern and measure.[3] As a consequence of this intangible quality, measurement efforts have often struggled with both of the key necessities of research—reliability and validity. To be honest, few outcomes, particularly those with real value and importance are easy to directly measure, particularly in the short-term. However, I and many other researchers would contend that all outcomes, even the most abstract and challenging, can be reliably and validly measured.

For those a little rusty on their research methods, here is a quick refresher course. Reliability implies consistency. For example, when research is consistent, that is, reliable, the measurement tool one uses will yield the same result time after time when measuring the same thing under the same circumstances and provide the same result regardless of who is collecting the data. Since, for example, I am interested in being able to measure the well-being outcomes that accrue from engagement with museum experiences, I will want to be sure that any measurement tool I create can be applied to any museum experience and that the resulting measurements provide consistent results time after time. If a measurement tool is designed to only measure the specific outcomes likely to occur as a consequence of engagement with a specific exhibition or program, those results might be quite interesting but cannot be generalized beyond that unique situation and therefore lack reliability. Although reliability is clearly a high standard to meet, particularly when dealing with something as ephemeral and inherently highly individualized as enhanced well-being, social science researchers committed to quality measurement have devised a wide array of mechanism for ensuring reasonable standards of reliability can be met.[4]

Validity is equally, if not an even more important requirement of sound measurement. A measure is valid if it measures what it's supposed to. That seems straightforward but is not. Validity, it turns out, is far more difficult to achieve than is reliability. Using a simplistic example, a thermometer is a very reliable way to measure a person's body temperature, but it is not a valid tool for measuring intelligence.

Just because you can accurately and reliably measure something does not mean that measurement means anything. And even when something can be found that most agree generally measures an intangible outcome like well-being, that measure may not be a valid outcome measure for a specific event or experience.[5] This has been a major problem with all of the past efforts to determine whether museums effected well-being, a flaw my methodology seeks to avoid. But before explaining how I have attempted to avoid that problem, first let me clarify why I think so many past efforts at measuring well-being have erred in this key area, in other words, lacked validity.

Over the years, most efforts to measure whether some activity or enterprise effects well-being have relied on tangible outcome measures like employment, divorce statistics, or annual health assessments. Putting aside the question for the moment of whether these types of indicators accurately capture positive well-being, no one would question that they are clearly metrics that can be reliably measured. However, as suggested above, reliability without validity is a bad bargain, and these measures dramatically fail to meet the test of validity for something like museum experiences. The reason why they fail the validity test is because there is no real way to draw a straight causal line between the activity of interest, in the current case the well-being created by a use of a museum, and any of these large, complex outcomes. Each of these outcomes is the result of dozens upon dozens of conditions, many of which interact and are co-dependent. In other words, whether someone is employed, married, or healthy cannot be explained by any single causation, particularly not one as limited in time and space as a two-hour visit to a museum on one day of a person's life. The likelihood of this experience seriously and directly impacting any of these kinds of outcomes is infinitesimally small. And yet, time and time again these are exactly the measures of well-being social scientists have used when trying to assess the value of museums.[6] Even if it was possible to find a correlation between one of these measures and museum-going, it is virtually impossible to know whether such a correlation, or for that matter a lack of correlation, was meaningful for the simple reason that the relationship between museum-going and these types of outcomes are just too distant and intertwined with other associated variables such as family background, level of education, personality, and countless other individual practices and events to be diagnostic. Remember, to be valid, one has to use measures that directly measure what they are supposed to measure, which in the current case is the impact of a museum experience.

RELIABLY AND VALIDLY MEASURING MUSEUM-GENERATED WELL-BEING

So, how did I go about trying to validly and reliably measure the enhanced well-being museum experiences generate? The first, and perhaps most critical task I faced was ensuring that the measures of well-being I used were truly and appropriately measuring well-being, both in general and specifically as pertained to museum experiences (i.e., valid measures). To be valid, my measures needed to actually capture this construct I have called well-being. This, it turns out, has long been a problem for most social scientists. As outlined earlier in the book, for several decades now social scientists have framed well-being using a flawed theoretical model—one framed entirely in psychology rather than equally grounded in basic biology. This, in my opinion, has resulted in a variety of problems, including measures that only focus on a single dimension of human well-being, such as happiness, physical health, or financial health.[7] Metrics built on a sounder, combined biological and psychological theoretical foundation are needed to accurately and validly measure museum experience–generated well-being. Such metrics recognize the foundational needs that all humans share—needs related to their personal, intellectual, social, and physical existence.

Equally problematic—and far too often—researchers have depended upon generic, second-hand measures of well-being, for example, the important but flawed effort in the UK to assess the well-being value of museum-going by connecting it to annual measures of happiness and physical health.[8] As suggested in the previous section, such indices of well-being are overly distant and highly unlikely to allow researchers to be able to draw direct causative links between them and a singular event like museum use.

Thus, the metrics I needed to accurately measure the enhanced well-being generated by museum experiences could not be some generalized, borrowed index of well-being but rather one or more measures that specifically captured the well-being-related outcomes desired by the public and known to be able to be directly associated with a particular museum experience. They needed to be measures capable of encapsulating the entire spectrum of outcomes highlighted in earlier chapters—feelings of joy and wonder, an improved sense of identity, the perception that one has a better understanding or awareness of the world, feelings of being more closely aligned and connected with those one loves, as well as a feeling of physical rejuvenation and comfort with one's surroundings. These are the types of well-being-related outcomes people regularly believe they achieve by using museums. Fortunately, I did not have to build such measures from scratch. A theoretically and empirically sound reservoir of just such measures within the museum literature already existed, though they were not historically labeled as such.

Over the past fifteen years or so, a range of researchers have theorized and measured the reasons people utilized museums. This research has yielded a compendium of tools for accurately and reliably capturing both the reasons why people said they chose to engage in a museum experience as well as the benefits those same people claimed they received as a consequence of their having engaged in a museum experience.[9] As detailed in earlier chapters, the public's use and outcome expectations can be readily described as falling into four broad categories of well-being-related "outcomes"—*personal*, *intellectual*, *social*, and *physical*—and there are measures for each of these outcome categories.[10] Of course, these were not always thought about in terms of well-being, and certainly not well-being as I have defined it here in this book.[11] Nonetheless, well-being outcomes they are, and I was able to directly utilize these previously developed and tested outcome measures to determine the degree to which each of the four dimensions of enhanced well-being was achieved.

However, in order to ensure true validity, I needed to apply a second important understanding coming out of the museum literature, the issue of the timing of data collection. Disproportionately, most research related to museum use outcomes has involved collecting data from users immediately following their experiences, for example, as they exited an exhibition or the museum. Although superficially a reasonable proposition, since the experience should still be fresh in mind and capturing people while still physically and temporally within the bounds of the experience is obviously convenient, it is actually a bad idea. Several decades of research have shown that the benefits of museum experiences are not immediately apparent to users. If you ask people to tell you what the benefit of their experiences were as they are figuratively just walking out the door, they will give you answers, but those answers will invariably be distorted and not completely accurate. It is not that people are purposefully giving bad answers; it is just that the effects of museum experiences take time to develop.[12] Some benefits require a little distance to appreciate, others just take time to develop, and some benefits are time dependent. For example, the great conversation about your experience you had with a loved one a week after your visit is not something you can know about or evaluate as you are walking out the door of the museum. Although I cannot say with certainty whether the optimum time delay is one week, two weeks, or two years, my research and those of others would suggest that one should wait at least two to four weeks, post experience, before collecting data.[13]

Pilot Study

With these methodological understandings in place, I created a simple instrument capable of measuring how much well-being a particular museum experience generated. Based on my and others' research, it was possible to not only capture outcomes in each of the four key well-being-related domains—personal, intellectual, social, and physical—but to do so using generic statements equally applicable across a wide array of museum uses (both physical and virtual), and across any topic area such as art, history, science, or nature. As my research on identity-related visit motivations has suggested, each of these four categories is likely to have several nuanced dimensions to them, and thus each requires not a single but multiple questions.[14] However, there does not need to be dozens of questions per dimension; if done carefully and thoughtfully, it is possible to capture each dimension with just a couple of questions.[15] For this pilot study, I used just two questions for each of the four categories, for a total of eight questions. Data was collected a minimum of two to four weeks after a museum experience, with each person asked to rate not only whether their museum experience resulted in a particular outcome, but more importantly, for how long any specific outcome lasted—an hour or two, a day, a week, or two or more weeks?

I have now collected preliminary data from hundreds of museum users at six types of museums across three countries.

Included in this initial pilot study was the Museum of Life + Science—an indoor/outdoor nature and science museum located in the southeastern part of the United States; Billings Farm and Museum—a living history museum located in the northeastern part of the United States; History Nebraska—a more traditional history museum located in middlewestern part of the United States; Heureka—an interactive science center located outside of Helsinki, Finland, in Northern Europe; the Toronto Zoo, located in Toronto, Canada; and Myseum of Toronto, a museum that explores history through art and culture, both virtually and in spaces across the city of Toronto, Canada.

Not only do these six institutions represent at least three distinct national populations and different subject matter foci—including history, art, science, and nature—but they range in size and budget from small to large, serving variously a few thousand people per year to well over a million users per year. As stated above, my goal was to develop a measurement tool that not only validly measured enhanced well-being but did so reliably, allowing repeated measures within the same institution as well as parallel data collection across virtually any type of museum and any type of museum experience.

An online survey was created, and each institution communicated by email with prior users and encouraged/invited them to complete the survey several weeks post-museum experience. In addition to asking some basic demographic questions related to age, gender, and family income, each survey asked people to respond whether they felt they did or did not experience each of the various well-being-related outcomes as a consequence of their experience, and if so, for how long did they perceived that benefit lasted.

Pilot Results

I will not go into great detail about the results, but data was collected from each of these six sites; and the good news was that respondents overwhelmingly indicated positive outcomes. In fact, not only did most users self-report that they had indeed experienced one or in most cases multiple outcomes, most indicated that these outcomes lasted quite a while. Specifically, the average duration of the enhanced personal and social well-being experienced by users of these six museums was one week, while the average duration of enhanced intellectual and physical well-being was a little over a day. In other words, using a museum for a couple of hours resulted in considerable benefit for most users, benefits that lasted, for most, well beyond the immediate time period of the visit.

As expected, based on research related to the reasons people use museums,[16] reported outcomes not only varied across visitors to a single institution, but varied systematically across these six different types of museums. The observed differences had less to do with each museum's content and more to do with who they attracted and why. So, for example, museums known to disproportionally attract parents with young children (e.g., the Toronto Zoo, Museum of Life + Science, and Billings Farm and Museum) had inordinately high social well-being outcomes. On average, large majorities of users at these three institutions indicated that they experienced strong social-well-being-related outcomes, with these outcomes lasting two or more weeks in duration. By contrast, users of both History Nebraska and Myseum of Toronto indicated having only minimal enhancements to their social well-being. However, users of these latter two institutions indicated achieving significant amounts of intellectual well-being, with outcomes lasting much longer than it did for users at the other institutions. Personal well-being was highest at Myseum, followed by Billings Farm and Museum and the Toronto Zoo. Physical well-being outcomes were higher for zoo users than it was for users at any of the other five institutions. All six of these museums supported the public's well-being, but the exact profile of satisfaction achieved differed for each. Some supported more social well-being than others and some supported intellectual or personal or physical well-being more. However, the data suggested that each institution, in its own way, met the well-being-related needs of most of its users.

This is great news and important data. Arguably, this is the first time that these types of data have been successfully measured in a way that is both validly quantifiable and reliably comparable across institutions. But unfortunately, this type of data only goes so far; validity and reliability are a necessity, but they are not a sufficiency. Again, the purpose of this effort is not merely to generate data that will be publishable in a peer-reviewed journal but rather to persuade policy makers and the public of the value of museums. What my measures of well-being outcomes lack is a less-often discussed, but equally important, third aspect of quality research, a dimension I would call "credibility." If I stopped here, with this kind of data, a policy maker or John Q Public would likely look at what I have described above and say, "Well that's impressive, but don't movies and doctors also generate increased well-being? How does this data compare to those kinds of experiences? I am willing to concede, based on this evidence, that museums make a difference, but I am not willing to say that museum experiences are clearly more valuable than any other types of experience. After all, I feel pretty good after watching a good movie."

Value, it turns out, is always a relative thing. Determining something's value is not a decision that can be made in isolation. In order for someone to judge whether something is or is not valuable, he or she needs to be able to directly and fairly compare the worth of this new something to that of something else that already has a known worth. To be a credible measure of value, measurements need to have authority and clout; they need to convincingly show that something has equal, or ideally even more worth, than something else of known value.

CREDIBILITY

This is why it is not enough to be able to measure whether someone felt good after going through an exhibition. To be credible, one has to be able to say that these positive, museum-generated outcomes were not only good but better than the positive feelings someone got from going to a movie or spending a day in a school classroom. If you cannot make that kind of direct comparison, then what good is your measurement of value? Sure, it is important that more people now know more about stuff or had a good time with their kids, but couldn't they just as easily have gotten those same benefits by reading a book or going to the park? For years, most in the museum community, including to be honest me, thought it was sufficient to just present the outcome data of a major study to policy makers and the public, who then would look at the data and exclaim, "Eureka! Here's more money. I now see the worth of the museum experience." However, as suggested at the beginning of this book, to date there is no evidence that the public and policy makers have reacted in this way, that they have found previous efforts and data sufficiently credible to change their opinions about the value of museum experience.

Clearly if the goal is to establish "value," if the goal is to convince those in authority of the worth of what museums do, then the evidence must not only meet validity and reliability standards, it must equally, and perhaps most importantly, meet credibility standards. To do this, I would argue that measures of the value of museum experiences need to be expressed in the currency of public policy and day-to-day life—and that currency is *money*!

Like it or not, most political decisions related to value/worth ultimately revolve around, or perhaps more accurately, devolve to the issue of money. Inevitably, decision makers—be they governments or the public—at least in part judge the worth of institutions, and the tangible as well as intangible goods and services they provide, in financial terms. At issue is whether the benefits that accrue from the existence/use of any given institution or collection of institutions is worth the cost it takes to maintain and run it/them.

Exacerbating this tendency to monetize value has been the increasingly explicit effort on the part of policy makers at both the local and national levels to treat financing issues as a zero-sum game. For example, we have $X in the budget, do we give those dollars to health care, police, or other protection services, community services like trash collection and roads, or do we give it to the local museum?[17] Again, for better or worse it is generally assumed, though not always true, that it is possible to monetarily quantify the financial benefit of an added policeman, extra beds at the hospital, or potholes filled. By contrast, the lack of comparable financial arguments for the benefits generated by the public use of museums places museums at a political disadvantage. Again, without making a value judgment as to the appropriateness of such sentiments, it is fair to say that policy maker's perceptions of benefits expressed in terms that significantly diverge from their own needs and realities are easily dismissed as interesting but ultimately not convincing. Literally, and figuratively, the coin of the realm for policy makers is money. They have money to give and their job is to make decisions on how best and fairly to distribute that money. Unless the value of museum experience outcomes can be expressed in dollars (or Euros, Yuan, Pound, etc.), and thus directly compared with the cost it might take to deliver those outcomes, there is little hope that any policy maker, nor vast swaths of the general public, will ultimately know how to appropriately apportion funds to museums.

One important caveat I need to make here. When I frame the issue of museum value in monetary terms it is important to appreciate that what is important, ultimately, is not the actual dollar figure but the sense of value that dollar figure represents. Money enables people to quickly and reliably compare the worth of commodities, even wildly disparate goods and services such as a basket of apples, a haircut, or a visit to a museum. Institutions like museums have long understood the need to demonstrate that they make a significant monetary contribution to their community, but historically they have not been able to agree on what the nature of that contribution was, let alone what it was worth. I argue that community policy makers and the public already believe that these institutions are "good"; in fact, they intuitively understand that these types of institutions measurably enhance the overall well-being of the individuals who engage with them. What is currently lacking, though, is the ability of cultural institutions to make this value both explicit and tangible.

As the previous section attests, it is finally possible to not only explicitly define how museums benefit the public but also to reliably and validly measure that enhanced value. The final piece of the puzzle, then, is knowing how much the enhanced well-being created using museums is actually worth so that this value can be directly compared to the value created by other types of public goods and services.

Monetizing well-being is something that quite a number of others have been doing for more than a decade, including efforts to calculate the economic value of enhanced well-being within the workplace,[18] from good government,[19] public safety,[20] and of course, as is painfully evident under the current circumstances, from a well-functioning public health system.[21] Obviously, attaching a monetary value to increased well-being is far from impossible, but doing it well, read validly and reliably is quite challenging.

MONETIZING MUSEUM EXPERIENCES: CHALLENGES

Most efforts by economists to assign a monetary value to a product or service have used one of two approaches, respectively referred to as either a "use" or "contingent value" approach. Although both approaches are used, far and away the most common of these two approaches is the "use" approach, since this is easily the most direct way to assign value, even with something as seemingly intangible as well-being. Since virtually all goods and services come with a price tag, it makes sense that it should be possible to just use the value of what someone is willing to pay for something as the measure of its worth. For examples, one could just measure the "opportunity" costs of museum experiences, such as how much individuals paid for admission or how much time they spent engaged in the activity. The obvious assumption is that whatever the direct dollar value associated with that use was, that then would be equivalent to the value of the experience.

The second, slightly less straightforward but equally accepted approach is what is called "contingent valuation," where monetary values are estimated by making inferences about people's willingness to pay based on comparable but indirect market data or by literally asking people directly what they would be willing to pay for a particular good or service. Given that enhanced well-being can be tricky to encapsulate fully into something like an admission price, this approach has predominated for measures of well-being. So, by way of example, people might be asked how much they think having an enjoyable and educational day at the museum might be worth to them. Whatever price they assign is then assumed to be the value of that experience.

Conflating Price and Value

The good news is that both of these approaches have been tried before with museums. The bad news is that all of these earlier efforts to assign value to museum experiences—whether based on the use approach (e.g., admission costs or time spent) or the contingent valuation approach (e.g., asking people to place a value on their perceptions of the value of a museum experience)—have always resulted in gross underestimates of museum value.[22] Arguably the primary reason for this undervaluing is directly attributable to the fact that neither the public nor economists have historically had an accurate sense of either the "real" costs associated with delivering museum experiences nor for that matter how to operationally define the actual benefits those museum experiences delivered.

A major challenge to accurate estimates of museum value arises from the way in which museum experiences have historically been priced, in particular, the cost of admissions to museums. Museum admission prices have always been artificially set well below their true value. A typical for-profit will calculate the full cost of a product or service and then charge the public anywhere from two to as much as five times that cost. The price museums charge the public for admission rarely comes close to even covering costs let alone generating a surplus (i.e., profit). This is not a criticism of museums but rather just an observation; there are clearly good reasons for this reality.

First, exhibitions and programs are virtually always heavily subsidized by government and private sector funding, and because museums do not need to fully recover their costs through admissions, they generally feel that it would be unethical to charge a price fully commensurate with actual production and delivery costs, let alone building in a profit margin. Related to the issue of ethics, and equally important when it comes to pricing decisions, museums (as nonprofits) have in fact been highly motivated to minimize rather than maximize the cost of their public offerings, all in an effort to encourage equity and promote broad access. These are all reasonable and good things about museums, and by way of example, in the United States the average cost of an adult museum admission ticket is just $10, though again real costs are much higher.[23] This generosity toward the public is normally not a problem, but it is when economists get involved in trying to assign monetary values to museum experiences based on these realities.

Again, without a value judgment implied, economists (and policy makers) tend to operate from a free-market perspective, assuming that the price of a commodity is always determined by the marketplace. In other words, value is, if not exclusively, determined by macroeconomic principles such as supply and demand. Thus, it is no surprise that when economists collect data from people about their perceived value of a museum experience, the public is likely to use the only frame of reference they know; they base their judgments on what they are used to paying in the marketplace for these experiences. As long as people are consistently charged $10 for a particular commodity, then when queried about the value of that commodity, they will consistently reply it must be worth about $10. Since all previous efforts to assign a value to the outcomes of museum experiences have always been explicitly connected with museums, unsurprisingly the public has consistently assumed the value must be commensurate with the artificially reduced market price they are used to paying for that museum experience—after all, you get what you pay for.

This problem has been exacerbated by the fact that neither economists involved in assessing the value of museums, nor for that matter museums themselves or the publics they serve, have historically been good at defining and articulating the actual benefits delivered by a museum experience. In the past, the outcomes used have been vague and frequently unclearly communicated to museum users. In the absence of clarity, people are left to make inaccurate guesses about value. Again, monetary value is always relative and based on beliefs about value. Unfortunately, many people have been consistently made to believe that something with a low cost is of low value, and thus they apply this mental shorthand to the value of museum experiences.[24]

Thus, accurately assigning a monetary value to museum experiences requires two things. First, it absolutely must begin with a clear articulation of the true nature of that benefit. Without clarity about the nature of the outcome, how can people accurately assess value? But complicating the ability to assign an accurate dollar value to this benefit, it is essential to fairly, read validly, measure that benefit free from the inherent bias that current museum admission pricing creates. For as stated by the grand old man of American finance, Warren Buffett, "Price is what you pay. Value is what you get."[25]

MONETIZING MUSEUM EXPERIENCES: SOLUTIONS

So, as I set out to validly and reliably monetize the value of enhanced well-being, I was committed to trying to avoid the above described pitfalls. The first problem I needed to solve was the problem of using generic, overly complex measures of well-being. I solved this by explicitly asking people to rate their museum-specific outcomes, outcomes I could validly and reliably measure. However, avoiding the museum admission cost problem required some careful thought. To avoid the inherent biases discussed in the previous section and ensure both validity and reliability, the approach that seemed to make the most sense was a contingent valuation approach.[26]

However, unlike previous efforts to contingently assign a dollar value to museum experiences, my approach was explicitly designed to ensure that I avoided the confounding influence of preexisting beliefs about the value of museums, in particular the historic undervaluing of museum experiences due to their artificially reduced costs. I achieved this by using a split sample approach[27]—independently assessing, from the same general population (not the same individuals at the same time), the perceived monetary value of a set of well-being-related benefits and the amount of that benefit individuals perceived they derived from a specific museum experience. By using such a sampling approach, I was able to derive reliable results about the perceived monetary value of each of the specific well-being outcomes—enhanced *personal, intellectual, social,* and *physical* well-being.

These independently collected values could then be combined with the independently perceived well-being outcomes, generated by specific museum experiences, to collectively calculate the perceived financial value of a museum experience. Since the two data sets were collected independently, both in time and context, each data set preserved its own inherent integrity.

Pilot Study

I collected data on the perceived financial value of outcomes in each of the four categories of well-being. Data was collected from the same populations as the first data set—museums of varying types located in the United States, Canada, and Finland.[28] A survey was constructed that asked each respondent to independently assign a monetary value to each of eight different, museum experience-appropriate well-being-related outcomes, each at four levels of intensity. In other words, there were a total of thirty-two separate responses, with each respondent asked to rate the dollar[29] value of each of the eight possible outcomes based on the duration of effect. How much would this be worth if it lasted an hour or less? How much would it be worth if the outcome lasted a day? A week? And how much would it be worth if this outcome lasted as long as two weeks or more? From this data I was able to calculate a mean dollar value for each of the four key outcome areas. As one might predict, perceived value increased as the duration of the effect of that outcome increased—the longer an outcome lasted, the greater was its perceived value.

Pilot Results

Again, I will not go into great detail about the results, but the valuation of each of the thirty-two possible indices of well-being, as expected, revealed the kind of variability one would expect for something as subjective as financial value. At one extreme, some individuals rated a particular outcome as of marginal value (e.g., one dollar or less); and at the other extreme, some people valued long-lasting outcomes as worth tens of thousands of dollars. Although the results for each of the thirty-two variables skewed toward lesser values, most responses were still in impressive territory, with the value of even short-term outcomes exceeding the typical cost of museum admission by a factor of two or more. Because of this skewing, rather than using the mean as the best indicator of central tendency, the median was a more accurate and appropriate measure. Interestingly and perhaps surprisingly, there were no significant differences in results between U.S., Canadian, and Finnish participants. As a consequence, it was justifiable to combine all of these monetization results into a single data set and derive a single value index for each of the four dimensions of well-being—a measure of value of enhanced, museum-specific personal, intellectual, social, and physical well-being that appears to be jointly held by the citizens of at least these three countries, and perhaps by others as well.

In general, the public's perceived value of these outcomes ranged from median lows of around $25 for an experience lasting an hour to valuations of around $200 or more for experiences lasting two or more weeks. Short-term physical well-being was the least valued outcome and short-term social well-being the most valued. Long-term personal well-being was the most highly valued outcome, and long-term intellectual well-being the least valued.

Calculating Overall Value

Together, data from these two surveys could be combined to directly compute the perceived monetary value of the museum experiences delivered by each of these six specific museums. Specifically, I could calculate the benefit for each individual who engaged in a particular museum experience, as well as the average, collective financial benefit of the entire population who had that experience.

In brief, the monetary value of a particular museum experience could be calculated by summing the average perceived level of benefit a person derived for each of the four categories of well-being-related outcome a person perceived they had. Data from the first survey described above determined whether a person perceived they had an outcome, and if so what the duration of that outcome was. Data from the second survey determined what the dollar value was for each of the four specific, time-dependent categories of well-being-related outcomes. In this way, the overall monetary value of a particular museum experience could be derived by collecting and combining data from two separate but related samples of users. First by calculating an average benefit by taking the mean of the total value of the sample and then multiplying that mean by the total number of people who engaged in that experience.

Based on the preliminary data collected as part of the pilot study with these six institutions, the average financial benefit of a day-long or partial day visit to one of these settings was calculated to be worth about $418, with values ranging from a low of $355/person to a high of $458/person. Even a short duration, virtual workshop was highly valued, with user data suggesting that this free-to-the-user workshop was assessed by users as delivering a value equivalent to $391.

THE ENHANCED WELL-BEING MUSEUMS DELIVER IS WORTH A LOT!

I began this book arguing that achieving a sense of well-being, particularly the well-being associated with personal intellectual, social, and cultural belonging—and the feeling that one has secured these benefits for one's family—is important to people, with previous research showing that attaining these outcomes are ultimately what allows a person to feel like they have lived a satisfying and successful life.[30] It is reassuring to discover that my research findings were consistent with this earlier research. The people in my study indicated that they perceived that the enhanced well-being accruing from a museum experience was worth a considerable amount of money—in fact roughly forty times more than what most people currently pay for these experiences.

My preliminary research shows that the value an individual perceives they derive from a museum experience ranges from a low for a few individuals of around $10 dollars/experience (roughly equivalent to the cost of admission) to a maximum by a few others of around $1,000 or more per experience, with an average museum experience being valued at somewhere around $418. Given the historic popularity of museum experiences, this would mean that a museum that was visited by several hundred thousand individuals would generate a value in the tens of millions of dollars. Even a relatively modestly utilized, but intense, experience such as a boutique museum workshop program that served less than two hundred individuals, as exemplified by one of the two Myseum of Toronto's workshops included in my pilot study, delivered a value worth more than a hundred thousand dollars. My calculations showed that the overall annual value of the museum experiences offered by the five institutions who sampled general visitors, ranged from a low of around $10 million to a high of over $500 million. Of course, these differences in value were reflective of the fact that these five institutions serve very different numbers of users each year; as I will discuss more below, there are more refined ways to make direct comparisons. Nonetheless, one thing is clear, in all cases, the net calculated value delivered by these institutions was highly significant. So, too, by extrapolation, is just how considerable must be the value of the museum experiences delivered by the tens of thousands of museums around the world. Importantly, with these kinds of dollar figures in hand, it is now possible to directly compare the economic value delivered by museum experiences with the economic value generated by other types of community services.

Comparing Value

In most societies, at the local level, health and education are two of the biggest social values, as well as social costs. For example, health care is one of the most highly valued community commodities. Of course, if someone is sick, then the value might be particularly high, but what about discretionary medicine, something like an annual check-up. In some ways, this kind of discretionary medical "well-being" boost is not unlike the discretionary "well-being boost" someone might opt to get from a museum visit. A study by Johns Hopkins University determined that the average cost of an annual visit to a doctor in the United States was around $160.[31] This is pretty close to the real market value of such visits since this is the price doctors on average charge to insurance companies. However, even if the actual cost was twice as much, this benchmark provides a valuable point of comparison with a museum experience. Given that the value of a single, annual use of a museum came in at about $418, we can see that museum experiences are clearly in the same ballpark, value wise, as an annual visit to the doctor, perhaps even slightly more.

What about education? Unfortunately, the financial benefits of education have typically only been framed in employment terms, specifically the amount of increased income each year of schooling generates over a lifetime of earnings. For example, it has been estimated that the typical college graduate earns around $650,000 more than the typical high school graduate over the course of a forty-year career.[32] In fact those extra years of college are equal to about an additional $20,000/year in earnings; or given that it now takes the average student somewhere between four and five years to complete an undergraduate college degree, it is about $4,000 to $5,000 per year in added benefit. Clearly, $4,000–$5,000/year in benefit is considerably greater than the $418/use benefit of a museum visit, but also clearly the time commitment is considerably greater too. Most museum experiences last only about two hours on average, plus another hour or so in travel time to and from. Going to college requires more like three thousand to four thousand hours. In other words, the benefit of going to college is on the order $1/hour, while the benefit of going to a museum is on the order $100 or more/hour.

A similar calculation can be done for secondary education. It has been estimated that the value of graduating high school is $6,500/year in additional earning power.[33] Again, amortized over a year of schooling, assuming an average about six hours/day in school and perhaps another hour each day doing homework, equals about 1,200 hours in a school year, which in turn is the equivalent to about $5/hour of benefit. Again, when framed in this way, museum-going seems like a pretty good value. Of course, no one has suggested that museum-going generates greater earning power than going to school, as this is an unreasonable comparison. What is needed to be truly comparable would be an assessment of how much improvement in a person's personal, intellectual, social, and physical well-being an hour or even a day of public education delivers, of which annual salary might be a factor but not totally, as research has consistently shown that there is not a one-to-one correlation between income and well-being.[34] Those calculations have yet to be undertaken, at least to my knowledge. The point is, the ability to assign a specific, and valid measure of the economic value museum experiences deliver makes it possible to even begin to have this conversation, and by so doing, dramatically changes how funding discussions can be conducted in the future. For example, museums might want to challenge schools to justify why keeping kids in the classroom, at an average projected benefit of $30/day, is a better investment then spending a day at a museum with a benefit equivalent to ten times that value.

Return on Investment (ROI)

I am guardedly optimistic that this new approach will make it possible to not only define and measure the financial benefit of museum experiences to a wide range of other cultural and civic experiences but increasingly make it possible for museum sector professionals, as well as the public and policy makers, to compare the value they derive from specific museum experiences. The key to both of these possibilities lies in a metric known as return on investment.

Return on investment (ROI) is one of the most common ways investors, and policy makers and funders, evaluate the efficiency of an investment or compare the efficiency of a number of different investments to each other.[35] ROI is a standardized way to measure the performance or value of something, thus allowing direct comparisons between similar, or even dissimilar, investments. ROI is determined by calculating whether the benefit (return) of something is greater than or less than what it cost to create that benefit (investment). The result is expressed as a percentage or a ratio with return always as the numerator and investment as the denominator. For example, a good, overall business ROI in the for-profit world is about 10 percent, or a return of $1.10 for every $1.00 spent. Returns in real estate are lower and most investors feel good about an average return of around 7 percent ($1.07 return per $1.00 invested). Of course, ROI can be larger in some areas, with advertising expected to bring a ROI of about 500 percent or better ($5 for every $1 spent). Of course advertising is not the full cost of something; there are also production costs, sales costs, management costs, and so on too.[36] Most nonprofits operate at a ROI of 10 percent or less, with anything over 20 percent considered excellent.[37]

So, using the data created by my pilot study, what kind of ROI did the individual museums in my pilot study have?[38] Although ROI varied by institution, overall the numbers were impressive. For example, the smallest museum, History Nebraska, with an annual budget in 2019 of around $600,000 generated value on the order of $10 million. This is an eye-popping 1,667 percent ROI. While the largest institution, Toronto Zoo with a 2019 annual budget of $30.3 million had an even greater 1,825 percent ROI—this was based on the creation of a total public value in enhanced well-being of more than US$550 million. The other institutions in my sample had equally impressive ROIs. For example, the ROI of the Finnish science center Heureka, with a total annual operating cost in 2019 of $13.5 million, was 1,274%. Even a living history museum such as Billings Farm and Museum, with enormous overhead and thus greater relative annual operating costs than most museums, had a more than enviable ROI of 674 percent. Although only a single, relatively small sample, the investigation of just a single, one-off workshop program offered by Myseum of Toronto also provided a very useful measure of impact. This limited, virtual program cost a relatively small amount of money to produce, with the two iterations of the workshop, costing Myseum a combined $4,589 to produce. However, this effort yielded a truly impressive ROI. Although only serving 197 people in total, the ROI was 2,112%; clearly worth the investment.

These kinds of ROI measurements should now make it possible for museum professionals, as well as the public and policy makers, to compare the value of museum experiences to other goods and services, both those delivered by the for-profit sector as well as those delivered by the non-profit sector. It should also make it possible for funders and museum professionals, should they desire to go there, to directly compare and contrast the value of specific museum experiences to each other or even compare the value created by different museums. The bottom line, at least based on this preliminary work, is that the value generated by museum experiences is truly impressive. It means, that on average, every dollar given to a museum is likely to generate something on the order $100 to $200 dollars in value to the community, and that is just the tip of the iceberg since these are average value delivered, not, as I will describe more fully below, the value delivered to those most in need. Those values are even higher.

MAXIMIZING THE VALUE DELIVERED

Those with even the most rudimentary understanding of how the mathematics of my formula for measuring value works should realize that there are two basic ways an institution can maximize the well-being-related value their museum experiences deliver. Overall value can be increased by the following: (1) increasing the total number of people utilizing the experience; and/or (2) increasing both the type and average perceived value of the benefits an experience generates, with longer lasting benefits having greater value. Quantity and quality are not in conflict here but represent complimentary dimensions of impact.

So, for many, I am sure it is reassuring that my measure of value incorporates traditional user number metrics; the assumption is that the greater the number of users an institution serves, the greater is the impact it delivers. However, it is also clear that numbers alone do not equal impact. Quality also matters. Regardless of how many people pass through one's halls, no matter how long people stand in front of an exhibition, no matter how many page clicks a website receives, if these experiences do not result in actual outcomes, outcomes lasting days and weeks, then the overall impact is significantly diminished. This also means that an institution can register significant value even if their user numbers are limited. As long as museum participants perceive that they derived great, long-lasting benefits from their experience, the resulting value is high. Obviously, these two ways of increasing value are not necessarily mutually exclusive, but all have costs associated with them. Thus, different institutions are likely to choose different approaches, with some favoring the quantity approach and others coming down on the side of quality.[39]

Even in the absence of the kind of data presented here, both quantity and quality strategies have long been used by institutions to try and enhance their impact. A common approach to the first strategy has been the bringing in of temporary exhibitions, most notably blockbuster exhibitions. A common approach to the second strategy has been the development of a range of special programs, often focused on special groups such as school groups, families, or aficionados. Determining the ultimate cost–benefit ratio of these two strategies will require further research. However, even with the greater clarity this approach affords, which strategy makes the most sense for any particular institution is likely be strongly influenced by institutional size, location, history, finances, and of course, mission. Importantly, ultimate value is highly dependent upon the nature of the audience and the quality and execution of the experience that is delivered.

My data also reinforces museum visitor data showing that different types of museum experiences afford different types of value to different people; museums cannot and should not be designed as one-size-fits-all institutions. Thus, not only must an institution decide whether to go for quantity or quality, so too must it decide what aspect of value they most want to focus on delivering—personal well-being, intellectual well-being, social well-being, or physical well-being. Despite the need to focus, this approach to measuring value emphasizes the importance of ensuring that every experience provides some measure of satisfaction within each of these four well-being dimensions, since value is generated not by any one area alone but through the sum of outcomes across all four areas of well-being.

Delivering Value to those Most in Need

The data from this preliminary research also revealed one other very important finding. The perceived monetary value of a museum experience significantly varied as a function of specific demographic variables, in particular race/ethnicity and income.[40] Individuals from non-majority populations (i.e., non-white) rated the value of their museum experiences as being significantly greater than did those from white, majority populations. Similarly, individuals with lower wealth (i.e., those with family incomes below the median community income) also rated the value of their museum experiences as being significantly greater than did individuals with family incomes above the median community level. These are both surprising and significant results.

Although it has been (fairly) argued that historically not all community members have equally shared in the potential benefits museum experiences deliver, the evidence from this work suggests that the historically most underrepresented individuals might actually be disproportionately benefiting from engaging in museum experiences. These findings relative to race/ethnicity are of particular interest due to the widespread concerns within the museum community about equity and inclusion. The limited data I am aware of support these findings. For example, I discovered as part of my decades-long research on the impact of the California Science Center that minority individuals rated the value of their science center experiences significantly higher than did majority populations.[41] I explained this phenomenon by suggesting that these individuals had fewer opportunities for enhancing such benefits than did their more privileged fellow users, thus the absolute value of the experience was greater.

My California Science Center data also showed a similar, negative relationship between value and income. As in this current research, those with the least financial means rated their museum experiences as disproportionately more valuable than did those with more affluence. As above, a possible explanation is that individuals with less means have fewer opportunities to enhance their well-being than do those with more means. Hence, if you are poor, an artificially reduced price option such as a museum represents a relatively a cost-effective way to enhance one's well-being, certainly as compared with other well-being-associated leisure activities such as moviegoing or foreign travel. In theory, museum experiences are relatively inexpensive, and thus more readily accessible, and thus relatively speaking, considered valuable.

These higher valuations by individuals with less privilege and financial means have important policy implications as it suggests a third strategy for how to enhance the value of the museum experiences a site offers. If minority and low-income individuals derive even greater value than do more affluent majority users, museums can enhance the overall value they deliver by specifically targeting these historically underrepresented groups. This also represents a significant argument for why museums should continue to receive public and private funding and subsidy—museum experiences deliver more value when they serve the entire community, not just those with means and privilege. In fact, when funds are used to make museum experiences available to those in greatest need, museums are able to deliver even greater returns on funders' investments.

As stated at the beginning of this book, the primary impetus for developing a sound measure of the value of museum experiences was my desire to provide a clear and unambiguous answer to the question of how museum experiences contribute to their communities and to the larger society. However, measures such as I have developed, though clearly useful, represent just one piece of what is required to persuade funders, policy makers, and the public of the true value of museums. My measure of value, like all such measures, are by necessity backward facing. They are a snapshot of what has been; they are not a vision of what is to come. When a museum director speaks to a potential funder, be that a governmental body or an individual donor, her goal is to convince these people or person that her museum is not some mere nicety but rather a societal necessity. Such conversations are not largely spent talking in the past tense; funding conversations are by their nature future-tense conversations.

The tool I have created allows that director to authoritatively brag about the benefits her past accomplishments have delivered. It allows her the perfect kick-off for this vital meeting by being able to convincingly demonstrate the value past appropriations/contributions have made. But she is not here at this meeting to talk about what she has accomplished in the past; no, what she wants to talk about is what she hopes to be able to accomplish in the future. She will want to be able to artfully and convincingly describe how she and her staff will use the new money she is seeking to plan and create even more exceptional and impactful outcomes for the public.

I believe the well-being focused approach I have advocated here in this book can provide the foundation for both parts of this funding conversation. It provides a way to validly, reliably, and credibly demonstrate the value of past accomplishments as well as provide the basis for describing an exciting and meaningful future. It provides a way to justify how museum experiences have benefited past users; and it creates a vision for the value museums hope to provide to the next generation in order to make their lives richer, healthier, more secure, and better. On to the future.

NOTES

1. "Value Creation." Quote Master. https://www.quotemaster.org/value+creation. Retrieved December 26, 2020.

2. Institute for Learning Innovation. Project team: J. Falk, J. Koke, and E. Vita. (2020–2021). *Science Museum Futures.* National Science Foundation #DRL-2041474. https://www.instituteforlearninginnovation.org/project/science-museum-futures/.

3. See, Falk, J. H. (2009). *Identity and the Museum Visitor Experience.* Walnut Creek, CA: Left Coast Press. See also, Holden, J. (2006). "Cultural Value and Crisis of Legitimacy." Demos. https://www.demos.co.uk/files/Culturalvalueweb.pdf. Retrieved July 2, 2020.

4. For example, Kaplan, D. (Ed.). (2000). *The SAGE Handbook of Quantitative Methodology for the Social Sciences.* Newbury Park, CA: Sage. See also, Maher, C., Hadfield, M., Hutchings, M., and de Eyto, A. (2018). "Ensuring Rigor in Qualitative Data Analysis." *International Journal of Qualitative Methods* 17(1), 160940691878636.

5. For example, Kaplan, D. (Ed.). (2000). *The SAGE Handbook of Quantitative Methodology for the Social Sciences.* Newbury Park, CA: Sage. See also, Maher, C., Hadfield, M., Hutchings, M., and de Eyto, A. (2018). "Ensuring Rigor in Qualitative Data Analysis." *International Journal of Qualitative Methods* 17(1), 160940691878636. And, Guba, E. G., and Lincoln, Y. (1989). *Fourth Generation Evaluation.* Newbury Park, CA: Sage.

6. For example, Clark, K. (Ed.). (2006). "Capturing the Public Value of Heritage: The Proceedings of the London Conference *25–26 January 2006.*" London: English Heritage.

Fujiwara, D., Kudrna, L., and Dolan, P. (2014). "Quantifying and Valuing the Wellbeing Impacts of Culture and Sport." Technical Report. London: UK Department for Culture, Media and Sport. https://assets.publishing.service.gov.uk/government/uploads/system/uploads/attachment_data/file/304899/Quantifying_and_valuing_the_wellbeing_impacts_of_sport_and_culture.pdf. Retrieved February 18, 2020.

Holton, E. (2018). "IMLS Announces National Study on Museums, Libraries, and Social Well-Being." Institute for Museum and Library Services, August 29, 2018. https://www.imls.gov/news/imls-announces-national-study-museums-libraries-and-social-wellbeing. Retrieved March 14, 2021.

Hull, D. (2011, February). "Assessing the Value and Impact of Museums." Technical Report. Belfast: Northern Ireland Assembly Research and Library Service Research Paper. http://www.niassembly.gov.uk/globalassets/Documents/RaISe/Publications/2011/Culture-Arts-Leisure/2911.pdf. Retrieved February 20, 2020.

Weinstein, M., and Bradburd, R. (2013). *The Robin Hood Rules for Smart Giving*. New York: Columbia University Press.

7. Some examples include the following:

Deniz, D. (2016). "Improving Perceived Well-Being through Improved Safety." *Procedia—Social and Behavioral Sciences* 2(6), 632–42.

Fujiwara, D., Kudrna, L., and Dolan, P. (2014). "Quantifying and Valuing the Wellbeing Impacts of Culture and Sport." Technical Report. London: UK Department for Culture, Media and Sport. https://assets.publishing.service.gov.uk/government/uploads/system/uploads/attachment_data/file/304899/Quantifying_and_valuing_the_wellbeing_impacts_of_sport_and_culture.pdf. Retrieved February 18, 2020.

Lindert, J., Bain, P., Kubzansky, L., and Stein, C. (2015). "Well-Being Measurement and the WHO Health Policy Health 2010: Systematic Review of Measurement Scales." *European Journal of Public Health* 25(4), 731–40.

Lohr, K. N. (2002). "Assessing Health Status and Quality-of-Life Instruments: Attributes and Review Criteria." *Quality of Life Research* 11, 193–205.

Patil, S., Patruni, B., Lu, H., Dunkerley, F., Fox, J., Potoglou, D., and Robinson, N. (2015). *Public Perception of Security and Privacy: Results of the Comprehensive Analysis of PACT's Pan-European Survey*. Brussels: Rand Europe.

Wood, D. A. and Wills, E. (2012). *Subjective Well-Being and Security*. Dordrecht, NL: Springer.

8. Fujiwara, D., Kudrna, L., and Dolan, P. (2014). "Quantifying and Valuing the Wellbeing Impacts of Culture and Sport." Technical Report. London: UK Department for Culture, Media and Sport. https://assets.publishing.service.gov.uk/government/uploads/system/uploads/attachment_data/file/304899/Quantifying_and_valuing_the_wellbeing_impacts_of_sport_and_culture.pdf. Retrieved February 18, 2020.

9. Falk, J. H. (2009). *Identity and the Museum Visitor Experience*. Walnut Creek, CA: Left Coast Press. See also, Falk, J. H. (2018). *Born to Choose: Evolution, Self and Well-Being*. London: Routledge. Packer, J. (2008). "Beyond Learning: Exploring Visitors' Perceptions of the Value and Benefits of Museum Experiences." *Curator: The Museum Journal* 51(1), 33–54. And, Phelan, S., Bauer, J., and Lewalter, D. (2018). "Visit Motivations: Development of a Short Scale for Comparison Across Sites." *Museum Management and Curatorship* 33(1), 25–41.

10. Falk, J. H. (2009). *Identity and the Museum Visitor Experience*. Walnut Creek, CA: Left Coast Press.

Falk, J. H. (2018). *Born to Choose: Evolution, Self and Well-Being*. London: Routledge.

Morris Hargreaves McIntyre (2004). *Tate through Visitor's Eyes*. Technical Report. Manchester, UK: Morris Hargreaves McIntyre.

Packer, J. (2008). "Beyond Learning: Exploring Visitors' Perceptions of the Value and Benefits of Museum Experiences." *Curator: The Museum Journal* 51 (1), 33–54.

Phelan, S., Bauer, J., and Lewalter, D. (2018). "Visit Motivations: Development of a Short Scale for Comparison Across Sites." *Museum Management and Curatorship* 33(1), 25–41.

11. Falk, J. H. (2018). *Born to Choose: Evolution, Self, and Well-Being*. New York: Routledge.

12. See, Anderson, D., Storksdieck, M., and Spock, M. (2006). "Long-Term Impacts of Museum Experiences." In J. Falk, L. Dierking, and S. Foutz (eds.), *In Principle, In Practice*, 197–215. Lanham, MD: AltaMira Press.

Falk, J. H., Scott, C., Dierking, L. D., Rennie, L. J., and Cohen Jones, M. (2004). "Interactives and Visitor Learning." *Curator* 47(2), 171–198.

Staus, N., Falk, J. H., Price, A., Tai, R. and Dierking, L. D. (in press). "Measuring the Long-Term Effects of Informal Education Experiences: Challenges and Potential Solutions." *Disciplinary and Interdisciplinary Research in Science Education.*

13. Falk, J. H., Koke, J., Price, A., and Pattison, S. (2018). *Investigating the Cascading, Long-Term Effects of Informal Science Education Experiences*. Informal Science, October 22, 2018. Technical Report. Portland, OR: Institute for Learning Innovation. https://www.informalscience.org/investigating-cascading-long-term-effects-informal-science-education-experiences-report.

14. Falk, J. H. (2009). *Identity and the Museum Visitor Experience*. Walnut Creek, CA: Left Coast Press.

15. Falk, J. H., Heimlich, J., and Bronnenkant, K. (2008). "Using Identity-Related Visit Motivations as a Tool for Understanding Adult Zoo and Aquarium Visitor's Meaning Making." *Curator* 51(1), 55–80.

16. See, Falk, J. H. (2009). *Identity and the Museum Visitor Experience*. Walnut Creek, CA: Left Coast Press.

Morris Hargreaves McIntyre (2004). *Tate through Visitor's Eyes*. Technical Report. Manchester, UK: Morris Hargreaves McIntyre.

Packer, J. (2008). "Beyond Learning: Exploring Visitors' Perceptions of the Value and Benefits of Museum Experiences." *Curator: The Museum Journal* 51 (1), 33–54.

Phelan, S., Bauer, J., and Lewalter, D. (2018). "Visit Motivations: Development of a Short Scale for Comparison Across Sites." *Museum Management and Curatorship* 33(1), 25–41.

17. For simplicity, dollars are used both figuratively and literally.

18. For example, Benjamin, D. J., Heffetz, O., Kimball, M., and Szembrot, S. (2014). "Beyond Happiness and Satisfaction: Toward Well-Being Indices Based on Stated Preference." *American Economic Review* 104(9): 2698–2735.

Fleurbaey, M. (2009). "Beyond GDP: The Quest for a Measure of Social Welfare." *Journal of Economic Literature* 47 (4), 1029–75.

Fox, J. (2012). "The Economics of Well-being." *Harvard Business Review*. https://hbr.org/2012/01/the-economics-of-well-being. Retrieved February 26, 2020.

Graham, C. (2011). *The Pursuit of Happiness: An Economy of Well-Being*. Washington, DC: Brookings Institution Press.

19. For example, Centre for Educational Research and Innovation (CERI). (2001). *The Well-Being of Nations: The Role of Social and Human Capital*. Paris: Organization for Economic Co-operation and Development.

Fleurbaey, M. (2009). "Beyond GDP: The Quest for a Measure of Social Welfare." *Journal of Economic Literature* 47 (4), 1029–75.

Fox, J. (2012). "The Economics of Well-Being." *Harvard Business Review*. https://hbr.org/2012/01/the-economics-of-well-being. Retrieved February 26, 2020.

Fujiwara, D., Kudrna, L., and Dolan, P. (2014). "Quantifying and Valuing the Wellbeing Impacts of Culture and Sport." Technical Report. London: UK Department for Culture, Media and Sport. https://assets.publishing.service.gov.uk/government/uploads/system/uploads/attachment_data/file/304899/Quantifying_and_valuing_the_wellbeing_impacts_of_sport_and_culture.pdf. Retrieved February 18, 2020.

Graham, C. (2011). *The Pursuit of Happiness: An Economy of Well-Being*. Washington, DC: Brookings Institution Press.

20. For example, Deniz, D. (2016). "Improving Perceived Well-Being through Improved Safety." *Procedia—Social and Behavioral Sciences* 2(6), 632–42. See also, Patil, S., Patruni, B., Lu, H., Dunkerley, F., Fox, J., Potoglou, D., and Robinson, N. (2015). *Public Perception of Security and Privacy: Results of the Comprehensive Analysis of PACT's Pan-European Survey.* Brussels: Rand Europe. And, Wood, D. A., and Wills, E. (2012). *Subjective Well-Being and Security*. Dordrecht, NL: Springer

21. For example, Lindert, J., Bain, P., Kubzansky, L., and Stein, C. (2015). "Well-Being Measurement and the WHO Health Policy Health 2010: Systematic Review of Measurement Scales." *European Journal of Public Health* 25(4), 731–40. See also, Lohr, K. N. (2002). "Assessing Health Status and Quality-of-Life Instruments: Attributes and Review Criteria." *Quality of Life Research* 11, 193–205. And, National Academies of Science, Engineering and Medicine. (2020). *Promoting Positive Adolescent Health Behaviors and Outcomes*. Washington, DC: The National Academies Press.

22. For example, Ashworth, J., and Johnson, P. (1996). "Sources of 'Value for Money' for Museum Visitors: Some Survey Evidence." *Journal of Cultural Economics* 20, 67–83.

Carmen, J. (2010). *Heritage Value: Combining Culture and Economics*. London: Arts and Humanities Council.

Carnwath, J. D., and Brown, A. S. (2014). *Understanding the Value and Impacts of Cultural Experiences—A Literature Review*. London: Art Council England. https://www.artscouncil.org.uk/sites/default/files/downloadfile/Understanding_the_Value_and_Impacts_.

Champ, P. A., Boyle, K. J., and Brown, T. C. (2003). *A Primer on Nonmarket Valuation.* Norwell, MA: Kluwer.

Choi, A., Ritchie, B., Papandrea, F., and Bennett, J. (2010). "Economic Valuation of Cultural Heritage Sites: A Choice Modeling Approach." *Tourism Management* 31(2), 213–20.

Clark, K. (Ed.). (2006). "Capturing the Public Value of Heritage: The Proceedings of the London Conference *25–26 January 2006*." London: English Heritage.

Crossick, G., and Kaszynska, P. (2016). *Understanding the Value of Arts & Culture. The AHRC Cultural Value Project*. Arts and Humanities Research Council. https://ahrc.ukri.org/documents/publications/cultural-value-project-final-report/

Hull, D. (2011). "Assessing the Value and Impact of Museums." Technical Report. Belfast: Northern Ireland Assembly Research and Library Service Research Paper. http://www.niassembly.gov.uk/globalassets/Documents/RaISe/Publications/2011/Culture-Arts-Leisure/2911.pdf. Retrieved February 20, 2020.

Johnson, P., and Thomas, B. (2000). *The Economic Impact of Museums: A Critique*. Technical Report. Durham, UK: University of Durham Business School.

Tohmo, T. (2004). "Economic Value of a Local Museum: Factors of Willingness-to-Pay." *Journal of Socio-Economics* 33(2), 229–40.

Scott, C. A. (2011). Measuring the immeasurable: Capturing intangible values. Marketing and Public Relations International Committee of ICOM (International Council of Museums) Conference Keynote Brno, Czech Republic 19th September 2011. https://citeseerx.ist.psu.edu/viewdoc/download?doi=10.1.1.1058.3671&rep=rep1&type=pdf. Retrieved February 18, 2020.

23. See, Smithsonian Institution (2007, April). "Going Free? Cooper-Hewitt National Design Museum and General Admission Fees." Technical Report. Washington, DC: Smithsonian Institution Office of Policy and Analysis. https://www.si.edu/Content/opanda/docs/

Rpts2007/07.04.Admissions.Final.pdf. Retrieved January 3, 2021. See also, Grant, D. (2019). "How Much Is Too Much? On the Difficulty of Calculating Museum Admission Prices." New Criterion.com, July 23, 2019. https://newcriterion.com/blogs/dispatch/how-much-is-too-much. Retrieved January 3, 2021.

24. Deval, H., Mantel, S., Kardes, F., and Posavac, S. (2013). "How Naive Theories Drive Opposing Inferences from the Same Information." *Journal of Consumer Research* 39(6), 1185–1201.

25. "Value Creation." Quote Master. https://www.quotemaster.org/value+creation. Retrieved December 26, 2020.

26. See, Benjamin, D. J., Heffetz, O., Kimball, M., and Szembrot, S. (2014). "Beyond Happiness and Satisfaction: Toward Well-Being Indices Based on Stated Preference." *American Economic Review* 104(9): 2698–2735.

Carson, R. T. (2001). "Resources and Environment: Contingent Valuation." *International Encyclopedia of the Social and Behavioral Sciences* 13272–75. https://www.sciencedirect.com/science/article/pii/B0080430767041966?via%3Dihub. Retrieved October 4, 2020.

Centre for Educational Research and Innovation. (2001). *The Well-Being of Nations: The Role of Social and Human Capital.* Paris: Organization for Economic Co-operation and Development.

Fleurbaey, M. (2009). "Beyond GDP: The Quest for a Measure of Social Welfare." *Journal of Economic Literature* 47(4), 1029–1075.

Fox, J. (2012). "The Economics of Well-Being." *Harvard Business Review.* https://hbr.org/2012/01/the-economics-of-well-being. Retrieved February 26, 2020.

Frey, B. S., Luechinger, S., and Stutzer, A. (2010). "The Life Satisfaction Approach to Environmental Valuation." *Annual Review of Resource Economics* 2(1), 139–60.

Fujiwara, D., and Dolan, P. (2016). "Happiness-Based Policy Analysis." In M. D. Adler and M. Fleurbaey (eds.), *Well-Being and Public Policy.* Oxford: Oxford University Press.

Graham, C. (2011). *The Pursuit of Happiness: An Economy of Well-Being.* Washington, DC: Brookings Institution Press.

Himmler, S., van Exel, J., and Brouwer, W. (2020). "Estimating the Monetary Value of Health and Capability Well-Being Applying the Well-Being Valuation Approach." *The European Journal of Health Economics.* https://doi.org/10.1007/s10198-020-01231-7. Retrieved August 22, 2020.

Lindert, J., Bain, P., Kubzansky, L., and Stein, C. (2015). "Well-Being Measurement and the WHO Health Policy Health 2010: Systematic Review of Measurement Scales." *European Journal of Public Health* 25(4), 731–40.

Lohr, K. N. (2002). "Assessing Health Status and Quality-of-Life Instruments: Attributes and Review Criteria." *Quality of Life Research* 11, 193–205.

Orlowski, J., and Wicker, P. (2015). "The Monetary Value of Social Capital." *Journal of Behavioral and Experimental Economic* 57, 26–36.

Sidney, J. A., Jones, A., Coberley, C., Pope, J., and Wells, A. (2017). "The Well-Being Valuation Model: A Method for Monetizing the Nonmarket Good of Individual Well-Being." *Health Services Outcomes Research Methods* 17, 84–100.

27. Fafchamps, M., and Labonne, J. (2017). "Using Split Samples to Improve Inference about Causal Effects." Working Paper, Stanford University. http://dx.doi.org/10.7910/DVN/Q0IXQY. Retrieved February 26, 2021. See also, Anderson, M., and Magruder, J. (2017). "Split-Sample Strategies for Avoiding False Discoveries." Working Paper. U.C. Berkeley. https://are.berkeley.edu/~jmagruder/split-sample.pdf. Retrieved February 26, 2021.

28. Due to timing, only five of the institutions participated in this data collection process.

29. Surveys used the local currency.

30. Falk, J. H. (2018). *Born to Choose: Evolution, Self, and Well-Being.* New York: Routledge.

31. Saloner, B., Polsky, D., Kenney, G., Hempstead, K., and Rhodes, K. (2015). "Primary Care Visits Available to Most Uninsured but at a High Price." Johns Hopkins Bloomberg School of Public Health, May 5, 2015. https://www.jhsph.edu/news/news-releases/2015/primary-care-visits-available-to-most-uninsured-but-at-a-high-price.html. Retrieved January 17, 2021.

32. Pew Research Center. (2011). "Is college worth it?" Pew, May 15, 2011. https://www.pewsocialtrends.org/2011/05/15/is-college-worth-it/#chapter-5-the-monetary-value-of-a-college-education?src=prc-number. Retrieved January 17, 2021.

33. Weinstein, M., and Bradburd, R. (2013). *The Robin Hood Rules for Smart Giving.* New York: Columbia University Press.

34. For example, Fox, J. (2012). "The Economics of Well-Being." *Harvard Business Review.* https://hbr.org/2012/01/the-economics-of-well-being. Retrieved February 26, 2020. See also, Itkowitz, C. (2016). "Harvard Researchers Discovered the One Thing Everyone Needs for Happier, Healthier Lives." *The Independent,* March 2, 2016. http://www.independent.co.uk/life-style/harvard-researchers-discover-the-one-thing-everyone-needs-for-happier-and-healthier-lives-a6907901.html. Retrieved March 2, 2016. And, Suttie, J. (2017). "How Does Valuing Money Affect Your Happiness?" *Greater Good Magazine,* October 30, 2017. https://greatergood.berkeley.edu/article/item/how_does_valuing_money_affect_your_happiness. Retrieved March 18, 2021.

35. Weinstein, M., and Bradburd, R. (2013). *The Robin Hood Rules for Smart Giving.* New York: Columbia University Press.

36. Peterson, R. (2018). "10 Experts Explain What Is a Good ROI and Why." BarnRaisers.com, May 28, 2018. https://barnraisersllc.com/2018/05/28/good-roi-experts-explain-industries/. Retrieved March 14, 2021.

37. Schmidt, M. (2021). "Return of Investment Metric ROI Measures Profitability." Solution Matrix, LTD. https://www.business-case-analysis.com/return-on-investment.html. Retrieved March 14, 2021.

38. Note: All calculations utilize U.S. dollars.

39. Ecologists have long recognized this dichotomy between quantity and quality, particularly with regard to reproduction. Referred to as "r" (quantity) and "K" (quality) strategies, each comes with its own unique costs and benefits. cf., Wikipedia, https://en.wikipedia.org/wiki/R/K_selection_theory. Retrieved February 20, 2020. See also Pianka, E. R. (1970). On r and K selection. *American Naturalist,* 104 (940): 592–97.

40. NOTE: Demographic variability in my preliminary research data did show significant differences as a function of both race/ethnicity and income but the sample size for this preliminary investigation was limited and thus caution needs to be exercised in interpreting results. Further investigation using a much larger sample size is needed to fully verify these preliminary findings.

41. Falk, J. H., and Needham, M. (2011). "Measuring the Impact of a Science Center On Its Community." *Journal of Research in Science Teaching* 48(1), 1–12.

9

Creating Future Value—Big Steps

> Engineering and mechanical thinking drove the last economic era; the next era will be driven by biology and what we are starting to refer to as the global well-being economy, which includes all the various aspects of well-being.
>
> —Bob Johansen[1]

The future for museums is murky. In the time that elapsed between when I conceptualized and received a contract to write this book and now, when I am writing it, so much has changed. In the midst of the worst global pandemic in a century, many professionals wonder if museum experiences will ever again return to how they once were. By necessity, most of the examples and data presented in this book were based on museum experiences as they existed pre-pandemic. Many now think that the world of tomorrow will never again be as it was. If this is true, how generalizable and useful are the ideas presented up to now? Will enhanced well-being still be a primary value delivered by museums? Of course, no one can truly predict the future, but no one who cares about what will happen in the future can afford not to try.

The first thing to know about the future is that it begins today. Although the future is never a straight line from the present, tomorrow's events, including those involving museums, will by necessity build on current realities. In these final two chapters I will build on what I have discussed up to this point and provide suggestions for how to build a better future for museums. This chapter will focus on the big steps, the ambitious re-envisioning of purpose, mission, and strategy that most museums will need to employ if they are to remain relevant and successful in the remaining decades of the twenty-first century. The next and final chapter will focus on the smaller but no less important tactical steps museum professionals can take toward ensuring that whatever shape or form museum experiences take in the future, those experiences will be engaging, personally meaningful, and well-being enhancing. First, though, a brief foray into current realities.

MUSEUMS TODAY

We currently live in a world characterized by volatility, uncertainty, complexity, and ambiguity (VUCA).[2] Navigating VUCA is no easy task as it regularly threatens to overturn any and all established ways of behaving. Wave after wave of VUCA is now battering individuals, organizations, and even whole societies, and all are reeling under the stresses created by the resulting, seemingly, never-ending "churn."

The current COVID-19 pandemic has been a period of immense disruption (more disruptive to some individuals and some sectors than others). Unfortunately, the individuals most impacted have been those at the lowest rungs of society; while among the hardest hit business sectors have been the leisure sector—travel and tourism, restaurants, entertainment venues, and of course, museums. Museums worldwide were forced to repeatedly close their doors for weeks and months and many institutions experienced unprecedented financial challenges. As suggested at the beginning of this book, some have predicted that perhaps as many as one-third of all the museums will not survive this global event.[3] Thus it is understandable that many in the museum community believe that this current crisis is going to be the "hinge event"—the one that forever changes the world, creating a clear distinction between realities, pre- and post-crisis. History suggests otherwise. Events like the current pandemic are unlikely to, in of themselves, dramatically reshape society. The most likely scenario is an altered, but not entirely remade world. There will of course be changes, but those changes are most likely to come from an acceleration of changes that were already happening before the pandemic.[4] There will also be things that will not change. Let us first explore what is likely to change.

WHAT WILL CHANGE

As we move into the third decade of the twenty-first century, there are a host of problems/issues that will threaten human well-being, and in the process force museums and other institutions to adapt and respond. Many will be totally unanticipated, but at least four do not require a crystal ball to predict; all are already clearly visible and already demanding attention.

- Equity and justice issues
- Technological change
- Climate change
- Global health issues

Equity and Justice

There has always been a gap between the rich and the poor, the haves and have-nots, but that gap has become increasingly large and increasingly intolerable. Wealth—the measure of an individual's or family's financial net worth—provides many privileges. Wealth makes it easier for people to seamlessly transition between jobs, respond in emergency situations, and invest in one's own health and betterment. Wealth is also a generational factor. Parents with wealth are better positioned to ensure the future success of their children and adults with wealth are better able to take care of themselves as they age. The current unequal distribution of wealth is not solely due to economic factors; current inequalities are also a legacy of racial, ethnic, religious, and colonial histories and policies. There is every reason to believe that the worldwide push back against these disparities and inequalities is likely to accelerate in the coming years. With this pushback, as already is apparent, will come further breakdown in public trust of institutions.[5] The drive for greater institutional access and equity is the through-line that connects many if not most of today's social movements, including Black Lives Matter, Me Too!, SARS (Nigeria's Special Anti-Robbery Squad) protests, and the rise of populism around the world. All are, in one way or another, reactions to the failure of institutions to fully meet the public's well-being-related needs; all are expressions of a desire for institutions to move beyond exclusively meeting the needs of the few to meeting the needs of all.

Technological Change

Few alive today can ignore the disruptions caused by the rapid and inexorable spread of digital technologies. The development of ever more effective forms of automation and artificial intelligence are already beginning to have a major impact on employment and international commerce as well as daily life. Still flying below the radar, but soon to rear its head will be the ethical, legal, social, and economic implications of genetic engineering technologies that will soon make it possible to change who gets to live, in what ways, and for how long. These, and other yet to be unveiled technologies, promise to impact virtually every facet of human life. For example, the relentless growth of automation and artificial intelligence is likely to further exacerbate current disparities in the distribution of wealth, as technology allows more and more jobs to be accomplished by machines rather than people. Predictably, those in society with the most intellectual and social capital will benefit from these changes and those with less will not, though all will be forced to accommodate to the inexorable intrusion of technological capabilities and malignancies into ever more areas of personal life.

Climate Change

There can be no denying that earth's climate is changing, creating predictably unpredictable living conditions for earth's inhabitants. The exponential increase in human-initiated release of carbon into the atmosphere has dramatically disrupted historical weather patterns, replaced by extreme events—unending hot summers, record-breaking polar temperatures, torrential rain, unrelenting drought, and monster storms—all of which are creating an existential threat to the well-being of all life on earth. Despite our hubris, humans will not be able to escape the coming disruptions of earth systems. All current human societies are adapted to the conditions that have existed for the past ten thousand years. These conditions will soon be gone as changing climate rapidly alters historic sea levels, ocean currents, temperatures, and rainfall patterns; disrupted will be the very foundations of human existence with the specter of wide-scale disruptions to food supplies, living spaces, economies, and geopolitical relationships. For example, the migration/immigration issues that roiled Europe and the United States much of the past two decades will only be exacerbated by climate change. Instead of tens of thousands of migrants, the world will likely see millions, perhaps even billions of people on the move. Where will they go? How will societies respond?

Global Health

As indicated, this book was written during the largest global pandemic in a century. Though currently there is optimism that this specific health threat might be tamed, any respite gained is likely to be short-lived. Most health experts predict that these kinds of pandemics will continue to occur, with the frequency of pandemics increasing and the numbers of people killed increasing as well.[6] In the coming years, as humans increasingly encroach upon hither-to isolated environments, combined with the ever-increasing rapidity with which people travel the globe, the evolution and worldwide spread of a panoply of novel, virulent diseases will become increasingly common.[7] Much as COVID-19 wreaked havoc on the world economy, so too will these future events. It is predicted that current behaviors like mask wearing could become standard practice, so too, could regular bouts of social distancing. The nature and severity of these events are of course unpredictable, but what is predictable is that they will happen and that they will alter how institutions respond to and accommodate people's concerns about their most fundamental well-being-related needs.

WHAT WILL NOT CHANGE

Despite the unprecedented tsunami of VUCA bearing down on humanity, humans themselves, will not markedly change. At their core, humans are shaped by their efforts to satisfy their fundamental well-being-related needs—the needs of a group of highly intelligent, bipedal apes that evolved to live in small hunter-gathering groups, each group fiercely striving to protect its own limited resources and ensure its own survival. Despite all the profound cultural shifts that occurred in the past few millennia, as well as the likely seismic shifts described above that will afflict humanity in the next few years, the fundamental needs and desires of humans will remain remarkably constant.

This constancy is what allows us to watch movies from fifty years ago and still relate to the main characters. This is why the same is true of the characters who populate the myths and stories of ancient Mesopotamia, Greece, China, Australia, India, Africa, and the Americas. Although the cultural customs and realities of these long-gone figures may at times strike us as unusual, the needs and desires of these heroes and heroines of the past remain completely recognizable and understandable. All describe people seeking love and companionship. All describe people with recognizable emotions such as pain, suffering, jealousy, and joy. All are peopled with individuals seeking to triumph over their circumstances. All describe people with concerns about their physical health and security. All describe people with the distinctive human qualities of curiosity, wile, and grit. All human stories, both those of the past and those of the present, reveal the fundamental, deep inner workings of humanity, in particular the never-ending need to fulfill personal, intellectual, social, and physical well-being.

Inherent in this reality lies a strategic and timeless formula for the future, an asset-based formula. For as suggested in chapter 1, the solutions we seek for the challenges that vex museums will not come from focusing on weaknesses and deficits but rather by focusing on strengths and assets. This is easy to say but harder to accomplish. As events of the past two decades make clear, the challenges posed by the increasingly VUCA world of the twenty-first century will continue to challenge the survival of museums. The long-term success and sustainability of museums will require two things—a clear focus on purpose and a willingness to embrace a more flexible and nimble approach to strategies and tactics that increasingly shifts the institution's priorities away from serving just the individual needs of the few to one that focuses more on serving the collective well-being needs of the many.

PURPOSE AND MISSION

As the preceding eight chapters have documented, museums are remarkably adept at enhancing the public's personal, intellectual, social, and physical well-being. This is an asset that can be built on; this is where the future of museums should begin. How best to leverage this unique and worthwhile, thus highly valuable societal benefit into a successful and sustainable future? Enhancing well-being should not only remain the core outcome of future museum experiences but arguably should become the focus of the museum's purpose and mission as well.

There are many approaches to defining institutional purpose and mission. I have come to appreciate the approach of business thought leaders Jim Collins and Jerry Porras,[8] as it is a research-based approach predicated on evidence of what really works. Collins and Porras's approach particularly diverges from traditional strategic-planning methods in how they frame both purpose and mission. In this approach, "purpose" is intended to represent the fundamental vision of the organization, the major, long-term, guiding goal of the organization. Purpose should be a fifty-to-one-hundred-year "shoot for the stars" aspiration for the future. An institution's purpose statement represents the world it hopes to help to make.

By contrast, "mission," though still an aspirational statement, is designed to be a more specific, shorter term, achievable goal. In place of, or in addition to a mission statement, Collins and Porras prefer to include a a shorter-term aspiration they call a Big Hairy Audacious Goal (BHAG), as it is designed to both create clarity about the organization's immediate activities, that is *strategies* and *tactics*, as well as serve as a simple, inspirational, galvanizing, easily remembered, but above all, daring statement about what this organization is really working to achieve. By design, there is no guarantee that an institution will achieve its BHAG, but it is a goal worth trying to achieve. Missions are like the series of mountains an organization needs to climb to reach its purpose. As mountains are climbed, as missions are accomplished, the institution needs to set its sights on the next mountain to be climbed and revise its BHAG. In his most recent book, Jim Collins and his coauthor Bill Lazier provide the following "tests" for what defines a good BHAG:[9]

- Does everyone in the organization find the BHAG exciting?
- Is the BHAG clear, compelling, and easy to grasp?
- Does the BHAG connect to the purpose of the organization?
- Is the BHAG undeniably a goal, not a verbose, hard-to-understand, convoluted, impossible-to-remember mission or vision "statement"?
- Do you have substantially less than a 100 percent chance of achieving the BHAG yet at the same time believe your organization can achieve the BHAG if fully committed?
- Would you be able to clearly tell if you achieved the BHAG?

Unfortunately, most museum's purpose and mission statements fall far short of this ideal, and even those that do have invariably defined the museum's purpose and mission within a twentieth-century context rather than a soon-to-be mid-twenty-first-century context. For example, most museums still cling to purposes couched in terms of twentieth-century intellectual academic framings such as art, science, or history. Instead, today's museums need to address the confluence of pressing social, economic, cultural, and environmental issues outlined above. Each of the four highlighted "challenges" directly speak to issues of societal well-being and each require a multi-disciplinary solution that transcends the traditional, disciplinary academic silos of yesteryear.

How should museums position themselves relative to these concerns? The time has come for museums to reexamine old assumptions and goals in order to adapt and create more responsive ways of bringing value to the world. I believe the future of museums will increasingly depend upon how well they are able to shape and revise their purposes and missions to directly accommodate and proactively address the trends and issues critically affecting the world.

Clearly, museums, and the museum experiences they create, are not in a position, to unilaterally ameliorate global challenges. Museum experiences will not tame pandemics, stem the tide of climate change, slow the pace of technological change, nor even in and of themselves level the economic and social playing field; but they can moderate these challenges for billions of people. Museums can commit their considerable talents and resources to supporting enhanced societal well-being. As argued by Lonnie Bunch III, Secretary of the Smithsonian Institution, at a recent meeting of the American Alliance of Museums,

> What I want to hear from museums in their vision statements is about the greater good, and that greater good is more than service to audiences, it's about helping a country find truth, find insight, find nuance, and in many ways, what I hope that cultural institutions like this can do is that they're better suited than most to define reality and to give hope.[10]

That is exactly what they should do—one individual, one family, and one community at a time. Specifically, what museums can do is focus their energies on promoting curiosity and helping people solve problems they face. They should also, each in their own way, work to promote joy and fellowship, safety and security, while working to alleviate undue pain and suffering. They should be places designed to allow more people, more of the time, to live meaningful, fulfilled, and successful lives.

Each and every museum needs to determine how they feel they can best accomplish the good they seek to do in the world, the purpose they aspire to accomplish. There cannot and should not be a single museum purpose and mission, but rather there needs to be tens of thousands of unique purposes and missions. How can your museum frame a purpose and mission/BHAG that will speak simultaneously to the unique affordances and assets of your institution while at the same time clearly speaking to the needs of the larger society?

Here are four examples of purposes and BHAGs that might be of use. I have selected not only museum examples but ones that I hope will provide a broader, more generic sense of the possible.

Merck (multinational pharmaceutical company)

Purpose: We are in the business of preserving and improving human life. All our actions must be measured by our success in achieving this.

BHAG (set in 1930): Transform this company from a chemical manufacturer into one of the preeminent drug-making companies in the world.

Treehouse (regional non-profit):

Purpose: We envision—and strive to create—a world where every child that has experienced foster care has the opportunities and support they need to pursue their dreams and launch successfully into adulthood.

BHAG: Within five years, King County youth in foster care will graduate from high school at the same rate as their peers.

Institute for Learning Innovation (international, learning research and development non-profit)
Purpose: We believe that lifelong, free-choice learning is key to individual and collective well-being and a better, more equitable, and just future for all.
BHAG (set in 2021): Make lifelong, free-choice learning a universally accepted idea by 2031.

Museum of Life + Science (regional science and nature museum)
Purpose: We envision a world where people generate and embrace evidence to advance understanding, improve lives, and shape the future.
BHAG: Create an entire generation of curious and evidence-driven kids in Durham (North Carolina)

Each of these purposes speak to building a better world; each expansively positions the organization in ways designed to improve societal well-being. Even the narrowest, that of Treehouse, is framed around helping individuals to live better, more successful lives. The four BHAGs are equally aspirational, all related to the organization's purpose, but appropriately, all are far more focused and organization specific. I included Merck as the one for-profit BHAG because, unlike most corporate BHAGs that seek to become the biggest and baddest company on the block, Merck's BHAG spoke to the need for shifting its focus away from that of a generic chemical company to that of a more specialized company, one focused on producing a single type of product, pharmaceuticals, that it could do equal to or better than any other company. Perhaps some museums might want to consider a similar shift away from a generic focus on art, history, or science to one more focused on supporting a specific aspect of enhanced public well-being, a focus that would allow them to be equal to or better at delivering this form of well-being than any other organization in their community.

Treehouse's BHAG is an example of a specific and measurable goal. Leaving aside for the moment whether high school graduation is truly the singularly important key to a successful life that many in society now consider it, abolishing the significant disparity in high school graduation rates between youth in foster care and their peers makes a compelling target. One could readily imagine the existence of equally tangible, challenging but achievable goals a museum might accomplish.

Both the Museum of Life + Science and the Institute for Learning Innovation's BHAGs are more expansive and less easily measured, but each in its own way defines a very specific strategy for moving their organizations one step closer to achieving their purpose; each of these are "how" statements. In the case of the Museum of Life + Science, they have clarified that the "how" is to ensure that everything they do fosters curiosity and empowers children to become better at using evidence-based approaches.

While the Institute for Learning Innovation has zeroed in on the idea that a critical first step in transforming the learning landscape of the future is to help people better understand and appreciate the prevalence and fundamental importance of the lifelong free-choice learning they do every day of their lives; that free-choice learning, more than formal education, is the key to life success. Most museums could benefit from a similar process of tangibly defining "how" they intend to achieve their purpose and then committing themselves to the relentless pursuit of that singular goal.

Once the purpose and mission/BHAG of the organization has been defined, then the strategies, and ultimately tactics can be defined. Organizations can have multiple strategies, each supported by multiple tactics, but every strategy's sole purpose should be to fulfill the mission, to achieve the organization's BHAG.

(BIG STEP) STRATEGIES

For more than a century, most museums have utilized content-focused, one-of-a-kind exhibitions and programs housed in large iconic buildings as their predominant approach to fulfilling their purpose and mission. There is no question that this approach, this strategy, has historically been fundamental to what many have thought of as the essence of the museum experience. Exhibitions and programs, as well as large buildings, may continue to be the best strategic approach in the future, but then again, they may not be.

Museums exist for more than the creation of exhibitions and programs. As described above, they should exist to fulfill a purpose, to have an impact on society.[11] The recent pandemic forced most museums to shift their strategies. In the face of shuttered buildings, most focused on delivering online, virtual experiences. Other institutions found themselves engaged in providing other types of non-building-related programming out in the community.[12] Collectively, these activities have helped the museum community appreciate that they are, and need to be, more than just exhibitions and buildings serving individuals, that their expertise can be applied to serving the broader community and fulfilling their mission in more ways than previously thought or done. This, I believe, is the silver lining that the COVID-19 pandemic revealed.

Every person today *and tomorrow* will possess basic well-being-related needs. In the future, as in the past, every person, each in his or her own way, will actively seek ways to satisfy their curiosity and wonder, will strive to enhance their personal sense of fulfillment, their ability to have choice and control over their world, to feel a sense of belonging and social acceptance, and a visceral need to ensure that their physical health and safety, and that of their loved ones, is secure. These needs have not diminished in today's constantly disrupted and topsy-turvy world; these needs are likely to be even more keenly felt and sought after.

In other words, if delivering public well-being is the goal, how can museums best fulfill this goal? The following are some thoughts on how museums might want to strategically think about delivering enhanced personal, intellectual, social, and physical well-being to a broader and more collective constituency.

Personal Well-Being

The ability to deliver personal well-being—wonder, interest, enjoyment, and curiosity, the fostering of a sense of personal power and identity—are historically museum strengths. This is a niche that much of the public already perceives museums are good at. Now is the time to extend and build on that strength and create new products and services designed to enhance personal well-being. People will increasingly be looking for ways to enhance their sense of competence, self-awareness, and self-efficacy. People will always be interested in what is new, what is different, what is valuable, and what is important; and museums can continue to play a role in defining these realities for people. In a world inundated with information, resources capable of providing quality, thoughtfully curated information will always be at a premium. Also, at a premium will be authentic and valid ways to discover more about oneself and how one fits into the world. The good news is that the work of building identity, what philosopher Jerrold Siegel called "identity work," is a never-ending job,[13] and there will always be a market for it. The bad news is that this form of personal well-being is, in reality, difficult to achieve. Many will claim they can provide increased self-knowledge and self-fulfillment, but few will, or can, actually deliver on this promise.

Many of the societal changes described earlier might result in more people than ever in search of places to support identity work. Advances in automation and implementation of guaranteed minimum incomes are just on the horizon, meaning that machines will do more tasks, and fewer people will need to work and/or actually be able to find work. People have always found meaning through work; historically it was hunting and gathering, and then it was farming, and then the production of goods and services. How will people continue to find meaning in life when work no longer can fill that role? History suggests that individuals with increased leisure time desire personal well-being even more than those with less leisure time. Given these trends, it is reasonable to predict that the provision of personal well-being could well become one of the largest growth industries of the mid-twenty-first century.

For years, museums have been among the best in the world at supporting the identity work of millions of people. Too often in the past, museums merely made it possible for people to use their resources for identity work but did not actively facilitate the journey.[14] In the years ahead, though, museums will need to not only come up with new methods and likely a diversity of approaches for helping people on their identity quest, but they will have to proactively work on providing this kind of support. The search for identity is an age-old problem, but as more people have the capability and desire to use their time for this purpose, it will also mean that what historically sufficed for help with identity work will also need to change as the people in need of assistance in their their identity-seeking journey will be beginning from an ever-greater diversity of backgrounds and cultural traditions. Museums will need to be able to accommodate and support more than just Western identities but other identity traditions as well.

In the past, identity work was almost exclusively inward facing, with the search for self-actualization often being synonymous with selfishness. The future of identity work does not need to be this way. Museums could foster a form of identity work that is outward facing, personal growth and development that comes from helping to serve the needs of others. I would like to believe that this approach to personal well-being will predominate in the future. Museums should figure out how to invent this and other new approaches. What is needed is some serious research and development (R&D) in this area; now is the time for museums to utilize whatever financial reserves they possess, individually or ideally collectively, to figure out how to invent the personal well-being products and services of the future.

Intellectual Well-Being

Although the future will certainly involve more artificial intelligence, as well as more technology-enabled support for learning and planning, the role of human intelligence and pursuit of knowledge is unlikely to decline anytime soon. The lifelong learning business is already one of the fastest growing industries in the world, and it is almost certainly going to continue expanding throughout the twenty-first century. In fact, it is this boom in demand for lifelong learning that likely was the primary driver of the museum community's rapid growth in the final decades of the twentieth century.[15] As the public seeks to acquire the intellectual capital they need to navigate a rapidly changing world, organizations capable of providing this kind of intellectual well-being will not only be in high demand but will need to continually evolve to keep up with the public's constantly changing needs and requirements. One predictable trend, one which traditional education institutions like schools have not accommodated well despite rhetoric to the contrary, is the public's increasing desire for more personalized, individual need-driven experiences. The past was about mass-produced educational offerings and standardized degrees; the future will increasingly be about competencies and an ever-increasing utilization of free-choice learning resources.[16] Similar to personal well-being, this is an area in which museums already have credibility, at least with many in the population. This reputation and wealth of experience can be mined to build the next generation of free-choice learning products and services to enhance intellectual well-being.

Another area of intellectual well-being in which museums currently possess cache in is in public literacy. Unfortunately, most museums continue to focus on dated notions of art, history, or science literacy. These antiquated definitions of literacy are predicated on the belief that somehow an individual can possess some basic canon of knowledge sufficient to ensure lifelong proficiency, a definition of literacy as out-of-step with current realities as are the nineteenth- and twentieth-century textbooks from which these ideas derive. Yes, in the future all citizens will need to possess basic literacy, but since no one can possibly know all there is to know, let alone all one is likely to need to know, the essential measure of literacy will be the competence to face novel issues as they arise, understand enough about those issues to be able to ask good questions, determine which resources to access, know how to access those resources and sort through vast quantities of often discrepant information in order to ultimately make sound decisions. As people focus more and more on solving immediate problems, obtaining the just-in-time knowledge required to make informed, evidence-based choices and decisions will become ever more essential. Whether the problems are climate change, social injustice, technological change, or personal health, all require quality information, all require lifeling, free-choice learning. Museums can play a role in supporting twenty-first-century literacy, but they need to rethink what literacy means and how best to support its achievement. As stated above, now is the time to leverage the existing credibility and expertise the museum community holds, to get out in front of these evolving trends before someone else gets there first. Stated directly, now is the time to invest the necessary research and development to allow this transformation to occur.

That is not to say museums cannot and should not continue to retain expertise in the ideas of the past—including art, history, natural history, and science—but doing so needs to be in service of something other than ivory tower scholarship. Consistent with the trends outlined above, also predictable will be the growth of myriad special-interest hobbyists. Serving the needs of these hobbyists can also be an appropriate museum purpose, but the resources devoted to this purpose needs to be proportional to their presence in society. Today, rather than either school or museums, most people utilize the internet to fulfill these often highly specialized free-choice learning needs, but that does not mean it will or need always be the case. What museums could offer, at least currently, that the internet lacks is authority and the personal attention required to guide learning and support the development of mastery in specific topic areas. Whether this is the ideal niche for museums is not clear, but somewhere in the likely growing public thirst for knowledge and learning lies a role for museums.

Social Well-Being

Social well-being, long appreciated as an important dimension of the museum experience, although historically deemed less important than personal and intellectual well-being, may ultimately be the primary value of the museum of the future. Museums can become engines for achieving greater social cohesion by proactively fostering improved understanding between individuals and groups. Museums can be the place where people learn what it means to be part of one's own cultural group, as well as the place where they learn what it means to be part of a different cultural group. In this way, museums can be places where different parts of the community come together to learn from and about each other, a place where, given its scarcity in the broader society, trust can be built. Trust and neutrality may turn out to be the single most important commodities museums offer their communities. Many museums have been striving to do this kind of work for years now, but it is likely that many more will find this effort to be a driving purpose.

Meanwhile, as the push for greater equity and inclusion accelerates in the coming years, more and more people will come to appreciate why a more equitable and just world is in everyone's best interests. Historic inequities do not just harm those at the bottom, they harm everyone. The current pandemic provides a clear example of why this is true. The global society cannot achieve the safety of "herd immunity" unless all people are vaccinated, including and particularly the majority of the population with the least financial means and security. It is not just that everyone deserves to enjoy the social benefits and well-being that experiences like the use of museums create but rather that denying these benefits to large sectors of society undermines the ability of all to fully enjoy these benefits. Broadening audiences is not just the right thing to do it is a necessary thing to do.

Given that clearly there is not a singular community nor a single culture that everyone can and should feel a sense of belonging to, it follows that if the goal of the museum is to help support a sense of belonging to one's community and culture, then the museum will need to work on broadening not only the communities and cultures it already serves, but equally those they currently fail to serve. To achieve greater plurality, in the future museums will need to actively move away from the one-size-fits-all models they primarily now employ in both their exhibitions and programs. If we are honest, we have to admit that there never was one size that fits all, only one size that fit some! In the coming years museums will need to increasingly diversify their offerings, ensuring that the multiple products and services they offer, not individually but collectively, satisfy the personal, intellectual, and increasingly the social needs of the various populations living within their communities. The goal should not be, as it was in the past, to find the one "perfect" solution and then scale that solution up to the many. Rather, in the future, museums and other similar organizations will need to increasingly create dozens upon dozens of solutions; each individual solution targeted to satisfying the needs and realities of one specific population. Only by creating these many solutions will museum professionals be able to fully and collectively meet the needs of the many.

Humans will always want to feel engaged with others, will always want to feel needed and appreciated. The challenge for museums will be designing new products and services that fulfill these basic social well-being needs. For some it may still involve visits to a museum and experiences within exhibition-like contexts, but for many others this may not be the solution. The time is now to expand and diversify museum offerings, to invent the multiple ways of supporting individuals, families, and small and large groups in building social community. There is no mystery in what these kinds of well-beings look like when successful. The mystery is in how best to deliver these outcomes to new and more diverse generations of potential museum users.

Finally, museums will also likely continue to strive to be places where multiple generations can find common ground, learn from one another, and provide mutual strength and enrichment. The world of the future will still require places where parents and children, grandparents and grandchildren, or adult couples can bond and forge relationships. Although the ability to conduct this type of social re-creation within a physical space has now been constrained by the current pandemic, the deeply felt human need for spaces and places in which this kind of bonding can take place will remain. The details of how best to support physical mingling may need to morph, but the desire for physical mingling will not disappear and represents a strategic opportunity for museums in the future.

Physical Well-Being

In a VUCA world, few things will be more valued than institutions that afford people a sense of security, both in their immediate surroundings and in the larger world they inhabit. At the most basic level, people want to engage in activities that make them feel comfortable and safe. Clean and secure facilities for users have long been basic requirements for present-day leisure, cultural, learning, and socially related organizations; but in a world where public health and safety concerns become front of mind, the standard for what constitutes clean and secure will become more stringent. Although it is possible that the current paranoia about infection from touching germ-infested surfaces could subside in the years to come, these fears are unlikely to return to pre-pandemic sensibilities. All organizations will need to invest more time and resources in ensuring these fundamental physical well-being-related needs are satisfied, but mere satisfaction will only represent the baseline of acceptability, not a competitive advantage. To be competitive, organizations will need to offer experiences that tamp down concerns while affording opportunities for physical and mental rejuvenation. As are many organizations currently, museums might consider partnering with health and spiritual care organizations to reassure and support the public's desire for improved physical well-being.

Meanwhile, in the larger world, disruptions caused by climate change, environmental pollution, and diminished biodiversity will become increasingly important areas of public concern. People will be looking for ways that they can individually help solve these problems and gravitate to institutions that support collective, meaningful actions. Museums can leverage their current positive public standing and credibility to be part of a coalition of institutions that allow people to feel like they are making a difference, helping both themselves and others within their community address each new pressing problem as it arises. Being part of collective environmental problem remediation efforts could become a major area of endeavor for many museums in the future.[17]

Another major trend that museums can possibly capitalize upon will be the growing desire of the public for unique, place-based experiences. One way to accomplish this would be for museums to redouble their commitment to making their buildings and programs uniquely reflect their local geography and culture in everything they do, from programming to food services. An alternative approach would be to abandon buildings and move out into the community; providing users with unique experiences in their own settings and homes—now that would truly be placed-based! Regardless of whether experiences remain centralized or become increasingly decentralized, the public is going to increasingly demand that all experiences be truly unique, personalized, and customized to not only their own needs but also the realities of their local history and situation.

Finally, just as in pre-pandemic days, an increasing number of museums discovered that appealing to some of the most fundamental physical well-being-related needs such as eating, drinking, and finding mates provided a vehicle for connecting with and satisfying public well-being, so it will again in the future. Likewise, the rapid proliferation of museum programs aimed at young singles will likely once again become popular, assuming appropriate health precautions are taken. However, these historic ways of supporting enhanced physical well-being should not be the only ones museums focus on. There are myriad dimensions to physical well-being and the potential opportunities for museums to support these are only limited by the creativity, ingenuity, and of course the hard work of those who work in museums.

MOVING FORWARD

No matter what purpose, mission, or strategy museums opt to take, the need to measure and account for the value of museums will persist. Clarity in describing the good that museums do, in particular the enhancement of collective, societal well-being, promises to provide a sound and persuasive argument, particularly when it is measured and presented in the monetized policy language that decision-makers understand. The approaches outlined in chapter 8 were predicated on the historic ways in which museums enhanced people's well-being, but if the approach to enhancing well-being changes, and with it the specific types of well-being supported, then the measurements too will need to change. What cannot change, though, is the tight fit between the specific types of well-being enhanced and the value measurements applied to that enhanced well-being. As long as this approach is adhered to, then the results, as attested to by my pilot research measurements of museum return on investment, will allow museums to convincingly make the case for the value of museum experiences. To maximize the effectiveness of this case, museums need to speak with one voice. The more consistently and aggressively all within the sector account for the value of museums, the more convincing the argument will be and the greater the influence on policy and funding it will have.

Also made evident in the previous chapter was that different museums have different strengths and affordances, and that the public proactively utilizes museums accordingly. Some museums have been particularly adept at supporting intellectual well-being while others are known for fostering social well-being. Not only do these differences currently exist, it is likely and desirable that such differences exist in the future. The goal should not be to homogenize the museum community but rather to ensure that each institution be distinguished in its own right and excellent at what it does. Ideally, each institution will need to make some hard choices. For as the internationally renowned business strategist Michael Porter once said, "Strategy is as much about deciding what an organization is not doing as it is about what the organization is going to do. An organization's [purpose, mission and] strategy should not try to serve the varied needs of different segments of customers in an industry. No organization could possibly pull this off. They get stuck in the middle."[18] Successful organizations make choices, hard choices, and then execute those choices.

The data in chapter 8 also revealed—both data from how the general public perceived their well-being-related needs and aspirations and the data on the types of well-being-related benefits the public perceived they derived from museum experiences—that most people, most of the time, seek well-being needs and benefits that encompass not just one but typically all four dimensions of well-being. Thus, the goal of museums, regardless of strengths, should not be to totally focus on facilitating but a single dimension of their user's well-being to the exclusion of other needs. All museums must at least acknowledge and strive to facilitate enhanced well-being across all four of the dimensions of well-being-related need and value.

The reason for this conclusion is that although it is clearly possible to distinguish and separate an individual's well-being into the dimensions of personal, intellectual, social, and physical well-being, rarely are these four dimensions of well-being fully discrete and separable. At any given moment, a person's perceptions of his physical and mental health, are directly related to his perceptions about the health of his current social relationships. Equally, a person's sense of the strength and quality of her personal identity are influenced by her current feelings about how she is perceived by others as well as how she currently feels about her level of choice and control over events in her life. In short, well-being is experienced holistically; with each separate dimension of well-being contributing to overall perceptions of well-being.

If there is any generalization one can make about how museums should address the future, it is the need for systemic thinking.[19] Not every aspect of well-being needs to be equally emphasized; but given that all four dimensions of well-being operate holistically, all four aspects of well-being must be at least minimally supported and measured. Museums should ensure that they employ such thinking, both in how they frame their purpose and mission statements as well as in how they strategically seek to accomplish those missions. The "big" strategic steps outlined in this chapter represent only part of the solution. It is equally important to focus on the small, more tactical steps required to ensure that every museum experience offered, no matter the approach taken, is as effective as possible.

NOTES

1. Johansen, B. (2012). *Leaders Make the Future: Ten New Leadership Skills for an Uncertain World*, second edition, p. 6. San Francisco: Berrett-Koehler.

2. See "Volatility, Uncertainty, Complexity and Ambiguity (VUCA)." https://en.wikipedia.org/wiki/Volatility,_uncertainty,_complexity_and_ambiguity. Retrieved May 16, 2021.

3. American Alliance of Museums (AAM). (2020). "United States May Lose One-Third of All Museums, New Survey Shows," July 22, 2020. https://www.aam-us.org/2020/07/22/united-states-may-lose-one-third-of-all-museums-new-survey-shows/. Retrieved October 23, 2020. See also, Siegel, N. (2020). "Europe's Museums Are Open but the Public Isn't Coming." *New York Times*, October 19, 2020. https://www.nytimes.com/2020/10/19/arts/design/europe-museums-covid.html?login=email&auth=login-email&login=email&auth=login-email. Retrieved October 23, 2020. And, Zongker, B. (2020). "U.S. Museums Face Financial Woes, Get More Visitors says American Association of Museums." Art Daily/Associated Press. https://artdaily.cc/news/46649/U-S--Museums-Face-Financial-Woes--Get-More-Visitors-Says-American-Association-of-Museums-#.XtU2C0FlByx. retrieved June 1, 2020.

4. Zakaria, F. (2020). *Ten Lessons for a Post-Pandemic World.* New York: W.W. Norton. See also, Christakis, N. A. (2020). *Apollo's Arrow: The Profound and Enduring Impact of Coronavirus on the Way We Live.* New York: Little, Brown, Spark. And Mickletwait, J., and Wooldridge, A. (2020). *The Wakeup Call.* New York: HarperCollins

5. Brooks, D. (2020). "America Is Having a Moral Convulsion." *The Atlantic*, October 5, 2020. https://www.theatlantic.com/ideas/archive/2020/10/collapsing-levels-trust-are-devastating-america/616581/. Retrieved December 29, 2020.

6. Berger, M. (2020). "COVID-19, 'Not Necessarily the Big One,' WHO warns." *Washgington Post*, December 29, 2020. https://www.washingtonpost.com/world/2020/12/29/coronavirus-2020-the-big-one-who-pandemics/. Retrieved December 29, 2020.

7. See Madhav, N., Oppenheim, B., Gallivan, M., Mulembakani, P., Rubin, E., and Wolfe, N. (2017). "Pandemics: Risks, Impacts, and Mitigation." In D. T. Jamison, H. Gelband, and S. Horton (eds), *Disease Control Priorities: Improving Health and Reducing Poverty*, third edition. Washington, DC: The International Bank for Reconstruction and Development / The World Bank. https://www.ncbi.nlm.nih.gov/books/NBK525302/. Retrieved December 31, 2020.

8. Collins, J., and Porras, J. (1994). *Built to Last: Successful Habits of Visionary Companies.* New York: HaperBusiness. See also, Collins, J., and Lazier, B. (2020). *BE 2.0 (Beyond Entrepreneurship 2.0).* New York: Penguin Portfolio.

9. Collins, J., and Lazier, B. (2020). *BE 2.0 (Beyond Entrepreneurship 2.0).* New York: Penguin Portfolio, p. 125.

10. Bunch, L. (2020). "Racism, Unrest, and the Role of the Museum Field," (special session). *American Alliance of Museums Virtual Annual Meeting and MuseumExpo.* https://www.aamus.org/2020/06/09/racism-unrest-and-the-role-of-the-museum-field/. Retrieved June 6, 2021.

11. For example, Gurian, E. (1988). "Museums as a Social Responsible Institution." In E. Gurian (2006). *Civilizing the Museum: The Collected Writings of Elaine Heumann Gurian*, 69–74. London: Routledge. See also, Weil, S. (1999). "From Being about Something to Being for Somebody: The Ongoing Transformation of the American Museum." *Daedalus* 128(3), 229–58. Korn, R. (2018). *Intentional Practice for Museums.* Lanham, MD: Rowman & Littlefield. And, Spock, M. (2020). "Museums: Essential or Non-Essential." Wunderkammer, May 7, 2020. https://wunderkammer.blog/2020/05/07/museums-essential-or-non-essential/. Retrieved May 20, 2020.

12. For example, Carlsson, R. (2020). "Community Engagement with Fun Palaces." MuseumNext, May 29, 2020. https://www.museumnext.com/article/community

-engagement-with-fun-palaces/. Retrieved May 13, 2021. See also, Merritt, E. (2021). "Serving the Needs of the Community during a Pandemic." Center for the Future of Museums. American Alliance of Museums, April 12, 2021. https://www.aam-us.org/2021/04/12/serving-the-needs-of-the-community-during-a-pandemic/. Retrieved May 13, 2021.

13. Siegel, J. (2005). *The Idea of the Self: Thought and Experience in Western Europe since the Eighteenth Century*. Cambridge: Cambridge University Press.

14. Rounds, J. (2006). "Doing Identity-Work in Museums. *Curator* 49(2), 133–50.

15. Falk, J. H., and Sheppard, B. (2006). *Thriving in the Knowledge Age: New Business Models for Museums and Other Cultural Organizations*. Lanham, MD: AltaMira Press.

16. See Falk, J. H., and Dierking, L. D. (2019). "Reimagining Public Science Education: The Role of Lifelong Free-Choice Learning." *Disciplinary and Interdisciplinary Research in Science Education* 1(1), 10–18. https://doi.org/10.1186/s43031-019-0013-x. See also, Falk, J. H. (2020). "Inventing a Public Education System for the 21st Century. In J. Calvo de Mora and K. J. Kennedy (eds.), *Schools and Informal Learning in a Knowledge-Based World*, 46–61. Boca Raton, FL: Taylor & Francis Group.

17. As it already is for some today; compare https://museumsforfuture.org/.

18. Porter, M. E. (1996). "What Is Strategy?" *Harvard Business Review* 74(6), 74, 61–78.

19. See Csapó, B., and Funke, J. (2017). *The Nature of Problem Solving: Using Research to Inspire 21st Century Learning*. Paris: The Organisation for Economic Co-operation and Development (OECD).

10

Principles for Designing Better Museum Experiences

When the roots are deep, there is no reason to fear the wind.

—African Proverb

Virtually everyone is familiar with the famous Chinese proverb "A journey of a thousand miles begins with a single step." Though thought to have originated with the Taoist sage Lao Tzu more than 2500 years ago, the sentiment is as true today as it almost certainly was then. As outlined in the previous chapter we need to think big and plan strategically, but nothing gets done unless one starts with the small, first steps. This chapter focuses on how to make those small steps toward creating well-begin-focused museum experiences.

The principles on creating quality museum experiences that I present here represent insights gained from my nearly fifty years of studying how and why people use museums. Although I clearly did not always think about these practical ideas through the lens of enhanced well-being, the validity of these ideas shines through as each of these ten principles can be readily slotted into one of the four areas of human well-being-related need.

Currently museum experiences take many forms and cover innumerable topics, and in the future, these experiences are likely to become even more diverse, potentially morphing into totally new and yet to be envisioned forms. However, no matter what the content or style of delivery of a museum experience is, no matter if physical or virtual, the well-being-related needs of the people for whom those experiences are designed, the users of museum experiences are unlikely to appreciably change. People are people, and what it is that makes people feel satisfied and supported has remained remarkably stable over the years. Successful museum experiences, any museum experience, must first and foremost satisfy and support the well-being-related needs of users. For this to happen, each and every museum experience should strive to accomplish ten things, Ten Principles of Quality Museum Experiences:

1. Connect to User's Life
2. Allow Users to Make the Experience Their Own
3. Maximize Opportunities for Choice & Control
4. Surprise and Delight
5. Make the Experience Feel Safe and Secure
6. Design for Social Interaction
7. Make the Experience Comfortable and Convenient
8. Give Users a Reason to Do It Again
9. Connect with Other Experiences
10. Support Sharing

These ten principles are the key to creating user-focused, user-satisfying museum experiences; experiences that will engender loyalty and frequent and repeated use.[1] I have opted not to sort these principles into the four dimensions of personal, intellectual, social, and physical well-being. Instead, I have organized them in a more natural, chronological order roughly following what I refer to as the Museum Experience Cycle. In museums, as in life, well-being is not cleanly parsed and distinct but typically a blend of differing needs and desires; each need and resulting action emerging and assuming priority as, and when required.

THE MUSEUM EXPERIENCE CYCLE

The core of the museum experience is driven by a desire to enhance well-being, but few people are consciously aware of these core motivations. Thus actual experiences, including particularly the ways in which people themselves, or museum professionals and social scientists as well, talk about these experiences typically reflect the cultural biases and linguistic vernacular of the time. Also, key is that the museum experience can be defined and described by others such as museum staff or researchers like me, but ultimately it is a very personal, internal process, a process owned and enacted by each and every user.

The museum experience plays out over time and thus I and others have often used a sequential lens in describing the experience, variously focusing on pieces of the experience occurring either before, during, or after the experience. This framing can be a useful way to organize better practice, but one should always remember that there is really no beginning or ending. The museum experience is never totally linear; it is always more of a continuous and cyclical phenomenon. I have illustrated the continuous, cyclical, and ongoing nature of the museum experience in figure 10.1, with particular reference to leisure use of museums.

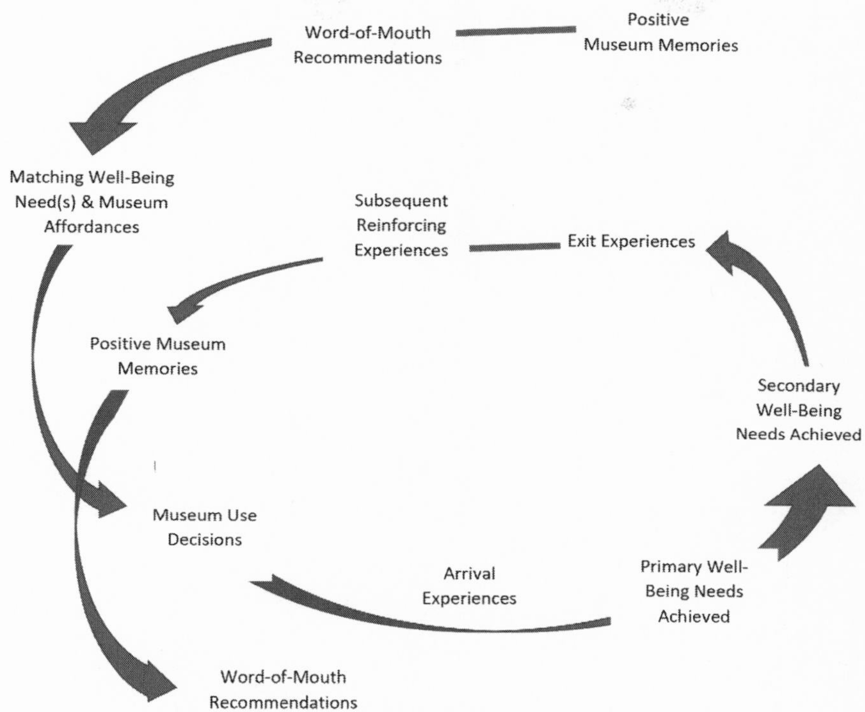

Figure 10.1. The Museum Experience Cycle. *Source:* John H. Falk

As suggested in the figure, every museum experience begins and ends with memories, typically positive, that propel the person on to additional steps in the process. For someone to choose to engage in a museum experience, at some point in their life they need to have first become aware of museums, and through that experience come to believe that engaging in future experiences offered by a museum will be positive. In short, before someone is likely to voluntarily engage in a museum experience in the future, they need to somehow perceive that this future experience will represent a positive way to support one, or some combination of their personal, intellectual, social, and physical well-being-related needs.

For some, this initial awareness of museums arrives through a school-based fieldtrip; but for most, this introduction happens as part of a family experience.[2] Regardless, in order for any given individual, on any given day, to choose to partake in a museum experience requires that that person, or someone close to that person, first know that such experiences exist and that those experiences have the potential for meeting well-being-related needs. Without that knowledge, without those positive prior museum experiences, no one would ever choose to engage in a future museum experience. So even though most of the research on museum experiences is based on data collected within the "box" of the museum, those experiences always have a history that predates arrival at the "box."

The vast majority of the hundreds of millions of people who engage in museum experiences do so as part of a leisure experience. All these people are actively trying to fill their leisure time with activities that they believe will support their various well-being-related needs. Of course, as I have described earlier, most people do not frame their decisions in this way. Rather, they talk about a desire to do something positive with their family, or have an educational and fun experience, an interest in seeing a particular object, exhibit, or website, or a desire to spend time in a stimulating but different space, somewhere that will allow them to get away from the pressures and noise of their daily life.[3] However, these self-related motivations are, at their core, well-being related motivations.

When trying to decide how to spend their leisure time, people wrack their brains for good matches between their perceived leisure needs and the affordances of the various leisure venues and experiences they can think of that might best fulfill those needs—perhaps a need for excitement, or the need for exercise, or the need for intellectual stimulation, or the need to do something with and for someone else. If they have had past, positive experiences with museums, if someone they care about has piqued their interest in a museum through word of mouth,[4] then, and only then, might it occur to them that engaging in a museum experience could be a possible "solution" to this leisure decision-making challenge. The bottom line is that virtually all the individuals who utilize museums do so with prior knowledge, experience, and most importantly, expectations about what they will experience.

However, in the absence of such a match between perceived need and perceived ability to satisfy that need based on the person's sense of what a museum experience has to offer, no one would ever choose to engage in a museum experience. What this means is that decisions to engage in museum experiences are totally dependent upon people's lived experiences. People with positive past experiences related to museums are highly likely to choose to engage in future experiences related to museums. Individuals with limited or negative past experiences related to museums are highly unlikely to choose to engage in experiences related to museums. It is as simple as that.

Central to the above framings is the idea that the past is indeed prologue to the future. Only people who perceive, based upon past lived experiences (which includes word-of-mouth experiences) that a good match exists between their current needs and their sense of what a museum experience affords, ultimately choose to engage in museum experiences. Once entered into the experience, past interests and motivations primarily drive the experience, though of course every new experience uniquely adds to the individual's sense of what a museum experience is and how it satisfies their (well-being-related) needs. Also explicitly called out in this model is the important role played by reinforcing experiences that occur after a museum use. Because of the way the human mind works, these subsequent events often become inextricably entwined with a person's memory of a museum experiences, and thus are just as important as anything that happened technically during the museum experience itself.

Importantly, though not explicitly labeled in my diagram, satisfaction acts as a mediating process between each of these events in the diagram. Individuals will only be receptive and willing to continue on to the next step in the process if they find each preceding step in the process satisfying.

With this brief overview in mind, on to talking further about each of the Ten Principles of Quality Museum Experience. In each section, I will also provide in a box, some current illustrations of these principles in practice. The source of each suggestion is noted and gratefully acknowledged in an accompanying footnote. I need to be clear, though, by calling out these particular examples I do not in any way want to suggest that these are necessarily the only examples or even the best examples of these principles; I know there are many others in the field doing exemplary work. The highlighted examples are merely the ones I and others I communicated with were aware of and personally found notable.

CONNECT TO USER'S LIFE

Although museums often create experiences to accomplish specific goals, such as illustrating the oeuvre of a particular artist, facilitating understanding of a particular scientific idea or principle, or expanding awareness of and appreciation for a particular historical time and place, these goals only have meaning to the extent that they actually connect, in some way, to the users' prior knowledge, experience, interests, and most particularly, their motivations for engaging in a museum experience on any given day. Finding out more about a topic and learning more about that topic—be it art, science, history, nature, or culture—are far from the only reason people engage in museum experiences. As described at length in this book, people engage in museum experiences for a wide range of reasons; all of which ultimately relate to enhanced well-being. Hence quality museum experiences need to be designed in ways that not only allow for but celebrate and encourage multiple reasons for using them, including reasons that deepen and enhance the user's personal, intellectual, social, and/or physical well-being.

Even when learning is the primary motivation of visitors, typically, but not always, falling within the domain of intellectual well-being, museum professionals should always be aware that learning too is about identity and making personal meaning, and hence, personal well-being.[5] People disproportionately use museums to reinforce their current understanding of the world.[6]

The hallmarks of great museum experiences are that they invite participation by diverse people with diverse backgrounds, interests, and motivations. However not only should the actual experiences themselves invite such diversity, so too should the descriptions and promotions of the experience. Whether on websites, brochures, in paid and unpaid advertising, or through social media, museums should seek to communicate with different potential audiences, encouraging multiple reasons for engaging in experiences. The days of mass marketing and one-size-fits-all approaches are gone. Today it is all about niche marketing and targeted messaging.

The San Antonio Museum of Art (SAMA) conducted a series of in-depth visitor research studies to determine who does and does not utilize their institution and why. Based on that work, they now offer a variety of programming specifically designed to reach a wide variety of specific audiences identified by the institution as critical to their mission. This includes less affluent members of the local Latinx and Black communities who historically were less frequently engaged with the museum. These audiences are specifically targeted on their website, through school and community organization programming, and proactively via word-of-mouth.[1]

The Tyne and Wear Archives and Museums in Northeastern England have long utilized a particularly innovative way to entice users to use the twelve museums and galleries located throughout their region, a district supported by five local area authorities. Through funding from the Arts Council of England they created a website that allows users to "[f]ind out what's on at museums in the North East." Potential users can explore a variety of personally relevant "trails," all of which begin with the phrase "I like . . ." These phrases enable potential users to find museum experiences tailored to their specific needs and interests that particular day, as well as to plan their specific visit (or visits).

Heureka, the Finnish science centre, has made an effort to engage more young adults. Appreciating that this audience is always looking for excuses to party, they went with it and created adult nights they called "H18." As described by the current director, "[u]sually it would be 'K18' meaning 'forbidden (K for Kielletty) for minors,' but we rephrased it with this H18—'Heureka 18' (in Finnish the pronunciation is close in a funny way). At any rate, these evenings are standing out with science programs. One of the very first evenings was called 'The Great Sex and Space Journey,' and we made that journey with investigating journalists and a group of photo-documentarists—very avant-garde, many hipsters, and, yes, sex toys photographed in jelly look like spaceships."[2]

1. Suggested by Lynn D. Dierking, Institute for Learning Innovation, Beaverton, Oregon.
2. Suggsted by Mikko Myllykoski, Heureka, Vantaa, Finland.

ALLOW USERS TO MAKE THE EXPERIENCE THEIR OWN

Although perceiving that an experience will fulfill one's self-related and well-being-related needs is clearly essential to choosing to engage in that experience, it is not sufficient. For someone to decide to partake in a museum experience, they also will need to factor in things like convenience, cost, time requirements, the ability of the specific experience to meet their specific interests and needs, and of course, the opinions and needs of others in their social group. Increasingly, people use institutional websites for this purpose, often focusing only on the specific parts of a website designed to answer the specific issues/needs they hope to satisfy.[7]

Historically, many websites disproportionately focused on providing prospective users with information on hours and amenities, but increasingly these bits of information are essential but insufficient. Institutions need to increasingly make it possible for users to actively co-create their museum experience. As Graham Black argued, "To remain relevant to [the museum's historic core] audience in the 21st century, in a society that is changing at web-speed, requires a profoundly different, much more participatory, museum experience—one that involves creating new and more meaningful opportunities for engagement."[8] Co-creation can and should happen at all points in the museum experience, but it needs to begin early. Museums need to enable people to plan and create, modify, and customize their experiences in ways that best meet their specific needs and interests.

At its core, co-creation and engagement is about empowering and respecting the user, of elevating the importance and status of "process" to being at least the equal of "product," if not the more important of the two. Inherent in this view of co-creation is not only that users deserve to have a significant voice in the content and delivery of the experiences they engage in but enshrining in the museum experience creation process the belief that users possess unique and valid insights and expertise, an authority comparable to, though different from, the authority possessed by the museum. Ensuring that voice and authority is extended to users is not only essential for ensuring maintenance of existing audiences but also imperative for broadening museum audiences, for allowing ever more diverse publics to enter into and benefit from museum experiences.

The Santa Cruz Museum of Art and History is one of the pioneers of co-created museum experiences. As stated on their website, "The MAH is of, by, and for Santa Cruz County because our creative community ignites something new here every day." Their website even includes an infographic-style "Theory of Change" that highlights this commitment to co-construction of experiences.[1]

---

1. Suggested by Amparo Leyman Pino, Yellow Cow Consulting, San Francisco, California.

A spin-off from MAH is the non-profit OF/BY/FOR ALL created by Nina Simon. Its approach starts with a simple equation: OF + BY = FOR. Arguing that the most powerful way to become relevant FOR diverse communities is to become representative OF them and co-created BY them. As stated on their website, "Rather than guessing what an unfamiliar community might want or need, we encourage you to get to know that community. To spend time in that community. To listen and learn from them. And then, with community partners at the table, to figure out how you can most meaningfully work together to achieve each of your goals."[2]

The Swedish Museum of Mölndal bills itself as a museum of cultural and local history, as well as a meeting place for visitors of all ages. Importantly, this museum lets each user examine and tell their own story about any of the thousands of objects they keep in open storage. These stories become part of the collections record. In addition, they open their exhibitions unfinished, so that the users themselves can finish them.[3]

In Dublin, Ireland, the Science Gallery has created what they call the Leonardo Group, which brings together individuals from a range of backgrounds—science, technology, the arts, media, education, and business—to act as a "brain trust" for the museum. These individuals generate themes for new exhibitions and programs, as well as approaches to social media and marketing. *Leonardos* frequently do more than just brainstorm ideas; often they directly contribute to programs in their area of interest and provide the connections to make it happen. In addition to adults, Science Gallery also has a Young Leos program that offers similar opportunities to adolescents.[4]

A more techy example of co-creation comes from the Museum of English Rural Life and their unorthodox social media tactic of challenging their followers to take a photo of an animal from their collection and photoshop that image into other paintings. Beginning with a badly painted cow being photoshopped into everything from Michelangelo's *The Creation of Adam* to Picasso's *Guernica,* the @TheMERL and a host of imitators have branched out to other paintings, objects, and of course animals.

2. Suggested by Martin Brandt Djupdræt, see https://www.ofbyforall.org/approach
3. Suggested by Elaine Heumann Gurian, Arlington, Virginia.
4. Suggested by Amparo Leyman Pino, Yellow Cow Consulting, San Francisco, California.

MAXIMIZE OPPORTUNITIES FOR CHOICE AND CONTROL

All living things like to be able to control events in their world, but people, due to conscientious awareness, are masters at exercising control over events in their lives.

Having choices and planning one's experiences, and through this planning ensuring control over one's life, is a major aspect of intellectual well-being. This is why giving people the opportunity for exercising agency and control over their experiences is so essential. Starting at the very first moment of a museum experience, and continuing throughout the entirety of the experience, users need to be able to exercise choice and control, and that is true regardless of whether the experience is physical or virtual.

As I have tried to make clear above, much has happened before a person ever actually arrives at a museum or types in the museum's URL. If it is a physical visit, people have to actually get to the museum. Not only do they need a way to get to the museum, whether they use public or private transportation, they will need to be able to determine how best to navigate their way to their destination. If they drive, they will also likely need the skill and luck required to park at or near the site. Getting to the site, though, is not enough. They also will have to be able to figure out how to get to the front door, and once through the front door, how to orient and figure out where to go and what to do next. Since most people who physically visit a museum arrive as part of a group, there is also the logistics of getting multiple people from point A to point B. As Henry David Thoreau long ago quipped, "The man who goes alone can start today; but he who travels with another must wait till that other is ready and it may be a long time before they are ready."[9] These may seem like trivial issues, but they are not. Sometimes these preparatory issues can consume a major portion of a day. These should not just be the user's problem, they need to also be the museum's problem. The museum should be an active partner in helping users plan and execute all facets of their museum experience; even those aspects of the experience that exist outside the museum's "envelope."

When people do arrive, they do not arrive empty-handed or without needs. Although occasionally museums have users who, like some professionals or hobbyists, arrive with but a single goal in mind and sufficient comfort with and knowledge of the setting to know exactly how and where to go to satisfy that goal; most museum users are much more open to whatever they encounter. However, even the most "open" user arrives with prior knowledge and interests, and most importantly, with well-being-related agendas for what they hope to experience. As discussed earlier, these prior interests, knowledge, and expectations have a profound impact on what is actually experienced. Every user looks for things of interest and things that are familiar. Every user seeks to find ways in which their museum experience can help them satisfy their entering visit expectations and motivations.

Nothing is more appreciated than having museum staff recognize and support one's expectations and motivations, since ultimately the user's agenda is the most important agenda. If you know and respect your users' expectations and interests, if you support their agenda, they will support yours!

A number of museums have utilized research on user motivations to specifically design experiences focused on the differing needs and motivations of users. Some notable examples of such institutions include the Art Gallery Ontario, Toronto; Thanksgiving Point Museums, Lehi, Utah; Museum Catherijneconvent, Amesterdam; Minnestrista Cultural Center, Muncie, Indiana; and Red Butte Garden Museum, Salt Lake City, Utah. By way of example, the volunteers and floor staff at the Monterey Bay Aquarium are trained to be on the alert for visitors with differing needs and interest. They do not assume that all visitors want or expect the same experience, so they begin by finding out what interests the user rather than presuming what *should* interest them. Armed with knowledge about what the user is interested in, the volunteers and staff provide suggestions that match these interests and needs, increasing the likelihood that users will accomplish the agenda they hoped to accomplish during their visit.

When developing the exhibit *Whodunit? The Science of Solving Crime*, staff at the Fort Worth Museum of Science and History worked with the education department at Texas Christian University to conduct a front-end evaluation for the exhibit. One question was related to how visitors would like the exhibit framed: Would they like to take on the role of detective and solve a crime? Would they like to learn about historical crimes and how they were solved? Would they like to learn about the various aspects of forensic science (fingerprinting, ballistics, blood spatter analysis, etc.), and learn how these were used to solve crimes? The front-end evaluation helped the museum learn how most visitors wanted to experience the exhibit, particularly through the lens of detective and helping to solve a crime, and then the designers took these ideas and built them in as the organizing theme for the exhibit.[1]

A more traditional way of organizing experiences to meet users' needs is demonstrated by the Préhistomuseum, Liège, Belgium. Already during the planning phase of the visit, users can customize their use experiences to meet the audience-specific needs of families, individuals, or special groups. While families are helped to discover age-appropriate experiences for their children, professionals and hobbyists are given more detailed information and guidance appropriate to their interests and priorities.[2]

1. Suggested by Charlie Walter, Mayborn Museum Complex, Baylor University, Waco, Texas.
2. Suggested by François Mairesse, Sorbonne, Paris, France.

SURPRISE AND DELIGHT

Despite the fact that every user arrives with his or her own unique agenda and expectations, there are some expectations that virtually all users share in common.

All hope that their experience will be "special"; something over and above the norm. They want to be delighted and surprised. Why bother if the experience is going to be dull and just like every other daily experience? Not everything can be surprising or delightful of course, but those that are, for the individual, are likely to be valued and thus memorable.

Museums should endeavor to make each user feel like they got to see, or do, or experience something that few others have. That is what sets museum experiences apart from so many other leisure and educational experiences. You can go to school any day, but it is not every day that you get to go to a museum! You can watch a television show or read a book any old time, but going to a museum and seeing real things in well-crafted contexts is out of the ordinary and special.

The unusual and rare, the novel and the unexpected, the strikingly beautiful and valuable; these are the things museum have to offer that few others do. These are the things that people seek out museums to see, do, and experience. The challenge, though, is how to create these kinds of wonderous experiences not just once but continually.

The City Museum, in Saint Louis, Missouri, is truly a unique museum. It is a private museum run by an artist, and every time one goes it feels like they have expanded or modified it some way. Also, unlike many museums, the City Museum encourages visitors to explore and ramble around without a map—in fact, a small sign at the admissions desk says, "We don't have maps. We want you to get lost!" Taking seriously the idea of surprise—even hoping people get scared, uncomfortable, or even "lost"—makes this museum an unusual and delightful user experience.[1]

In the same vein is the quirky Museum of Jurassic Technology, in Los Angeles, California. One of my favorite examples from this museum is the film loop you start watching only to discover that it is not really a loop at all but seemingly endless with the narrator just going on and on and on. And they give you tea and a cookie for free to sit around and watch the loop or anything else you might be interested in.

One particularly interesting example of surprise and delight was incorporated into the design of the Dinosphere exhibit at the Children's Museum of Indianapolis. Visitors entering this repurposed CineDome theater discover a totally immersive world of dinosaurs, complete with the scent of rain forest and dinosaur dung, changing times of day, and even simulated rainstorms with moisture and thunder and lightning. Also part of this exhibition is the now iconic sculpture of an Alamosaurus that crashes out of the exhibit and emerges on the outside of the museum—visible to all who drive by the museum.

1. Suggested by Paul Orselli, and also Elaine Heumann Gurian, Arlington, Virginia.

The Minneapolis Institute of Art is one of a number of museums that have begun playing with smartphone technologies to afford their visitors interactive and surprising experiences. As visitors explore the various galleries of the art museum, they can use a free cellphone app called *Riddle Mia This* to engage with dozens of puzzles that transform the galleries into a giant escape room. For example, in one particular example, holding up the phone's camera to an abstract painting reveals a hidden message, "What does Ludwig see?" The answer to that riddle lies in another artwork, then another. Who knew?

MAKE THE EXPERIENCE SAFE AND SECURE

As suggested by Abraham Maslow more than a half century ago, in the absence of physical well-being, in particular feelings of safety and security, little else of consequence is going to happen. Museum experiences, both physical and virtual ones, need to be free of threat.

In physical settings, safety obviously begins outside the building where people do not want to feel like they need to look over their shoulder as they walk to and from their vehicles or the nearest Metro or bus stop. But even within the building, people want to feel secure about their surroundings. Most museum users, anxious to avoid losing their way, hope and expect the museum to provide direction and way-finding support. Adults who come with young children expect their children to be safe from dangerous objects and people, and they definitely want to ensure that their children do not get lost. These concerns are often unspoken, and often subconscious, but they are real and not to be ignored.

In today's crazy world, where stress is on the rise, more and more people are looking for leisure experiences that are refreshing and recharging. Museums have increasingly been seen as places that fulfill this role. For example, in the wake of the traumatic events of 9/11, U.S. museums saw a marked uptick in attendance[10] and preliminary evidence suggests that, where possible, museums were used to fulfill a similar need amid the traumas of the COVID-19 pandemic.[11] Although it is always challenging to know what the future will be like, it seems a reasonable guess that things will not be getting markedly calmer and less stressful anytime soon. Being able to spend time in a safe and tranquil space, whether physical or virtual, is likely to be something users value for years to come.

At places like interactive science centers and children's museums, children are constantly on the move and engaged in all manner of hands-on, whole-body activities. The chances for an accident may be one in a million, but many of these institutions regularly see close to a million children each year making the chances of such odds occurring almost a certainty. At the Sciencenter in Ithaca, New York, and At-Bristol in the U.K., staff place user safety at the top of their priorities. Staff continually have conversations about safety and brainstorm ways to manage and reduce risk in an effort to anticipate and as much as humanly possible prevent even those one-in-a-million events from happening.[1]

Health and safety during the COVID pandemic have been high priorities for all museums. Here is just one example of how that effort has been communicated, one that highlights that despite the inconsistencies, and often counterproductive policies of government, quality institutions develop their own policies and procedures designed to engender user trust and above all, safety.

> "Providing a safe, accessible and healthy environment in which our visitors can play and learn is a top priority for the Children's Museum of Phoenix. The following information is intended to answer questions you might have about specific Museum procedures and priorities, and will also provide you with some good general tips.
>
> **PLEASE NOTE:**
> In light of Governor Ducey's lifting of mask mandates and COVID restrictions for the state, we wanted to let everyone know that **the Children's Museum of Phoenix will continue to require masks for visitors 3 years of age and up when visiting the Museum until further notice.** We will also continue our social distancing protocols and capacity limitations. While we respect the Governor's right to lift these restrictions, as a business owner we choose to err on the side of caution and continue our COVID-related safety protocols until we determine that it is safe to revise them. The Museum makes these decisions in counsel with our advisory panel of doctors and medical experts and we will continue to monitor the situation on an ongoing basis. Thank you for your understanding."[2]

Moving museum educational programming online in response to the closures was initially fraught with challenges both technical and social. With the Zoom platform being the most common and easily adopted, the real risk of "Zoombombing" quickly emerged which had the potential to expose unwitting virtual attendees to some serious racist, misogynist, homophobic content and rants.[3] As museums' maturity with the platform evolved, and the platform provider implemented improved security and safety measures, simple protocols

---

1. Krafft, K., and White, H. (2014). Keeping visitors safe around exhibits. *ASTC Dimensions.* https://www.astc.org/astc-dimensions/keeping-visitors-safe-around-exhibits/. Retrieved May 9, 2021.
2. https://childrensmuseumofphoenix.org/plan-your-visit/health-safety-and-accessibility/. Retrieved May 9, 2021.
3. Cold, K. (2020). *Don't be surprised, be an ally: Better security planning for virtual programs.* https://www.aam-us.org/2020/10/09/dont-be-surprised-be-an-ally-better-security-planning-for-virtual-programs. Retrieved May 10, 2021.

were enough to significantly mitigate the issue and protect attendees. Measures including signup, passwords, a registered rather than free account, and virtual waiting rooms significantly reduced the risks, but these still needed to be implemented in coordination with staff policies and procedures. Birmingham Museums, a U.K. collective of nine institutions, has one of the most accomplished set of guidelines and security measures,[4] which not only describe technical measures but also behavior, programming protocols and that espouse the need for explicit online programming training, including what to do in the event of a "bad actor" accessing a program.

4. Birmingham Museums. (2020). *Digital engagement guidelines and online safety policy.* https://www.birminghammuseums.org.uk/schools/virtual-sessions/digital-engagement-guidelines-and-online-safety-policy. Retrieved May 10, 2021. Suggested by Nik Honeysett.

DESIGN FOR SOCIAL INTERACTION

People are social creatures and so are most museum experiences; particularly in-person museum experiences. Well over 90 percent of all museum visitors come as part of a social group,[12] thus ensuring that these experiences are maximally designed to support groups, rather than just individuals, is fundamental to maximizing users' well-being.

A vast array of articles and book chapters have been written on how to design museum experiences in ways that facilitate the social well-being of museum users, including useful summaries in both *The Museum Experience Revisited* and *Learning from Museums*. Because families make up a significant percentage of visitors to most types of museums, a common exhibition design recommendation is to ensure that displays are designed in ways that allows parents to effectively facilitate their children's experiences. For example, create exhibitions and displays at heights that allow them to be seen from both an adult's and a child's level. Make interactive experiences accessible to groups rather than just one person at a time. Ensure that the content and experiences offered are comprehendible by and engaging to both children and adults.

The core idea behind all such recommendations is that what all visitors, whether visiting as part of a family group or an all-adult group, see, do, and remember are primarily those museum experiences that they share with others. Since virtually all museum experiences are in this way socially mediated, making sure that social well-being concerns are woven into the fabric of all aspects of the experience is essential. Take for example museum acoustics. Given the critical role of conversation in museums, and the essential importance in mean-making played by inter-group conversations, it is essential that the museum not be so noisy as to make conversation impossible. No one wants to have to shout at their companions in order to be heard.

As long as they genuinely support the social agendas and needs of visiting groups and individuals, having staff and/or volunteers engage with users is highly desirable. Museum professionals can have a tremendous impact on the quality of the museum experience. When real people are integrated into museum experiences, visitors often can discover things otherwise inaccessible to them. In fact, some of the most memorable museum experiences are those in which people have had an opportunity to engage with others—live artisans, musicians, scientists, and interpreters. And this is not just true for children, but is equally true for adults, including and particularly it seems for seniors.

Although no longer new, or even totally novel, for 27 years, in more than 41 countries throughout Europe, the Americas, Africa, and Asia, the Dialogue in the Dark exhibition remains one of the world's most life-changing social and physical experiences. In absolute darkness, museum visitors are guided by blind guides through a one-of-a-kind exhibition experience. Museum visitors are pushed out of their comfort zone as they need to totally depend upon another person who is the master of this totally dark environment. These strangers become not only guides but mentors for how people can experience and conquer the foreign, threatening, and totally novel world of blindness. Millions of visitors have learned the value of trusting others as they are led through the exhibition by thousands of blind individuals, and by so doing, learn to see in the darkness.[1]

The USS Constitution Museum in Boston realized that as a history museum for families they needed to be more interactive; they needed to create more opportunities for both adults and children to personally and physically engage with the content. They decided to help families actually become part of the exhibition. For example, family members were allowed to climb into the hammocks that sailors would have slept in. Adults could experience just how small the hammocks were, while children could see what it felt like to swing back and forth while trying to sleep. Families were also invited to eat lunch like a typical late-eighteenth/early-nineteenth-century sailor sitting on the ships deck to a meal of hard tack and beans.[2]

The Durham, North Carolina–based Museum of Life + Science is an indoor/outdoor museum located in the southeastern part of the United States. In an effort to ensure that families are able to enjoyably spend time together

1. https://www.dialogue-se.com/what-we-do/dialogue-in-the-dark/. Retrieved May 9, 2021.

2. Suggested by Lynn Dierking.

year-round, the museum created *Into the Mist*, an extensive playscape continuously enveloped in clouds of mist. *Into the Mist* is designed as a space that caters to both children and adults. Children can climb and explore, while adults can sit and chill; all while enjoying the opportunity to keep cool during a hot and humid North Carolina summer afternoon.[3]

3. Suggested by Barry Van Deman.

MAKE THE EXPERIENCE PERSONAL AND COMFORTABLE

It is sad to say, but most museums have virtually no idea who, specifically, is using their experiences on any given day, and even worse, most consistently fail to even bother to try and know. Every person is unique, and people appreciate when their individuality is recognized. One of the legacies of the nineteenth/twentieth centuries' Industrial Age roots of current museum practice is the impersonal, one-size-fits-all nature of most current museum experiences. People everywhere highly value being considered unique and important, and successful museum experiences ensure that every person feels acknowledged and special; that the museum is concerned with their individual well-being; including their personal, intellectual, social, and physical well-being.

Today's museum users expect some basic level of hospitality and service from their museum experience, particularly the increasingly sophisticated and experienced professional class. They come expecting an enjoyable experience. Museum use is not considered an "extreme sport." Museum users are not looking to "rough it," they do not desire to be physically challenged, and they do not want to feel confused or stressed. They want the experience to be intellectually and socially engaging but relaxed. They are not expecting luxury, but they do expect the facilities to be clean and well-maintained. They expect that food is of high-quality and reasonably priced. They also expect there to be a well-stocked gift shop with items unlike those that can readily be found at the local mall or even on the internet.

Today's users also expect staff to be friendly, available, and helpful when needed and by and large absent and inconspicuous when not needed. In the best of circumstances, they want staff to be able to not just meet their needs but rather anticipate and, ideally, even exceed their needs.

In fact, independent of a visitor's specific self/identity-related visit motivations, all people share a need to have all aspects of their well-being at least minimally satisfied during their museum experience. Even "Explorers" and "Professionals/Hobbyists" typically find themselves engaging with other people and thus need to have opportunities for positive social interactions. All have physical requirements—the need to use the restrooms, the need to rest and eat and recharge their caloric batteries. When users are unable to have these basic needs met, they will at a minimum truncate their use, and at worst, will perceive the experience as unpleasant.

Few museums do "customer service" quite like Science North, in Sudbury, Ontario, Canada. Every staff member is hired and trained to ensure that, first and foremost, every user is made to feel accepted and comfortable. The moment you walk into Science North you are welcomed. Everywhere you go, there is a smiling, friendly young person there to greet you and to eagerly assist in your experience. Repeat visitors are recognized and welcomed by name. Even for first-time users, every effort is made to make them feel totally comfortable and at home.

Another approach to making users feel comfortable is the quirky Museum of Jurassic Technology, in Los Angeles, California. Every visitor is offered tea and a cookie for free and encouraged to just sit around, eat, chat, and take as much time as they wish as they wander around the museum.[1]

Located in the center of Amsterdam, ARTIS thinks of itself as a meeting place where people can come closer to nature and debate and learn about how to better appreciate, understand, and treat nature. ARTIS's offerings are vast. They have interior and exterior exhibits, such as a butterfly building (which provides many visitors with a taste of warmth and tropical weather in a northern, cold land), playgrounds, more traditional zoo experiences as well as a central park with playgrounds for multiple ages, cafes with quality food, an aquarium, a small animal house where the animals run free, a petting zoo, and classrooms. In short, there is a little something for everyone, with amenities to accommodate eating, shopping, looking, listening, and conversing—all in a safe and inviting environment.[2]

1. Suggested by Elaine Heumann Gurian, Arlington, Virginia.
2. Suggested by Sarah van Haastert, Gallagher and Associates, Washington, DC.

GIVE USERS A REASON TO DO IT AGAIN

The easy thing is to create an experience that someone will engage with once. More important and harder is creating museum experiences that people can and will want to engage with again and again. Too many current museum experiences reinforce feelings of "been there, done that." Too many current museum experiences, be they physical or virtual, are designed to support interactions with but a single possible correct response, exhibits with a single message, and the presentation of rare and special objects that allow but a single way to engage with them. Is it any surprise that more than half of all museum visitors never return to the same museum twice,[13] feeling like they indeed have seen what there is to see and done what there is to do?

Museum experiences need to be open-ended experiences, experiences that have multiple possible responses, solutions, messages, and possible endings. Museum experiences need to create opportunities for personal growth and development, for every use to engender new beginnings, new ways of seeing and doing. There is no surprise and wonder if it is always the same. At the conclusion of every museum experience, the user should feel like she or he has progressed but not completed his or her journey; he or she should feel satisfied but not fulfilled. Each use should spur the user to want more, to do it again. And again. And again. Individuals who feel like their well-being has been enhanced will naturally gravitate to doing an activity again and again, after all, enhanced well-being is hard to come by. The key is ensuring that users can clearly see how and why they should repeat an activity, that it feels readily accessible, and of course, mentally, physically, emotionally, and financially worth their while.

The FRida und freD children's museum in Graz, Austria is an example of an institution that has deliberately set out to ensure it is always fresh and surprising. Focusing on children ages four to twelve and their families, as well as schools and larger groups, the museum reinvents itself and its experiences every six months, in the process literally becoming a new museum twice a year.[1]

Institutions have found interesting ways to make their museum experiences keep giving day after day. One of these ways is by creating on-going programs with formal education institutions. At the extreme, schools have even been located within the physical museum, such as at the California Science Center, Los Angeles, and the Henry Ford Museum, Dearborn, Michigan. A similar concept is the "my primary school is at the museum" project organized by faculty at Kings College, London. The pilot study involved two primary schools and one nursery school taking up residence at one of three museums across the UK—the National Waterfront Museum in Swansea, Tate Liverpool, and Arbeia Roman Fort, South Shields, England. In all these represent ways traditional boundaries between institutions are being eliminated and museum experiences are being extended by weeks, months, or even years.[2]

---

1. Suggested by Amparo Leyman Pino, Yellow Cow Consulting, San Francisco, California.
2. Suggested by Elaine Heumann Gurian, Arlington, Virginia.

CONNECT THE MUSEUM TO OTHER EXPERIENCES

Museums do not exist in a vacuum. Regardless of their focus—art, history, biodiversity, science, cultural identity, or children—museums are just one institution within an entire ecosystem of institutions focused on that topic or issue. Most museum experiences are short, ephemeral experiences—a couple hours out of a day, a week, a month, a year, or even a lifetime. To be effective, to be of lasting benefit to the individuals who engage in the experience, museum experiences need to be a means to an end, not an end in of themselves. Museum experiences need to be a bridge, meaningfully connecting what happens within the experience to both a person's prior and future well-being-related experiences. People try to link what they are seeing and doing with the experiences they have had in the past. People equally try to link what they have seen and done at the museum to what they are seeing and doing post-experience. Experiences, ideas, and objects that connect with people's past and future experiences are most likely to be perceived as meaningful, and only things that are meaningful are memorable.

Although virtually all users enter a museum experience with expectations and hopes of coming away enriched and with their well-being enhanced, none arrive with the expectation that this is the final stop on their life journey—either personally, intellectually, socially, or physically. All hope the museum experience will be an effective way to facilitate not just their immediate well-being, but ideally their longer term well-being as well, though of course, few, if any, believe that this will be the ultimate solution. In other words, museum experiences are valuable experiences to the extent they facilitate people's on-going journeys, that they build on and support the past and prepare for and propel people into a better, happier, safer, and more successful future.

The Minnesota Historical Society is trying to reach the next generation of museum users through an institution-wide effort to improve service to twenty-first-century learners, particularly digital natives. They are working to better integrate new media, particularly social media, into their exhibitions and programs on site; but equally, if not more importantly, they are working to improve their virtual resources in ways that allow users to take advantage of the rich expertise and resources of the museum. For example, visitors to the museum's website can now research their family history or learn about historical Minnesotans through an index of birth certificates, another one of death certificates, and also through an online people finder.

The Nelson-Atkins Art Museum in Nebraska is one of a number of museums that partners with local agencies and educational institutions to support the needs of the country's newest residents. With art at the foundation, the museum offers a range of programs designed to enhance language skills, develop cultural and social investment, prepare people for the citizenship test, and support new immigrants in helping to build workforce skills and employment. As these new individuals settle into their new homes, they come to see the museum not as a distant, unrelated resource but as one that is central and specific to their lives and needs.

Originally created by Heureka in Finland but adapted to the realities of Australia, the Museum of Discovery (MOD) engages users both physically and virtually with an experience called "Seven Siblings from the Future." This interactive experience tells the story of how seven different individuals (siblings) in the year 2050 respond to the inheritance of a plot of land from their grandmother. Through the eyes of each of these fictional siblings, users discover the conflicting realities and trade-offs inherent in land use decision making today and likely in the future. In fact, the real genius of the experience is that it provides a vehicle for users to directly connect these issues to their own lives and in the process discover a lot about themselves and their own views and biases.[1]

One of the more exceptional examples of how museum experiences can be directly connected to users' lives, initially presented in chapter 6, is the effort by the open-air history museum Dem Gamble By, Aarhus, Denmark, to create an environment where elderly Alzheimer patients can relive the sights, sounds, and even smells of their past. By immersion within this re-created environment, these individuals are not only able to reconnect with their past but also build bridges to their present-day families and current care-givers.[2]

1. Suggested by Paul Martin, Arizona State University, Tucson, Arizona.
2. Suggested by Martin Brandt Djupdræt, Den Gamle By, Aarhus, Denmark.

KEEP ON GIVING

As described throughout this book, one of the things that has historically distinguished museum experiences is how frequently they result in long-lasting memories and enhanced well-being. Even when little or no follow-up occurs, people tend to positively recall their museum experiences. When queried, most museum users readily and without hesitation connect what they did during a museum experience with other events and experiences they have had, often connecting experiences that happened weeks or even months and years apart. In other words, the fact that these events were temporally and spatially removed from the actual museum use only reinforces that most people, unlike most museum professionals, do not conceptualize these events primarily through a "museum experience" lens but rather through a "life experience" lens. However, just because museum experiences are often perceived as meaningful and yield positive, long-term impacts (and memories), does not mean that they could not be even better if museums purposefully and systematically attempted to extend experiences beyond traditional physical and temporal boundaries. Historically, though, few museums have actually committed to such efforts.

Considerable research now supports how important it is to support post-use experiences.[14] These subsequent, related experiences serve to reinforce and build on and cement prior experiences and can be particularly helpful in ensuring that more experiences become more memorable more often. After all, even the most memorable experiences tend to fade with time if they are not continuously recalled and refreshed through associations with new experiences.[15] In the absence of purposeful follow-up and reinforcement by the museum, many of the details of most people's museum experiences tend to fall away with time, leaving only a broad-brush recollection of the most salient things the person saw or did.[16] This may be okay, but it is far from ideal. To ensure that users continue to think positively and specifically about their museum experiences long after the initial experience, there is no substitute for follow-up, and then additional follow-up, and then even more follow-up. Follow-up is the ticket for building both fidelity and loyalty, particularly if the follow-up is targeted to support and extend the user's original interests, experiences, and user motivations.

Founded in 2015, the Museum of Homelessness (MoH) is a community-driven social justice museum created and run by people with direct experience of homelessness. It tackles the problems of homelessness and housing inequality by amplifying the voices of its community through research, events, workshops, campaigns, and exhibitions. MoH also provides opportunities for users to continue to directly support the homeless community after a visit through bursaries, mentoring, training, and opportunities for users to directly work with and support the homeless community.[1]

A number of institutions have found ways to extend the museum experience in both time and space by collaborating with, and even co-locating, other types of organizations within themselves, for example public libraries. By co-locating a library adjacent to or within the museum, institutions like the Children's Museum, Indianapolis, Indiana, and Sun Prairie, Wisconsin library and museum are helping to obliterate traditional boundaries between museum experiences and other comparable experiences and in the process extending the museum experience by weeks, months, or even years.[2]

With support from researchers at the University of Queensland; the Taronga Zoo, Sydney, Australia; Territory Wildlife Park, Darwin, Australia; Wellington Zoo, New Zealand; and the Bronx Zoo, New York, they developed a series of web-based "action resources" designed to reinforce, complement, and extend each zoos' on-site conservation messages and support visitors' translation of

1. Suggested by Elaine Heumann Gurian, Arlington, Virginia.
2. Suggested by Elaine Heumann Gurian, Arlington, Virginia.

environmental behavioral intentions into actions after a visit. Although challenging, these web resources did indeed support on-going conservation-related activities and behaviors on the part of museum users.[3]

3. Ballantyne, R., Packer, J., Hughes, K., and Gill, C. (2018). "Post-visit Reinforcement of Zoo Conservation Messages: The Design and Testing of an Action Resource Website. *Visitor Studies* 21 (1), 98–120. See also, Hughes, K. (2011). "Designing Post-Visit Action Resources for Families Visiting Wildlife Tourism Sites." *Visitor Studies* 14(1), 66–83.

SUPPORT SHARING

People like to share their experiences with others, particularly experiences that are positive and well-being enhancing. Museums should go out of their way to make it easy for past users to share their positive museum experiences with others.

When friends and family share their positive museum experiences with someone, that sharing will motivate that person to want to use the museum themselves; often in the near future.

For the vast majority of people, their awareness of the existence and potential value of a particular museum experience arrives via this kind of word-of-mouth endorsement.[17] Even a generation ago, word-of-mouth was the most important mechanism by which individuals formed opinions about their world.[18] With the advent of the internet and social media, that reality has only increased. Recent research has shown that 90 percent of Americans consider "recommendations from friends" to be the most worthwhile form of promotion.[19] In fact, not only do nine out of ten U.S. adults regularly or occasionally *seek* advice about products or services in this way, even more, 95 percent, regularly or occasionally *give* advice about products or services to others through word-of-mouth, increasingly online.[20] Museums need to make it easy for users to create and disseminate word-of-mouth recommendations.[21] The social, unsolicited nature of most word-of-mouth information gives it credibility, social validity, and authenticity, presumably because it comes from individuals with first-hand experience but no vested interest in what they are recommending. Thus, the more museums can encourage and make it easy for people to tell their friends and relatives about their museum experiences, the greater will be the number of people who decide to engage themselves in museum experiences.[22]

However, the fact that word-of-mouth recommendations from family and friends represents the single and overwhelmingly dominant way that people today learn about and decide to use museums also creates a problem for museums. These types of word-of-mouth recommendations tend to be quite insular—person A communicates with their friends and family who in turn communicate back to their friends and family. However, if someone is outside this loop, if they and their friends and family never utilize museums, then they will never be touched by this type of word-of-mouth communication. To broaden one's audience beyond the "usual suspects" requires proactively building community, proactively supporting word-of-mouth sharing outside of one's normal circle of friends and family. Unless that happens, new audiences will never be enticed to give museums a try. Museums need to make it possible for all in the community to see how museum experiences could meet their needs and then be supported in sharing those discoveries with their networks of friends and family. Obviously this is easier said than done; but it is not only possible, it is essential as it is the only way museum experiences will ever come to be something all community members find accessible and desirable.

It has become common practice for museums to encourage their users to post comments, pictures, and endorsements of social media. However, efforts by institutions to build special interest constituencies are notable. For example, the Children's Discovery Museum of San Jose, California, has a special membership program for grandparents, which includes free admission for two adults and all their grandchildren. This is a great way for grandparents to both meet their needs and support their wallets. And evidence is that grandparents eagerly share and promote this opportunity with other grandparents in their networks.[1]

Another similar example, but for an entirely different constituency, is exemplified by Explora, Albuquerque, New Mexico, which has built a strong partnership with the New Mexico Autism Society. Collaboratively, these two partners have created a series of special programs and opportunities for this special needs community, including dedicated hours when families with children on the autism spectrum can visit and use the museum. Participants are encouraged to not only take advantage of the offerings but to share their experiences with others in special needs community to build awareness and extend opportunities.[2]

Another, simple example of allowing users to share their experiences, this time with each other and museum staff, was created by Daniel Spock, at the time director of the Minnesota Historical Society's History Center (MHC). Visitors to the MHC wear buttons in the galleries to show that they have paid admission. In the past, on their way out, visitors would throw away their buttons, and often these discarded buttons would end up as litter both inside and outside the museum. Spock's team designed a simple voting mechanism so that instead of

1. Suggested by Amparo Leyman Pino, Yellow Cow Consulting, San Francisco, California.

2. Suggested by Amparo Leyman Pino, Yellow Cow Consulting, San Francisco, California.

littering, visitors could toss their buttons into one of several bins to "vote" for whichever exhibit was their favorite that day. This simple participatory activity invited people to share their opinions and give staff feedback instead of trash.[3]

In 2020, Heureka, located in Vantaa outside of Helsinki, joined the Finnish Museum Card system. This card system has been a tremendous success for museums throughout the country, increasing the number of museum visits in Finland by more than 50 percent over the five years of its existence. Over two hundred thousand of these cards were sold in 2019 at a cost/card of about 69 € in 2019 (about $80 U.S.). Cardholders get free access to 327 Finish museums. Survey research conducted by Heureka revealed that in 2018, when they were not part of the museum card system, only about 2 percent of their visitors had a museum card. Within months of joining the system, nearly a quarter of their visitors were cardholders. More importantly, being part of the museum card system has created a mechanism for Heureka, and other museums throughout Finland, to directly communicate with a large percentage of the nation's adults, including individuals who never physical or virtually visit. This communication channel proved particularly valuable during the recent COVID-19 pandemic when the card system was used as a vehicle for helping to disseminate messages and updates related to public health, and in so doing helped to reinforce for the public the value of museums.[4]

3. Simon, N. (2012). "Principles of Participation." In G. Anderson (ed.), *Reinventing the Museum: The Evolving Conversation on the Paradigm Shift*, second edition, 334–55. Lanham, MD: AltaMira Press.

4. Suggested by Mikko Myllykoski, Heureka, Vantaa, Finland.

CONCLUSION

I clearly believe that museums have value and that they can have a bright future. A positive future, though, is not guaranteed and will not happen without significant effort. The key I believe lies in the museum's unique capacity to enhance societal well-being.

I want to end this chapter and this book by calling out the ancient African proverb that I used as the epigram for this chapter. That proverb states: "When the roots are deep, there is no reason to fear the wind." The roots are your users. Ultimately, the true value of museums lies in how and why they are used, and by whom. Users of museums are what create valuable experiences; exhibitions, objects, programs, films, and presentations merely provide the opportunity and the context for value creation. At the end of the day, value is in relationships.

In everything museums do, including particularly the experiences they create, museums should celebrate the triumphs and successes of their users (and not the triumphs and successes of the institution). Thoughtful museum professionals understand this. Quality museum experiences do this throughout the experience, rewarding discovery, reinforcing ah-ha moments, and highlighting and supporting those special, emotionally laden moments when the user has achieved something special for him- or herself. But museums can and should do more.

The message of this book has been that everything people do, ultimately, is done in order to support and enhance their personal, intellectual, social, and physical well-being. It is simply human to seek things like comfort and safety, recognition, intellectual growth, and self-affirmation. Just as we look to our friends and family to be consistent and supportive, to appreciate and respect us, so too do we want the organizations we use to be consistent and safe, appreciative and respectful.

If museums can create experiences that consistently and genuinely support both individual and societal well-being. If they can design experiences that provide each and every user with the personal, intellectual, social, and physical supportive they so desperately desire. If museums can ensure that they are places where people and communities can come together with respect; places that celebrate each and every user. Then museums need not fear for their future.

NOTES

1. Service Management Group. (2018). *Five Things We Learned from Talking to More Than 1 Billion People.* https://www.smg.com/resources/detail/five-things-we-learned-from-talking-to-1-billion-people. Retrieved April 12, 2021.

2. For further details, see Falk, J. H. and Dierking, L. D. (2014). *The Museum Experience Revisited.* Walnut Creek, CA: Left Coast Press.

3. See, Falk, J. H. (2009). *Identity and Museum Visitor Experience.* Walnut Creek, CA: Left Coast Books.

4. Sernovit, A. (2007). "The Rising Importance of Word of Mouth." Damn, I Wish I'd Thought of That!, June 29, 2007. http://www.damniwish.com/2007/06/the-rising-impo .html. Retrieved December 27, 2011.

5. Wenger, E. 1998. *Communities of Practice: Learning, Meaning and Identity.* Cambridge: Cambridge University Press.

6. Falk, J. H., and Dierking, L. D. (2019). *Learning from Museums,* 2nd ed. Lanham, MD: Rowman & Littlefield.

7. Wambold, S., and Spellerberg, M. (2018). "Identity-Related Motivations Online: Falk's Framework Applied to US Museum Websites." *Journal of Digital & Social Media Marketing* 5(4), 353–69.

8. Black, G. (2018). "Meeting the Audience Challenge in the 'Age of Participation.'" *Museum Management and Curatorship* 33(4), 302.

9. Thoreau, H. D. (1854, 1948). *Walden: Or, Life in the Woods.* New York: Rinehart.

10. Gardner, J., and Henry, S. (2002). September 11 and the Mourning After: Reflections on Collecting and Interpreting the History of Tragedy. *The Public Historian,* 24(3), 37–52.

11. Ross Nelson, K. and Ashton, S. (in prep.). Normalcy as Respite? American Association of Museums. (pre-print).

Szanto, A. (2020)/ People need art in times of crisis. That's why museums should be amongt the first institutions to reopen for business – here's how. ArtNetNews. https://news-artnet-com.cdn.ampproject.org/c/s/news.artnet.com/opinion/andras-szanto-op-ed-reopening-museums-1832439/amp-page?fbclid=IwAR0G74_QiPefV2c311FSUS9JywuSryV3it6ZHO2L_96DmEmUU58jNJ1pcXs Retrieved December 21, 2020.

12. Falk, J. H. and Dierking, L. D. (2019). *Learning from Museums,* 2nd ed.. Lanham, MD: Rowman & Littlefield.

13. Falk, J. H. and Dierking, L. D. (2014). *The Museum Experience Revisited.* Walnut Creek, CA: Left Coast Press.

14. For example, Ballantyne, R., Packer, J., Hughes, K., and Gill, C. (2018). "Post-Visit Reinforcement of Zoo Conservation Messages: The Design and Testing of an Action Resource Website." *Visitor Studies* 21 (1), 98–120. See also, Hughes, K. (2011). "Designing Post-Visit Action Resources for Families Visiting Wildlife Tourism Sites." *Visitor Studies* 14 (1), 66–83. And, DeWitt, J., and Storksdieck, M. (2008). "A Short Review of School Field Trips: Key Findings from the Past and Implications for the Future." *Visitor Studies* 11(2), 181–97.

15. See Cooper, R. A., Kensinger, E., and Ritchey, M. (2019). "Memories Fade: The Relationship between Memory Vividness and Remembered Visual Salience." *Psychological Science.* DOI: 10.1177/0956797619836093.

16. Falk, J. H., and Dierking, L. D. (1996). "Recollections of Elementary School Field Trips." In D. Herrmann and M. Johnson (eds.), *The Third Practical Aspects of Memory Conference,* 512–26. University of Maryland: College Park. See also, Falk, J. H., Scott, C., Dierking, L. D., Rennie, L.J., and Cohen Jones, M. (2004). "Interactives and Visitor Learning." *Curator* 47(2), 171–98.

17. For further details, see Falk, J. H., and Dierking, L. D. (2014). *The Museum Experience Revisited.* Walnut Creek, CA: Left Coast Press.

18. Roper, G. (1988). "Roper poll." *Social Science Monitor* 10(4), 2.

19. Sernovit, A. (2007). "The Rising Importance of Word of Mouth." Damn, I Wish I'd Thought of That!, June 29, 2007. http://www.damniwish.com/2007/06/the-rising-impo.html. Retrieved December 27, 2011.

20. Sernovit, A. (2007). "The Rising Importance of Word of Mouth." Damn, I Wish I'd Thought of That!, June 29, 2007.http://www.damniwish.com/2007/06/the-rising-impo.html. Retrieved December 27, 2011.

21. Sernovit, A. (2007). "The Rising Importance of Word of Mouth." Damn, I Wish I'd Thought of That!, June 29, 2007. http://www.damniwish.com/2007/06/the-rising-impo.html. Retrieved December 27, 2011.

22. Hausmann, A. (2012). "The Importance of Word of Mouth for Museums: An Analytical Framework." *International Journal of Arts Management* 14(3), 32–43. See also, Huang, F.-C. (2020). "The Influence of Electronic Word of Mouth on Museum Cultural Products." *The Journal of Human Resource and Adult Learning* 16(1), 26–31.

References

NA. (2013). "Show Me the Value—A Discussion about Public Value and the Arts." Panel discussion sponsored by QPAC, Queensland, Australia. November 7, 2013. https://www.youtube.com/watch?v=_4Aw0pCDmHg. Retrieved February 13, 2021.

NA. (2020). "Autism in Museums: Welcoming Families and Young People." *Kids in Museums*. Beckenham: UK. https://kidsinmuseums.org.uk/resources/how-can-your-museum-better-welcome-families-and-young-people-with-autism/. Retrieved August 9, 2020.

NA. (2021). "Memory without a Brain: How a Single Cell Slime Mold Makes Smart Decisions." SciTechNews. February 26, 2021. https://scitechdaily.com/memory-without-a-brain-how-a-single-cell-slime-mold-makes-smart-decisions/. Retrieved February 27, 2021.

Abu-Schumays, M., and Leinhardt, G. (2000). "Two Docents in Three Museums: A Study of Central and Peripheral Participation." *Museum Learning Collaborative Technical Report #MLC-02*, p. 6. http://www.lrdc.pitt.edu/mlc/documents/mlc-02.pdf. Retrieved July 26, 2020.

Adami, C., Ofria, C., and Collier, T. C. (2000). "Evolution of Biological Complexity." *Proceedings of the National Academy of Sciences* (USA), 97, 4463–68).

American Alliance of Museums. (2020). "Museum Facts." https://www.aam-us.org/wp-content/uploads/2019/02/Museums-Facts-Infographic.pdf?utm_source=American+Alliance+of+Museums&utm_campaign=f0787b9159–MAD_2020_Advocate_Anywhere_Non Members&utm_medium=email&utm_term=0_f06e575db6–f0787b9159–37291589. Retrieved February 25, 2020

American Alliance of Museums. (2020). "United States May Lose One-Third of All Museums, New Survey Shows." July 22, 2020. https://www.aam-us.org/2020/07/22/united-states-may-lose-one-third-of-all-museums-new-survey-shows/. Retrieved October 23, 2020.

Anderson, D. and Shuichi, Y. (2020). "My Identity in the Garden—Self Reflections of Expatriates' Garden Visits." *Journal of Museum Education*, 45(2), 176–86.

Anderson, D., Storksdieck, M., and Spock, M. (2007). "Understanding the Long-Term Impacts of Museum Experiences." In J. H. Falk, L. Dierking, and S. Foutz (eds.), *In Principle, In Practice: Museums as Learning Institutions*, 197–215. Lanham, MD: AltaMira Press.

Anderson, M., and Magruder, J. (2017). "Split-Sample Strategies for Avoiding False Discoveries." Working Paper. U.C. Berkeley. June 30, 2017. https://are.berkeley.edu/~jmagruder/split-sample.pdf. Retrieved February 26, 2021.

Anderson, R. W. (1995). "Learning and Evolution: A Quantitative Genetics Approach." *Journal of Theoretical Biology* 175, 89–101.

ArtsCouncil UK. (ND). *Generic Learning Outcomes*. https://www.artscouncil.org.uk/measuring-outcomes/generic-learning-outcomes. Retrieved February 25, 2020.

Ashton, S., Johnson, E., Nelson, K. R., Ortiz, J., and Wicai, D. (2019). "Brace for Impact: Utah Is Conducting a Pilot Study to Show the Social Impact of the State's Museums." *MUSEUM*, May-June 2019, 26–31.

Ashton, S., Johnson, E., Nelson, K. R., Ortiz, J., and Wicai, D. (in prep.). "Social Impact at Thanksgiving Point." *Curator*.

Ashworth, J., and Johnson, P. (1996). "Sources of 'Value for Money' for Museum Visitors: Some Survey Evidence." *Journal of Cultural Economics* 20, 67–83.

Association of Science-Technology Centers. (2018). "Science Center Statistics—2017." https://www.astc.org/wp-content/uploads/2018/11/ASTC_ScienceCenterStatistics-2017.pdf. Retrieved February 25, 2020.

Australian Expert Group on Industry Studies (AEGIS). (2004). *Social Impacts of Participating in the Arts and Cultural Activities: Report on Stage Two—Evidence, Issues and Recommendations*. Sydney, AU: University of Western Sydney. https://www.stategrowth.tas.gov.au/__data/assets/pdf_file/0003/160833/Social_Impacts_of_the_Arts.pdf. Retrieved February 25, 2020.

Bachman, J. (2011). *STEM Learning Activity among Home-Educating Families*. Unpublished doctoral thesis. Corvallis: Oregon State University.

Bamberger, Y. (2008). "An Experience for the Lifelong Journey: The Long-Term Effect of a Class Visit to a Science Center." *Visitor Studies*, 11(2), 198–212.

Bamberger, Y., and Tali, T. (2007). "Learning in a Personal Context: Levels of Choice in a Free Choice Learning Environment in Science and Natural History Museums." *Science Education*, 91(1), 75–95.

Bandura, A. (1977). "Self-Efficacy: Toward a Unifying Theory of Behavioral Change." *Psychological Review* 84(2), 191–215.

Barber, N. (2012). "Why Atheism Will Replace Religion: The Triumph of Earthly Pleasures over Pie in the Sky." E-book, available at http://www.amazon.com/Atheism-Will-Replace-Religion-ebook/dp/B00886ZSJ6/.

Barber, N. (2012). "Why Did Religion Evolve?" *Psychology Today*. June 13, 2012. https://www.psychologytoday.com/blog/the-human-beast/201206/why-did-religion-evolve. Retrieved January 15, 2017.

Barrero, J. M., Bloom, N., and Davis, S. J. (2020). "COVID-19 Is Also a Reallocation Shock." University of Chicago, *Becker Friedman Institute for Economics Working Paper No. 2020–2059*. May 5, 2020. https://ssrn.com/abstract=3592953. Retrieved June 1, 2020.

Barrett, L. F. (2017). *How Emotions Are Made: The Secret Life of the Brain*. New York: Houghton Mifflin Harcourt.

Battaglia, A. (2020). "Museums in Crisis, Art Spaces Lobby New York State, and More: Morning Links from October 13, 2020." ARTnews. October 13, 2020. https://www.artnews.com/art-news/news/museums-in-crisis-morning-links-1234573525/. Retrieved November 3, 2020.

Baumeister, R., and Leary, M. (1995). "The Need to Belong: Desire for Interpersonal Attachment as a Fundamental Human Motivation." *Psychological Bulletin*, 117, 497–529.

Belcher, M. (1991). *Exhibitions in Museums*. Washington, DC: Smithsonian Institution Press.

Beliveau, J. (2015). *Audio Elements: Understanding Current Uses of Sound in Museum Exhibits*. Unpublished master's thesis. University of Washington, Seattle, Washington.

Belk, R. W. (1988). "Possessions and the Extended Self." *Journal of Consumer Research* 15, 139–69.

Benjamin, D. J., Heffetz, O., Kimball, M., and Szembrot, S. (2014). "Beyond Happiness and Satisfaction: Toward Well-Being Indices Based on Stated Preference." *American Economic Review* 104(9): 2698–735.

Berger, K., Penna, R. M., and Goldberg, S. H. (2010). "The Battle for the Soul of the Nonprofit Sector." *Philadelphia Social Innovations Journal*. http://www.philasocialinnovations.org/site/. Retrieved February 18, 2020.

Berger, M. (2020). "COVID-19, 'Not Necessarily the Big One,' WHO Warns." *Washington Post*. December 29, 2020. https://www.washingtonpost.com/world/2020/12/29/coronavirus-2020-the-big-one-who-pandemics/. Retrieved December 29, 2020.

Birmingham Museums. (2020). *Digital Engagement Guidelines and Online Safety Policy*. https://www.birminghammuseums.org.uk/schools/virtual-sessions/digital-engagement-guidelines-and-online-safety-policy. Retrieved May 10, 2021.

Black, G. (2018). "Meeting the Audience Challenge in the 'Age of Participation.'" *Museum Management and Curatorship* 33(4), 302–19.

Bollo, H., Bothe, B., Toth-Kiraly, I., and Orosz, G. (2018). "Pride and Social Status." *Frontiers of Psychology*. October 25, 2018. https://doi.org/10.3389/fpsyg.2018.01979.

Bonnellan, M. B., Trzesniewski, K. H., Robins, R. W., Moffitt, T. E., and Caspi, A. (2005). "Low Self-Esteem Is Related to Aggression, Antisocial Behavior, and Delinquency." *Psychological Sciences* 16(4), 328–35.

Bonnette, R. N., Crowley, K., and Schunn, C. D. (2019). "Falling in Love and Staying in Love with Science: Ongoing Informal Science Experiences Support Fascination for All Children." *International Journal of Science Education* 41(12), 1626–43. DOI: 10.1080/09500693.2019.1623431.

Bounia, A., Nikiforidou, A., Nikonanou, N., and Matossian, A. (2012). "Voices from the Museum: Survey Research in Europe's National Museums." EuNaMus Report No. 5. Linköping: Sweden, Linköping University Electronic Press.

Boutin, C. (2006). "Snap Judgments Decide a Face's Character, Psychologist Finds." *Princeton University Education News*. August 22, 2006. https://www.princeton.edu/news/2006/08/22/snap-judgments-decide-faces-character-psychologist-finds. Retrieved September 27, 2020.

Bradberry, T. (2016). "Why You Should Spend Your Money on Experiences, Not Things." *Forbes*. August 9, 2016. https://www.forbes.com/sites/travisbradberry/2016/08/09/why-you-should-spend-your-money-on-experiences-not-things/#70ab29366520. Retrieved June 21, 2020.

Bradley, R. D., Bradley, L. C., Garner, H., and Baker, R. (2014). "Assessing the Value of Natural History Collections and Addressing Issues Regarding Long-Term Growth and Care." *BioScience* 64(12), 1150–58.

Brooks, D. (2020). "America Is Having a Moral Convulsion." *The Atlantic*. October 5, 2020. https://www.theatlantic.com/ideas/archive/2020/10/collapsing-levels-trust-are-devastating-america/616581/. December 29, 2020.

Brown, R. L. (2013). "Learning, Evolvability and Exploratory Behavior: Extending the Evolutionary Reach of Learning." *Biological Philosophy* 28, 933–55.

Brown, S., and Gao, X. (2011). "The Neuroscience of Beauty." *Scientific American*. September 27, 2011. https://www.scientificamerican.com/article/the-neuroscience-of-beauty/. Retrieved June 21, 2020.

Bunch, L. (2020). "Racism, Unrest, and the Role of the Museum Field," (special session). *American Alliance of Museums Virtual Annual Meeting and MuseumExpo*. https://www.aamus.org/2020/06/09/racism-unrest-and-the-role-of-the-museum-field/. Retrieved June 6, 2021.

Bureau of Labor Statistics. (2020). *American Time Use Survey Summary, 2019*. Washington, DC: United States Department of Labor. June 25, 2020. https://www.bls.gov/news.release/pdf/atus.pdf. Retrieved August 9, 2020.

Buss, D. (2016). *Evolutionary Biology: The New Science of the Mind*, fifth edition. London: Routledge.

Butler, H. (2020). "Why Do Smart People Do Foolish Things?" *Scientific American*. October 3, 2017. https://www.scientificamerican.com/article/why-do-smart-people-do-foolish-things/. Retrieved October 31, 2020.

California Association of Museums. (ND). *Foresight Research Report: Museums as Third Places*. https://art.ucsc.edu/sites/default/files/CAMLF_Third_Place_Baseline_Final.pdf. Retrieved August 16, 2020.

Cameron, K. S. (2012). *Positive Leadership: Strategies for Extraordinary Performance*. San Francisco: Beret-Koehler Publishers.

Carlsson, R. (2020). Community engagement with Fun Palaces. MuseumNext. https://www.museumnext.com/article/community-engagement-with-fun-palaces/ Retrieved May 13, 2021.

Carmen, J. (2010). *Heritage Value: Combining Culture and Economics*. London: Arts and Humanities Council.

Carnwath, J. D., and Brown, A. S. (2014). *Understanding the Value and Impacts of Cultural Experiences—A Literature Review.* London: Art Council England. https://www.artscouncil.org.uk/sites/default/files/downloadfile/Understanding_the_Value_and_Impacts.

Carson, R. T. (2001). "Resources and Environment: Contingent Valuation." *International Encyclopedia of the Social and Behavioral Sciences*, 13272–75. https://www.sciencedirect.com/science/article/pii/B0080430767041966?via%3Dihub. Retrieved October 4, 2020.

CASE: The Culture and Sport Evidence Programme. (2010). *Understanding the Impact of Engagement in Culture and Sport: A Systematic Review of the Learning Impacts for Young People*.

Casey, N. (2013). "Art Made Edible at Magritte-Inspired Dinner Series at MoMA." Food: Gothamist.com. November 5, 2013. https://gothamist.com/food/art-made-edible-at-magritte-inspired-dinner-series-at-moma. Retrieved March 12, 2021.

Centre for Educational Research and Innovation (CERI). (2001). *The Well-Being of Nations: The Role of Social and Human Capital*. Paris: Organization for Economic Co-operation and Development.

Chamovitz, D (2012). *What a Plant Knows*. New York: Scientific American/Farrar Straus and Giroux.

Champ, P. A., Boyle, K. J., and Brown, T. C. (2003). *A Primer on Nonmarket Valuation.* Norwell, MA: Kluwer.

Champkins, M. (2013). "Generating Ideas: Drawing Inspiration from the Science Museum." London: Science Museum. July 22, 2013. https://blog.sciencemuseum.org.uk/generating-ideas-drawing-inspiration-from-the-science-museum/. Retrieved November 8, 2020.

Chatterjee, H. and Noble, G. (2016). *Museums, Health and Well-Being*. London: Routledge.

Chen, C.-L., and Tsai, C.-G. (2015). "The Influence of Background Music on the Visitor Museum Experience: A Case Study of the Laiho Memorial Museum, Taiwan." *Visitor Studies* 18(2), 183–95.

Cheng, J. T., Tracy, J. L., and Henrich, J. (2010). "Pride, Personality, and the Evolutionary Foundations of Human Social Status." *Evolution and Human Behavior* 31(5), 334–47.

Choi, A., Ritchie, B., Papandrea, F., and Bennett, J. (2010). "Economic Valuation of Cultural Heritage Sites: A Choice Modeling Approach." *Tourism Management* 31(2), 213–20.

Christakis, N. A. (2020). *Apollo's Arrow: The Profound and Enduring Impact of Coronavirus on the Way We Live*. New York: Little, Brown, Spark.

Clark, K. (Ed.). (2006). "Capturing the Public Value of Heritage: *The Proceedings of the London Conference 25–26 January 2006*." London: English Heritage.

Clawson, M., and Knetsch, J. (1966). *Economics of Outdoor Recreation*. Baltimore, MD: John Hopkins University Press.

Cloninger, C. R. (2004). *Feeling Good: The Science of Well-Being*. Oxford: Oxford University Press.

Cold, K. (2020). *Don't Be Surprised, Be an Ally: Better Security Planning for Virtual Programs*. https://www.aam-us.org/2020/10/09/dont-be-surprised-be-an-ally-better-security-planning-for-virtual-programs. Retrieved May 10, 2021.

Collins, J., and Lazier, B. (2020). *BE 2.0 (Beyond Entrepreneurship 2.0)*. New York: Penguin Portfolio.

Collins, J., and Porras, J. (1994). *Built to Last: Successful Habits of Visionary Companies*. New York: HaperBusiness.

Coren, S. (2004). *How Dogs Think*. New York: Atria.

Cronin, M. (2015). "What Are Museums' Economic Impact." *Citizen Times*. May 22, 2015. https://www.citizen-times.com/story/money/business/2015/05/22/evolving-art-calculating-museums-economic-impact/27774457/. Retrieved February 18, 2020.

Crossick, G. & Kaszynska, P. (2016). *Understanding the Value of Arts & Culture. The AHRC Cultural Value Project*. Arts and Humanities Research Council. https://ahrc.ukri.org/documents/publications/cultural-value-project-final-report/.

Crystal Bridges. (2013). "Crystal Bridges Museum of American Art and University of Arkansas Department of Education Reform Announce Results of a Study on Culturally Enriching School Field Trips." September 16, 2013. https://crystalbridges.org/blog/crystal-bridges-museum-of-american-art-university-of-arkansas-department-of-education-reform-announce-results-of-a-study-on-culturally-enriching-school-field-trips/. Retrieved March 19, 2020.

Csapó, B., and Funke, J. (2017). *The Nature of Problem Solving: Using Research to Inspire 21st Century Learning*. Paris: The Organization for Economic Co-operation and Development (OECD).

Csikszentmihalyi, M. (1990). *Flow: The Psychology of Optimal Experience*. New York: Harper Perennial.

Culture24. (2018). "Three-Part Study on the Role and Impact of Museum Lates: *A Culture of Lates; An International Culture of Lates; Late Like a Local*." London: Culture24.

February 2, 2018. http://museumsatnight.org.uk/festival-resources/news/our-research-reports-on-museum-lates-are-here/#.Wp5_eufLjIU. Retrieved November 20, 2020.

Dafoe, T. (2020). "Attendance Has Always Been a Narrow Way to Define Success: That's Why This Museum Is Using Data Science to Measure Its Social Impact." artnet news. February 19, 2020. https://news.artnet.com/art-world/oakland-museum-social-impact-1780698#.XlEnYoZUia0.twitter. Retrieved February 23, 2020.

Daley, B. (2014). "Indigenous Australians Offer a Broader Concept of Wellbeing." *The Conversation*. November 19, 2014. https://theconversation.com/indigenous-australians-offer-a-broader-concept-of-wellbeing-32887. Retrieved July 31, 2020.

Damasio, A. (2011). *Neural Basis of Emotions*. Scholarpedia 6(3), 1804. http://www.scholarpedia.org/article/Neural_basis_of_emotions. Retrieved December 8, 2016.

Darwin, C. (1859). *On the Origin of the Species by Means of Natural Selection*. London: John Murray.

Davies, S. (2008). "Intellectual and Political Landscape: The Instrumentalism Debate." *Cultural Trends* 17(4), 259–65.

Davis, T. (2019). "What Is Well-Being? Definition, Types, and Well-Being Skills." *Psychology Today*. January 2, 2019. https://www.psychologytoday.com/us/blog/click-here-happiness/201901/what-is-well-being-definition-types-and-well-being-skills. Retrieved June 21, 2020.

Deary, I.J. (2013). "Intelligence." *Current Biolog*, 23(16), R673–676.

del Bosque, I. R., and Martin, H. S. (2008). "Tourist Satisfaction: A Cognitive-Affective Model." *Annals of Tourism Research* 35 (2), 551–73.

Deniz, D. (2016). "Improving Perceived Well-Being through Improved Safety." *Procedia – Social and Behavioral Sciences* 2(6), 632–42.

Department of Culture, Arts and Leisure. (2010). *Experience of Museums in Northern Ireland: Findings from the Continuous Household Survey 2008/09*. Technical Report. March 11, 2013. https://data.gov.uk/dataset/2e47d924-19a2-417a-ae1a-7e76f7113eeb/experience-of-museums-in-northern-ireland-findings-from-the-continuous-household-survey-2008–09–dcal-research-findings. Retrieved February 25, 2020.

Dergisi, E. (2017). "Play and Flow: Children's Culture and Adult's Role." *Journal of Early Childhood Studies* 1(2), 247–61.

Desjardins, R. (2004). *Learning for Well-Being*. Stockholm: Stockholm University Institute for International Education.

Deval, H., Mantel, S., Kardes, F., and Posavac, S. (2013). "How Naive Theories Drive Opposing Inferences from the Same Information." *Journal of Consumer Research* 39(6), 1185–1201.

Devonis, D. C. (2014). *History of Psychology 101*. New York: Springer.

Diamond, J. (2012). *The World until Yesterday*. New York: Viking.

Diener, E. (Ed.). (2009). *The Science of Well-Being: The Collected Works of Ed Diener*. Dordrecht: Springer.

Diener, E. (2015). *Subjective Well-Being Scales*. https://internal.psychology.illinois.edu/~ediener/scales.html. Retrieved December 8, 2016.

Diener, E., and Biswas-Diener, R. (2008). *Happiness: Unlocking the Mysteries of Psychological Wealth*. Malden, MA: Blackwell.

Djupdræt, M. B. (2018). Historiebevidsthed hos demente. Erindringsforløb, velvære og identitetsdannelse på museer, *Kulturstudier* nr. 1. https://tidsskrift.dk/fn/article/view/106574.

Djupdræt, M. B., Fog, L., Kofod, L., Lindberg, H., Mathiassen, T. E., and Rasmussen, A. (2017). "Evaluation." In A. Hanson (ed.), *Reminiscence in Open Air Museums*, 47–49. Ostersumn, Sweden: Jamtli Forlag.

Djupdræt, M. B., and Lindberg, H. (2018). *Forskning viser, at erindringsformidling virker, Den Gamle by* [Yearbook]. Annual Report 2018, 83–87.

Doctrine of the Mean. Wikipedia. https://en.wikipedia.org/wiki/Doctrine_of_the_Mean. Retrieved August 2, 2020.

Dodge, R., Daly, A., Huyton, J., and Sanders, L. (2012). "The Challenge of Defining Wellbeing." *International Journal of Wellbeing* 2(3), 222–35.

Dolan, P. (2014). *Happiness by Design: Finding Pleasure and Purpose in Everyday Life*. London: Penguin.

Donald, M. (2012). "Evolutionary Origins of Autobiographical Memory Systems: A Retrieval Hypothesis." In D. Berntsen and D. C. Rubin (eds.), *Understanding Autobiographical Memory: Theories and Approaches*, 269–89. Cambridge: Cambridge University Press.

Durie, M. (1994). *Whaiora: Māori Health Development*. Auckland: Oxford University Press.

Eagleman, D. (2015). *The Brain: The Story of You*. New York: Pantheon.

Edelman, G., and Tononi, G. (2000). "Reentry and the Dynamic Core." In T. Metzinger (ed.), *Neural Correlates of Consciousness: Empirical and Conceptual Questions*, 121–38. Cambridge, MA: MIT Press.

Eid, M., and Larsen, R. J. (Eds.). *The Science of Subjective Well-Being*. New York: The Guildford Press.

Engelhart, A., Adamala, K., and Szostak, J. (2016). "A Simple Physical Mechanism Enables Homeostasis in Cells." *Nature Chemistry* 8(5), 448–53.

Faerber, L. S., Hofmann, J., Ahrholdt, D., and Schnittka, O. (2021). "When Are Visitors Actually Satisfied at Visitor Attractions? What We Know from More than 30 Years of Research." *Tourism Management* 84. https://doi.org/10.1016/j.tourman.2021.104284. Retrieved March 29, 2021.

Fafchamps, M., and Labonne, J. (2017). "Using Split Samples to Improve Inference about Causal Effects." Working Paper, Stanford University. http://dx.doi.org/10.7910/DVN/Q0IXQY. Retrieved February 26, 2021.

Falk, J. H. (1985). "The Impact of Novelty on Learning and Behavior in Museums and Other Informal Settings." In S. M. Nair (ed.), *Proceedings of the Centenary Meeting of the Bombay Natural History Society*. Bombay, India.

Falk, J. H. (1991). "Analysis of Family Visitors in Natural History Museums: The National Museum of Natural History." Washington, DC. *Curator* 34(1), 44–50.

Falk, J. H. (2008). "Identity and the Art Museum Visitor." *Journal of Art Education* 34(2), 25–34.

Falk, J. H. (2009). *Identity and the Museum Visitor Experience*. Walnut Creek, CA: Left Coast Press.

Falk, J. H. (2018). *Born to Choose: Evolution, Self, and Well-Being*. New York: Routledge.

Falk, J. H., Ballantyne, R., Packer, J., and Benckendorff, P. (2012). "Travel and Learning: A Neglected Tourism Research Area." *Annals of Tourism Research* 39(2), 908–27.

Falk, J. H., and Balling, J. D. (1982). "The Field Trip Milieu: Learning and Behavior as a Function of Contextual Events." *Journal of Educational Research* 76(1), 22–28.

Falk, J. H., and Dierking, L. D. (1992). *The Museum Experience*. Washington, DC: Whalesback Books.

Falk, J. H., and Dierking, L. D. (1995). “Recalling the Museum Experience.” *Journal of Museum Education* 20(2), 10–13.

Falk, J. H., and Dierking, L. D. (1996). “Recollections of Elementary School Field Trips.” In D. Herrmann and M. Johnson (eds.), *The Third Practical Aspects of Memory Conference*, 512–26. University of Maryland: College Park.

Falk, J. H., and Dierking, L. D. (2000). *Learning from Museums*. Lanham, MD: Rowman & Littlefield.

Falk, J. H., and Dierking, L. D. (2010). “The 95% Solution: School Is Not Where Most Americans Learn Most of Their Science.” *American Scientist* 98, 486–93.

Falk, J. H., and Dierking, L. D. (2014). *The Museum Experience Revisited.* Walnut Creek, CA: Left Coast Press.

Falk, J. H., and Dierking, L. D. (2019). *Learning from Museums,* second edition. Lanham, MD: Rowman & Littlefield.

Falk, J. H., Dierking, L. D., Rennie, L., and Scott, C. (2005). “In Praise of ‘Both-And’ rather than ‘Either-Or’ Thinking: A Reply to ‘Interacting with Interactives.’” *Curator* 48(4), 475–77.

Falk, J. H., Dierking, L. D., and Staus, N. L. (2020). “The Use of Ecological Concepts in the Social Sciences: Measuring the Productivity, Durability and Resilience of Learning ecosystems.” *Ecology and Conservation Science* 1(3): 555563. DOI: 10.19080/ECOA.2020.01.555563.

Falk, J. H., Dierking, L. D., Swanger, L., Staus, N., Back, M., Barriault, C., Catalao, C., Chambers, C., Chew, L.-L., Dahl, S. A., Falla, S., Gorecki, B., Lau, T. C., Lloyd, A., Martin, J., Santer, J., Singer, S., Solli, A., Trepanier, G., Tyystjärvi, K. and Verheyden, P. (2016). “Correlating Science Center Use with Adult Science Literacy: An International, Cross-Institutional Study.” *Science Education* 100(5), 849–76.

Falk, J. H., and Gillespie, K. L. (2009). “Investigating the Role of Emotion in Science Center Visitor Learning.” *Visitor Studies* 12(2), 112–32.

Falk, J. H., Heimlich, J., and Bronnenkant, K. (2008). “Using Identity-Related Visit Motivations as a Tool for Understanding Adult Zoo and Aquarium Visitor’s Meaning Making.” *Curator* 51(1), 55–80.

Falk, J. H., Koke, J., Price, A., and Pattison, S. (2018). *Investigating the Cascading, Long-Term Effects of Informal Science Education Experiences*. Technical Report. October 22, 2018. Portland, OR: Institute for Learning Innovation. https://www.informalscience.org/investigating-cascading-long-term-effects-informal-science-education-experiences-report.

Falk, J. H., and Meier, D. (in prep.). “Monetizing the Value of Museum Experiences: A Preliminary Study.” *Museum Management and Curatorship*.

Falk, J. H., and Needham, M. (2011). “Measuring the Impact of a Science Center on Its Community.” *Journal of Research in Science Teaching* 48(1), 1–12.

Falk, J. H., and Needham, M. D. (2013). “Factors Contributing to Adult Knowledge of Science and Technology.” *Journal of Research in Science Teaching* 50(4), 431–52.

Falk, J. H., Pattison, S., Meier, D., Livingston, K. and Bibas, D. (2018). “The Contribution of Science-Rich Resources to Public Science Interest.” *Journal of Research in Science Teaching* 55(3), 422–45.

Falk, J. H., Scott, C., Dierking, L. D., Rennie, L. J., and Cohen Jones, M. (2004). “Interactives and Visitor Learning.” *Curator* 47(2), 171–98.

Falk, J. H., and Sheppard, B. (2006). *Thriving in the Knowledge Age: New Business Models For Museums and Other Cultural Organizations*. Lanham, MD: AltaMira Press.

Falk, J. H., and Storksdieck, M. (2004). *Investigating the Long-Term Impact of a Science Center on Its Community*. Final Report to National Science Foundation. Annapolis, MD: Institute for Learning Innovation.

Falk, J. H., and Storksdieck, M. (2005). "Using the Contextual Model of Learning to Understand Science Learning from a Science Center Exhibition." *Science Education* 89, 744–78.

Falk, J. H., and Storksdieck, M. (2010). "Science Learning in a Leisure Setting." *Journal of Research in Science Teaching* 47(2), 194–212.

Faragher, E. B., Cass, M., and Cooper, C. L. (2005). "The Relationship between Job Satisfaction and Health: A Meta-Analysis." *Occupational and Environmental Medicine* 62,105–12.

Farver, J. A. M., Ghosh, C., Garcia, C. (2000). "Children's Perceptions of Their Neighborhoods." *Journal of Applied Developmental Psychology* 21, 139–63.

Feinstein, L., Hammond, C., Woods, L., Preston, J., and Bynner, J. (2003). *The Contribution of Adult Learning to Health and Social Capital*, Research Report 8. London: Centre for Research on the Wider Benefits of Learning.

Field, J. (2009). "Good for Your Soul? Adult Learning and Mental Well-Being." *International Journal of Lifelong Education* 28(2), 175–91.

Fink, G. (2016). "Stress: The Health Epidemic of the 21st Century." Elsevier Sci-Tech Connect. April 26, 2016. http://scitechconnect.elsevier.com/stress-health-epidemic-21st-century/#:~:text=Stress%3A%20The%20Health%20Epidemic%20of%20the%2021st%20Century.,our%20emotional%20and%20physical%20health%20can%20be%20devastating. Retrieved September 27, 2020.

Finn, P. (2006). "Bias and Blinding: Self-Fulfilling Prophecies and Intentional Ignorance." *The ASHA Leader* 11(8), 16–17, 22.

Fleurbaey, M. (2009). "Beyond GDP: The Quest for a Measure of Social Welfare." *Journal of Economic Literature* 47 (4), 1029–75.

Ford, M. R. (2016). *"Sharing Joy": Volunteers' Motivations at California's Crystal Cove State Park*. Unpublished masters capstone. Corvallis, OR: Oregon State University.

Forrest, R. (2014). *Design Factors in the Museum Visitor Experience*. Unpublished doctoral dissertation. University of Queensland, Brisbane, Australia.

Fox, J. (2012, January-February). "The Economics of Well-Being." *Harvard Business Review*. https://hbr.org/2012/01/the-economics-of-well-being. Retrieved February 26, 2020.

Freeman, W. (2000). *How Brains Make Up Their Mind*. New York: Columbia University Press.

Frey, B. S., Luechinger, and Stutzer, A. (2010). "The Life Satisfaction Approach to Environmental Valuation." *Annual Review of Resource Economics* 2(1), 139–60.

Fried, M. H. (1967). *The Evolution of Political Society: An Essay in Political Anthropology*. New York: Random House.

Fristrup, T. (Ed.) (2019). *Socially engaged Practices in Museums and Archives*. Jamtli Forlag. Fornvårdaren Serie No. 38.

Fujiwara, D., and Dolan, P. (2016). "Happiness-Based Policy Analysis." In M. D. Adler and M. Fleurbaey (eds.), *Well-Being and Public Policy*. Oxford: Oxford University Press.

Fujiwara, D., Kudrna, L., and Dolan, P. (2014). "Quantifying and Valuing the Wellbeing Impacts of Culture and Sport." Technical Report. London: UK Department for Culture, Media and Sport. https://assets.publishing.service.gov.uk/government/uploads/system/uploads/attachment_data/file/304899/Quantifying_and_valuing_the_wellbeing_impacts_of_sport_and_culture.pdf. Retrieved February 18, 2020.

Fukui, H., and Toyoshima, K. (2008). "Music Facilitates the Neurogenesis, Regeneration and Repair of Neurons." *Medical Hypotheses* 71(5), 765–69.

Fulkerson IV, R. (2020). "Houston Museum of Natural Sciences." http://www.hmns.org/visit/rent-the-museum/testimonials/. Retrieved August 9, 2020.

Gallagher, M. W., and Shane J. Lopez (2007). "Curiosity and Well-Being." *The Journal of Positive Psychology* 2(4), 236–48.

Gardner, J., and Henry, S. (2002). "September 11 and the Mourning After: Reflections on Collecting and Interpreting the History of Tragedy." *The Public Historian* 24(3), 37–52.

Geertz, C. (1973). *The Interpretation of Cultures*. New York: Basic.

George, A. (2014). "Hunters and gatherers." *New Scientist*, 221 (2962), 38. https://www.newscientist.com/article/mg22129620-700-stuff-humans-as-hunters-and-mega-gatherers/#ixzz6Q1SwlPCU. Retrieved June 21, 2020.

Gifford, R. (2014). *Environmental Psychology: Principles and Practice*, fifth edition. Colville, WA: Optimal Books.

Glaser, E. (2019). "Defining Critical Thinking." *The International Center for the Assessment of Higher Order Thinking (ICAT, US)/Critical Thinking Community*. https://www.criticalthinking.org/pages/defining-critical-thinking/766. Retrieved November 1, 2020.

Godrey-Smith, P. (2016). *Other Minds: The Octopus, the Sea, and the Deep Origins of Consciousness*. New York: Farrar Straus and Giroux.

Goleman, D. (2006). *Social Intelligence: The New Science of Human Relationships*. New York: Bantam Books.

Graefe, A. R., and Fedler, A. J. (1986). "Situational and Subjective Determinants of Satisfaction in Marine Recreational Fishing." *Leisure Science*, 8, 275–95.

Graham, C. (2011). *The Pursuit of Happiness: An Economy of Well-Being*. Washington, DC: Brookings Institution Press.

Gramling, C. (2016). "Hints of Oldest Life on Earth." *Science*. http://www.sciencemag.org/news/2016/08/hints-oldest-fossil-life-found-greenland-rocks. Retrieved August 31, 2016.

Grand, S. 1998). "Curiosity Created the Cat [the Relationship between Curiosity and Intelligence]." *IEEE Intelligent Systems and Their Applications* 13(3), 2–4.

Grant, D. (2019). "How Much Is Too Much? On the Difficulty of Calculating Museum Admission Prices." New Criterion.com. July 23, 2019. https://newcriterion.com/blogs/dispatch/how-much-is-too-much. Retrieved January 3, 2021.

Gray, P. (2008). "The Value of Play 1: The Definition of Play Gives Insights." *Psychology Today*. November 19, 2008. https://www.psychologytoday.com/us/blog/freedom-learn/200811/the-value-play-i-the-definition-play-gives-insights. Retrieved September 27, 2020.

Green, C. (Ed.) (2001). *Picasso's Les Demoiselles d'Avignon*. Cambridge, UK: Cambridge University Press.

Greene, J. P., Kisida, B., and Bowen, D. H. (2014). "The Educational Value of Field Trips." *Education Next* 14(1), 78–86.

Griffin, J. (1998). *School-Museum Integrated Learning Experiences in Science: A Learning Journey*. Unpublished doctoral dissertation. University of Technology, Sydney.

Groves, I. (2005). "Assessing the Economic Impact of Science Centers on Their Local Communities." Technical Report. Canberra, AU: Questacon—The National Science and Technology Centre. https://www.informalscience.org/sites/default/files/EconImpact-whole.pdf. Retrieved February 18, 2020.

Grubbs, J., Wright, P., Braden, A., Wilt, J., and Kraus, S. (2019). "Internet Pornography Use and Sexual Motivation: A Systematic Review and Integration." *Annals of International Communication Association* 43(2), 117–55. https://www.tandfonline.com/doi/abs/10.1080/23808985.2019.1584045?journalCode=rica20. Retrieved July 12, 2020.

Guastella, A., Mitchell, P., and Mathews, F. (2008). *Biological Psychiatry* 64(3), 256–58.

Guba, E. G., and Lincoln, Y. (1989). *Fourth Generation Evaluation*. Newbury Park, CA: Sage.

Gurian, E. (1988). "Museums as a Social Responsible Institution." In E. Gurian (2006), *Civilizing the Museum: The Collected Writings of Elaine Heumann Gurian*, 69–74. London: Routledge.

Hamblin, J. (2014). "Buy Experiences, Not Things." *The Atlantic*. October 7, 2014. https://www.theatlantic.com/business/archive/2014/10/buy-experiences/381132/. Retrieved October 25, 2020.

Hansen, A. (2016). Learning to Feel Well at Jamtli Museum: A Case Study. *Journal of Adult and Continuing Education,* 22(2), 168–83.

Hanson, A. (Ed.). (2017). *Reminiscence in Open Air Museums*. Ostersumn, Sweden: Jamtli Forlag.

Harmon-Jones, E., and Mills, J. (1999). *Cognitive Dissonance: Progress on a Pivotal Theory in Social Psychology*. Washington, DC: American Psychological Association.

Harris, K. J. (2015). *Leaving Ideological Social Groups Behind: A Grounded Theory of Psychological Disengagement*. Retrieved from http://ro.ecu.edu.au/theses/1587. Retrieved March 13, 2016.

Hawkley, L. C., and Cacioppo, J. T. (2007). "Aging and Loneliness: Downhill Quickly?" *Current Directions in Psychological Science* 16, 187–91.

Hawkley, L. C., Thisted, R. A., Masi, C. M., and Cacioppo, J. T. (2010). "Loneliness Predicts Increased Blood Pressure: Five-Year Cross-Lagged Analyses in Middle-Aged and Older Adults." *Psychological Aging* 25, 132–41.

Henrich, J., and Gil-White, F. J. (2001). "The Evolution of Prestige: Freely Conferred Deference as a Mechanism for Enhancing the Benefits of Cultural Transmission." *Evolution and Human Behavior* 22, 165–96.

Henrich, J., Heine, S. J., and Norenzayan, A. (2010). "The Weirdest People in the World?" *Behavioral and Brain Sciences* 33(2–3), 61–83.

Heritage Lottery Fund and Oxford Economics. (2010). *Investing in Success: Heritage and the UK Tourism Economy*. https://www.heritagefund.org.uk/sites/default/files/media/about_us/hlf_tourism_impact_single.pdf. Retrieved July 2, 2020.

Himmler, S., van Exel, J., and Brouwer, W. (2020). "Estimating the Monetary Value of Health and Capability Well-Being Applying the Well-Being Valuation Approach." *The European Journal of Health Economics*. https://doi.org/10.1007/s10198-020-01231-7. Retrieved August 22, 2020.

Holden, J. (2006). "Cultural Value and Crisis of Legitimacy." *Demos*. https://www.demos.co.uk/files/Culturalvalueweb.pdf. Retrieved July 2, 2020.

Holton, E. (2018). "IMLS announces National Study on Museums, Libraries, and Social Well-Being." Institute for Museum and Library Services. August 29, 2018. https://www.imls.gov/news/imls-announces-national-study-museums-libraries-and-social-wellbeing. Retrieved March 14, 2021.

Honekopp, J., Rudolph, U., Beier, L., Liebert, A., and Mueller, C. (2007). "Physical Attractiveness of Face and Body as Indicators of Physical Fitness in Men." *Evolution and Human Behavior* 28(2), 106–11.

Hooper-Greenhill, E. (2004). "Measuring Learning Outcomes in Museums, Archives and Libraries: The Learning Impact Research Project (LIRP)." *International Journal of Heritage Studies* 10(2), 151–74.

Hull, D. (2011, February). *Assessing the Value and Impact of Museums*. Technical Report. Belfast: Northern Ireland Assembly Research and Library Service Research Paper. http://www.niassembly.gov.uk/globalassets/Documents/RaISe/Publications/2011/Culture-Arts-Leisure/2911.pdf. Retrieved February 20, 2020.

Hunt, E. G. (2009). *Study of Museum Lighting and Design*. Unpublished honors thesis. Texas State University. San Marcos, Texas.

Hunt, E., and Collander, D. (2014). *Social Science: An Introduction to the Study of* Society, fifth edition. London: Routledge.

Hunter, S., and Jacobus, J. (1977). *Modern Art*. New York: Prentice-Hall.

Imafidon, E. (2012). "The Concept of Person in an African Culture and Its Implication for Social Order." *Lumina* 23(2), 1–19. https://ejournals.ph/article.php?id=7365. Retrieved August 2, 2020.

Itkowitz, C. (2016). "Harvard Researchers Discovered the One Thing Everyone Needs for Happier, Healthier Lives." *The Independent*. March 2, 2016. http://www.independent.co.uk/life-style/harvard-researchers-discover-the-one-thing-everyone-needs-for-happier-and-healthier-lives-a6907901.html. Retrieved March 2, 2016.

Jablonka, E., and Lamb, M. J. (2014). *Evolution in Four Dimensions*. Cambridge, MA: MIT Press.

Jacobsen, J. W. (2016). *Measuring Museum Impact and Performance: Theory and Practice*. Lanham, MD: Rowman & Littlefield.

Jakubowski, R. D. (2011). *Museum Soundscapes and Their Impact on Visitor Outcomes*. Unpublished doctoral dissertation. University of Washington, Seattle, Washington.

James, W. (1902/1985). *The Varieties of Religious Experience*. Cambridge, MA: Harvard University Press.

Jara-Diaz, S., Munizaga, M., Greeven, P., Guerra, R., and Axhausen, K. (2008). "Estimating the Value of Leisure from a Time Allocation Model." *Transportation Research Part B: Methodological* 42(10), 946–57.

Jaremka, L. M., Fagundes, C. P., Glaser, R., Bennett, J. M., Malarkey, W. B., and Kiecolt-Glaser, J. K. (2012). "Loneliness Predicts Pain, Depression, and Fatigue: Understanding the Role of Immune Dysregulation." *Psychoneuroendocrinology*; pii: S0306–4530(12)00403–9. doi: 10.1016/j.psyneuen.2012.11.016.

Jarrett, C. (2013). "The Psychology of Stuff and Things." *The Psychologist*, 26, 560–65.

Jaynes, J. (1976). *The Origin of Consciousness in the Break-Down of the Bicameral Mind*, 23. Boston: Houghton Mifflin.

Jenkins, A., and Mostafa, T. (2013). "The Effects of Learning on Wellbeing for Older Adults in England." *Ageing and Society* 35(10), 1–18.

Johnson, P., and Thomas, B. (2000). *The Economic Impact of Museums: A Critique*. Technical Report. Durham, UK: University of Durham Business School.

Jones, J. (2019). "Quantifying Our Museum's Social Impact." Medium.com. May 14, 2020. https://medium.com/new-faces-new-spaces/quantifying-our-museums-social-impact-e99bff3ef30e. Retrieved July 26, 2020.

Jung, C. G. (1992). *Psychological Types*. Collected Works. Princeton, NJ: Princeton University Press.

Jussim, L., and Harber, K. D. (2005). "Teacher Expectations and Self-Fulfilling Prophecies: Knowns and Unknowns, Resolved and Unresolved Controversies." *Personality and Social Psychology Review* 9, 131–55.

Kahneman, D. (2011). *Thinking, Fast and Slow*. New York: Farrar, Straus and Giroux.

Kaimal, G., Ray, K., and Muniz, J. (2016). "Reduction of Cortisol Levels and Participants' Responses Following Art Making." *Art Therapy* 33(2), 74–80.

Kaplan, D. (Ed.). (2000). *The SAGE Handbook of Quantitative Methodology for the Social Sciences*. Newbury Park, CA: Sage.

Kaplan, R., and Kaplan, S. (1989). *The Experience of Nature: A Psychological Perspective*. Cambridge University Press.

Kaufman, S. B. (2010). "Two Routes to Social Status." *Psychology Today*. August 6, 2010. https://www.psychologytoday.com/us/blog/beautiful-minds/201008/two-routes-social-status#:~:text=The%20bulk%20of%20the%20evidence%20suggests%20that%20pride,each%20form%20may%20have%20evolved%20along%20different%20paths. Retrieved July 26, 2020.

Keeler, J., Roth, E., Neuser, B., Spitsbergen, J., Waters, D. and Vianney, J.-M. (2015). "The Neurochemistry and Social Flow of Singing: Bonding and Oxytocin." *Frontiers of Human Neuroscience* 9, 518–25. https://www.ncbi.nlm.nih.gov/pmc/articles/PMC4585277/. Retrieved December 31, 2016.

Kelley, R. (2014). "The Emerging Need for Hybrid Entities: Why California Should Become the Delaware of 'Social Enterprise Law.'" *Loyola L.A. Law Review* 47, 619–55.

Kelly, J. (1996). *Leisure*, third edition. Boston: Allyn and Bacon.

Kenrick, D. T., Griskevicius, V., Neuberg, S. L., and Schaller, M. (2010). "Renovating the Pyramid of Needs: Contemporary Extensions Built upon Ancient Foundations." *Perspectives on Psychological Science* 5, 292–314.

Kim, J., Seto, E., Christy, A., and Hicks, J. (2016). "Investing in the Real Me: Preference for Experiential to Material Purchases Driven by the Motivation to Search for True Self-Knowledge." *Self and Identity* 15(6), 727–47.

Kirk, M., Rasmussen, K. W., Overgaard, S. B., and Berntsen, D. (2019). "Five Weeks of Immersive Reminiscence Therapy Improves Autobiographical Memory in Alzheimer's Disease." *Memory* 27(4), 441–54.

Kirsch, P. (2015). "Oxytocin in the Socioemotional Brain." *Dialogues in Clinical Neuroscience* 17(4), 463–76.

Kirshenbaum, S. (2011). *The Science of Kissing*. New York: Grand Central Publishing.

Korn, R. (2018). *Intentional Practice for Museums*. Lanham, MD: Rowman & Littlefield.

Koski, J., Xie, H., and Olson, I. (2015). "Understanding Social Hierarchies: The Neural and Psychological Foundations of Status Perception." *Social Neuroscience* 10(5), 527–50.

Kramer, M., and Alim, K. (2021). "Encoding Memory in Tube Diameter Hierarchy of Living Flow Network." *Proceedings of the National Academy of Sciences*. DOI: 10.1073/pnas.2007815118.

Kraut, R. (2015). "Aristotle on Well-Being." In G. Fletcher (ed.), *Routledge Handbook of Philosophy of Well-Being*. London: Routledge.

La Terra, M. (2017). "Guide to Dating in Melbourne." Culture Trip. August 29, 2017. https://theculturetrip.com/pacific/australia/articles/a-singles-guide-to-dating-in-melbourne/

Lackoi, K., Patsou, M., and Chatterjee, H. J. (2016). *Museums for Health and Wellbeing: A Preliminary Report*. London. National Alliance for Museums, Health and Wellbeing.

Lapa, T. Y. (2018). "Life Satisfaction, Leisure Satisfaction and Perceived Freedom of Park Recreation Participants." *Procedia – Social and Behavioral Sciences* 93, 1985–93.

Lawton, G. (2014). "Stuff: The First Things Humans Owned." New Scientist. March 26, 2014. http://www.newscientist.com/gallery/first-possessions/2. Retrieved June 21, 2020.

Lazarus, R. S. (1966). *Psychological Stress and the Coping Process*, 16. New York: McGraw-Hill.

Lee, B. K., and Shafer, C. S. (2002). "The Dynamic Nature of Leisure Experience: An Application of Affect Control Theory." *Journal of Leisure Research* 34(2), 290–310.

Lee, B. K., Shafer, C. S., and Kang, I. (2005). "Examining Relationships among Perceptions of Self, Episode-Specific Evaluations, and Overall Satisfaction with a Leisure Activity." *Leisure Science*, 27, 93–109.

Lee, K., and Kim, I. (2005). "Estimating the Value of Leisure Time in Korea." *Applied Economics Letters* 12(10), 639–41.

Leinhardt, G., Crowley, K., and Knutson, K. (Eds.). (2002). *Learning Conversations in Museums*. Mahwah, NJ: Lawrence Erlbaum Associates Publishers.

Lester D. (1990). "Maslow's Hierarchy of Needs and Personality." *Personality and Individual Differences* 11, 1187–88.

Leung, D. S. Y., and Liu, B. C. P. (2011). "Lifelong Education, Quality of Life and Self-Efficacy of Chinese Older Adults." *Educational Gerontology* 37(11), 967–81.

Lieberman, D. E. (2013). *The Story of the Human Body*. New York, Pantheon. http://humanorigins.si.edu/human-characteristics/brains. Retrieved August 9, 2013.

Lindert, J., Bain, P., Kubzansky, L., and Stein, C. (2015). "Well-Being Measurement and the WHO Health Policy Health 2010: Systematic Review of Measurement Scales." *European Journal of Public Health* 25(4), 731–40.

Lohr, K. N. (2002). "Assessing Health Status and Quality-of-Life Instruments: Attributes and Review Criteria." *Quality of Life Research* 11, 193–205.

Lovelock, J. E. (1972). "Gaia as Seen through the Atmosphere." *Atmospheric Environment* 6(8), 579–80.

Lovern, L. (2008, January). "Native American Worldview and the Discourse on Disability." *Philosophy of Disability*, 9(1). http://pieducators.com/sites/default/files/Native-American-Worldview-Discourse-on-Disability.pdf. Retrieved July 31, 2020.

Luke, J., Letourneau, S., Rivera, N., Brahms, L., and May S. (2017). "Play and Children's Museums: A Path Forward or a Point of Tension?" *Curator* 60(1), 37–46.

Lyengar, S. (2010). *The Art of Choosing*. New York: Hachette Book Group.

Ma, W. (2016). "The Essence of Life." *Biology Direct* 11(1). DOI: 10.1186/s13062-016-0150-5. Retrieved June 28, 2020.

Maas, K. (2008). *Social Impact Measurement: Towards a Guideline for Managers*. https://www.erim.eur.nl/fileadmin/default/content/erim/research/centres/erasmus_centre_for_strategic_philanthropy/research/publications/social_impact_measurement_voor_sso_nieuwsbrief%5B1%5D.pdf. Retrieved February 25, 2020.

Macphail, E. M. (1995). "Cognitive Function in Mammals: The Evolutionary Perspective." *Cognitive Brain Research* 3, 279–90.

Madge, C. (2019). *Autism in Museums: A Revolution in the Making*. Center for the Future of Museums. American Alliance of Museums. July 16, 2019. https://www.aam-us.org/2019/07/16/autism-in-museums-a-revolution-in-the-making/. Retrieved August 9, 2020.

Madon, S., Guyll, M., Spoth, R. L., Cross, S. E., and Hilbert, S. J. (2003). "The Self-Fulfilling Influence of Mother Expectations on Children's Underage Drinking." *Journal of Personality and Social Psychology* 84, 1188–205.

Maher, C., Hadfield, M., Hutchings, M., and de Eyto, A. (2018). "Ensuring Rigor in Qualitative Data Analysis." *International Journal of Qualitative Methods* 17(1), 160940691878636.

Mannell, R., and Iso-Ahola, S. E. (1987). "Psychological Nature of Leisure and Tourism Experience." *Annals of Tourism Research* 14, 314–31.

Margulis, L., and Sagan, D. (1986). *Microcosmos*. New York: Summit Books.

Markowsky, G. (2004). "Information Theory." *Encyclopedia Britannica*. https://www.britannica.com/science/information-theory/Physiology. Retrieved June 26, 2020.

Martin, W., and Russell, M. J. (2003). "On the Origin of Cells: A Hypothesis for the Evolutionary Transitions from Abiotic Geochemistry to Chemoautotrophic Prokaryotes, and from Prokaryotes to Nucleated Cells." *Philosophical Transactions of the Royal Society of London, B-Biological Sciences* 358(1429), 59–85.

Maslow, A. H. (1943). "A Theory of Human Motivation." *Psychological Review* 50(4), 370–96. *Handbook of Positive Psychology*, 195–206. Oxford: Oxford University Press.

Maslow, A. H. (1962). *Toward a Psychology of Being*. Princeton, NJ: Van Nostrand-Reinhold.

Maslow, A. H. (1964). *Religions, Values, and Peak Experiences*. London: Penguin Books Limited.

McGaugh, J. L. (2013). "Making Lasting Memories: Remembering the Significant." *Proceedings of the National Academy of Sciences U.S.A.*, 110(Suppl 2), 10402–407.

McKinley, K. (2017). "What Is Our Museum's Social Impact?" Medium.com. July 10, 2017. https://medium.com/new-faces-new-spaces/what-is-our-museums-social-impact-62525fe88d16. Retrieved July 23, 2020.

McLean, D. (2015). *Kraus's Recreation and Leisure in Modern Society*, tenth edition. Burlington, MA: Jones & Bartlett Publishers.

McLean, F. (1998). "Museums and the Construction of National Identity: A Review." *International Journal of Heritage Studies* 3(4), 244–52.

McLean, K. (1993). *Planning for People in Museum Exhibitions*. Washington, DC: Association of Science Technology Centers.

McLean, K. (1999). "Museum Exhibition and the Dynamics of Dialogue." *Daedalus* 128(3), 83–107.

Merritt, E. (2021). Serving the Needs of the Community During a Pandemic. Center for the Future of Museums. American Alliance of Museums. https://www.aam-us.org/2021/04/12/serving-the-needs-of-the-community-during-a-pandemic/. Retrieved May 13, 2021.

Merton, R. K. (1957). *Social Theory and Social Structure*, revised edition. New York: Free Press.

Mickletwait, J., and Wooldridge, A. (2020). *The Wakeup Call*. New York: HarperCollins.

Mileham, M. (2021). "Measuring the Social Impact of Museums: Call for Study Sites." American Alliance of Museums. February 2, 2021. https://www.aam-us.org/2021/02/02/measuring-the-social-impact-of-museums-call-for-study-sites/. Retrieved February 19, 2020.

Millie, K. (2019). "I Met My Love There." Review of Currier Museum of Art. https://www.tripadvisor.com/ShowUserReviews-g46152–d264427–r716453159–Currier_Museum_of_Art-Manchester_New_Hampshire.html. Retrieved August 9, 2020.

Mitchell, J. (1970). "Big Yellow Taxi." Crazy Crow Music / Siquomb Music Publishing.

Morris Hargreaves McIntyre (2004). *Tate through Visitor's Eyes*. Technical Report. Manchester, UK: Morris Hargreaves McIntyre.

Moussouri, T., (1997). *Family Agendas and Family Learning in Hands-On Museums*. Unpublished doctoral dissertation. University of Leiscester, Leicester, England.

Museums, Libraries and Archives Council. (2008). "Generic Social Outcomes." http://nia1.me/5pf. Retrieved February 18, 2020.

Naime, J. S. and Pandeirada, J. (2016). "Adaptive Memory: The Evolutionary Significance of Survival Processing." *Perspectives on Psychological Science* 11(4), 496–511.

Narushima, M., Liu, J., and Diestelkamp, N. (2016). "Lifelong Learning in Active Ageing Discourse: Its Conserving Effect on Wellbeing, Health and Vulnerability." *Ageing and Society* 38(4), 1–25.

National Academies of Science, Engineering and Medicine. (2020). *Promoting Positive Adolescent Health Behaviors and Outcomes*. Washington, DC: The National Academies Press.

National Academies of Science, Engineering and Medicine. (2020). *Sustaining the Future of the Nations' Biological Collections*. Washington, DC: The National Academies Press.

Neher, C., Duffield, J., and Patterson, D. (2013). "Valuation of National Park System Visitation: The Efficient Use of Count Data Models, Meta-Analysis, and Secondary Visitor Survey Data." *Environmental Management* 52(3), 683–98.

Nerurkar, A., Bitton, A., Davis, R. B., Phillips, R. S., and Yeh, G. (2013). "When Physicians Counsel about Stress: Results of a National Study." *JAMA Internal Medicine* 173(1), 76–77.

Newman, K., and Tourle P. (2011). *The Impact of Cuts on UK Museums: A Report for the Museums*. Technical Report. London: Museums Association.

Nieuwhof, A. (2017). *Olfactory Experiences in Museums of Modern and Contemporary Art*. Unpublished master's thesis. Leiden University, Leiden, Netherlands.

Orlowski, J., and Wicker, P. (2015). "The Monetary Value of Social Capital." *Journal of Behavioral and Experimental Economics* 57, 26–36.

Ostrower, F. (2003). "Trustees of Culture: Power, Wealth, and Status of Elite Arts Boards." *Contemporary Sociology* 32(6), 711–12.

Oxytocin. (2020). Wikipedia. https://en.wikipedia.org/wiki/Oxytocin. Retrieved November 15, 2020.

Packer, J. (2006). "Learning for Fun: The Unique Contribution of Educational Leisure Experiences." *Curator: The Museum Journal* 49(3), 329–44.

Packer, J. (2008). "Beyond Learning: Exploring Visitors' Perceptions of the Value and Benefits of Museum Experiences." *Curator: The Museum Journal* 51 (1), 33–54.

Packer, J. (2014). "Visitors' Restorative Experiences in Museum and Botanic Gardens Environments." In S. Filep and P. Pearce (eds.), *Tourist Experience and Fulfilment: Insights from Positive Psychology*, 202–22. London: Routledge.

Packer, J., and Ballantyne, R. (2012). "Comparing Captive and Non-Captive Wildlife Tourism." *Annals of Tourism Research* 39(2), 1242–45.

Packer, J., and Bond, N. (2010). "Museums as Restorative Environments." *Curator: The Museum Journal* 53 (4), 421–56.

Patil, S., Patruni, B., Lu, H., Dunkerley, F., Fox, J., Potoglou, D., and Robinson, N. (2015). *Public Perception of Security and Privacy: Results of the Comprehensive Analysis of PACT's pan-European Survey*. Brussels: Rand Europe.

Paul-Labrador, M. D., Polk, J. H., Dwyer, I., Velasquez, S., Nidich, S., Rainforth, M., Schneider, R., and Merz, C. N. (2006). "Effects of a Randomized Controlled Trial of Transcendental Meditation on Components of the Metabolic Syndrome in Subjects with Coronary Heart Disease." *Archives of Internal Medicine* 166: 1218–24.

Pchelin, P., and Howell, R. (2014). "The Hidden Cost of Value-Seeking: People Do Not Accurately Forecast the Economic Benefits of Experiential Purchases." *The Journal of Positive Psychology* 9(4), 322–34.

Peacock, S., and Patel, S. (2008). "Cultural Influences on Pain." *Reviews in Pain* 1(2), 6–9.

Pedretti, E., and Navas Iannini, A. M. (2020). *Controversy in Science Museums: Re-imagining Exhibition Spaces and Practices*. London: Routledge.

Perasso, E. (2017). "Eating at the Museum: When Food Is a Work of Art." Fine Dining Lovers. February 1, 2017. https://www.finedininglovers.com/article/eating-museum-when-food-work-art. August 9, 2020.

Perry, D. (1989). *The Creation and Verification of a Developmental Model for the Design of a Museum Exhibit*. Unpublished doctoral dissertation. Indiana University.

Perry, S. J. (1998). "A Study of Physical Appearance and Level of Attraction to the Opposite Sex." *Modern Psychological Studies* 6(2), 12–17.

Peterson, R. (2018). "10 Experts Explain What Is a Good ROI and Why." BarnRaisers.com. May 28, 2018. https://barnraisersllc.com/2018/05/28/good-roi-experts-explain-industries/. Retrieved March 14, 2021.

Pew. (2011). "Is College Worth It." May 15, 2011. https://www.pewsocialtrends.org/2011/05/15/is-college-worth-it/#chapter-5–the-monetary-value-of-a-college-education?src=prc-number. Retrieved January 17, 2021.

Phelan, S., Bauer, J., and Lewalter, D. (2018). "Visit Motivations: Development of a Short Scale for Comparison across Sites." *Museum Management and Curatorship* 33(1), 25–41.

Pianka, E. R. (1970). "On r and K selection." *American Naturalist* 104 (940): 592–97.

Plato. (375 BC). *The Republic*. http://www.literaturepage.com/read.php?titleid=therepublic&abspage=284&bookmark=1. Retrieved October 30, 2020.

Plomin, R., and Deary, I. J. (2015). "Genetics and Intelligence Differences: Five Special Findings." *Molecular Psychiatry* 20(1), 98–108.

Pogrebin, R. (2020). "Met Museum Prepares for $100 Million Loss and Closure Till July." *New York Times*. March 18, 2020. https://www.nytimes.com/2020/03/18/arts/design/met-museum-coronavirus-closure.html. Retrieved March 19, 2020.

Porter, M. E. (1996). "What Is Strategy?" *Harvard Business Review* 74(6), 74, 61–78.

Powell, R. B., Stern, M., and Frensley, T. (2020). "Identifying Outcomes for Environmental Education Programming in National Parks." In J. Thompson and A. Houseal (eds.), *America's Largest Classrooms: What We Learn from Our National Parks*, 245–58. Berkeley, CA: University of California Press.

Preko, A., Gyepi-Garbrah, T. F., Arkorful, H., Akolaa, A. A., and Quansah, F. (2020). "Museum Experience and Satisfaction: Moderating Role of Visiting Frequency." *International Hospitality Review* 34(2), 203–20.

Prum, R. O. (2017). *The Evolution of Beauty: How Darwin's Forgotten Theory of Mate Choice Shapes the Animal World—and Us*. New York: Doubleday.

Raven, D., Van Vucht Tijssen, L., and de Wolf, J. (Eds.). (1992). *Cognitive Relativism and Social Science*. Piscataway, NJ: Transaction Publishers.

Reeves, R., and Rodrigue, E. (2016). "Fewer Field Trips Mean Some Students Miss More than a Day at the Museum." Brookings. https://www.brookings.edu/blog/social-mobility-memos/2016/06/08/fewer-field-trips-mean-some-students-miss-more-than-a-day-at-the-museum/. Retrieved December 28, 2020.

Reio, T. G., and Sanders-Reio, J. (2020). "Curiosity and Well-Being in Emerging Adulthood." *New Horizons in Adult Education and Human Resource Development* 32(1), 17–27.

Rennie, L. J., and McClafferty, T. P. (1995). "Using Visits to Interactive Science and Technology Centers, Museums, Aquaria, and Zoos to Promote Learning in Science." *Journal of Science Teacher Education* 6(4), 175–85.

Roberts, A. (2018). *Evolution: The Human Story*, second edition. New York: Penguin Random House.

Rosenberg, A. (2020). "Will Coronavirus Kill-Off Movie Theaters?" *Washington Post*. https://www.washingtonpost.com/opinions/2020/03/19/will-coronavirus-kill-off-movie-theaters/. Retrieved August 30, 2020.

Ross Nelson, K., and Ashton, S. (in prep.). "Normalcy as Respite?" *Museum*. Washington, DC: American Association of Museums (pre-print).

Rounds, J. (2004). "Strategies for the Curiosity-Driven Museum Visitor." *Curator* 47(4), 389–412.

Rounds, J. (2006). "Doing Identity Work in Museums." *Curator* 49(2), 133–50.

Rudd, M., Vohs, K. and Aaker, J. (2012). "Awe Expands People's Perception of Time, Alters Decision Making, and Enhances Well-Being." *Psychological Science*, 23(10), 1130–36.

Rule, N., and Ambady, N. (2008). "Brief Exposures: Male Sexual Orientation Is Accurately Perceived at 50 ms." *Journal of Experimental Social Psychology* 44(4), 1100–1105.

Ryff, C. D. (1989). "Happiness is Everything, or Is It? Explorations On the Meaning of Psychological Well-Being." *Journal of Personality and Social Psychology* 57 (6): 1069–1081.

Ryff, C. D. (2014). "Psychological Well-Being Revisited: Advances in the Science and Practice of Eudaimonia." *Psychotherapy and Psychosomatics* 83(1), 10–28.

Salmi, H. (1998). "Motivation and Meaningful Science Learning in Informal Settings." Paper presented at the annual meeting of the National Association for Research in Science Teaching, April, San Diego, CA.

Saloner, B., Polsky, D., Kenney, G., Hempstead, K., and Rhodes, K. (2015). "Primary Care Visits Available to Most Uninsured but at a High Price." Johns Hopkins Bloomberg School of Public Health. https://www.jhsph.edu/news/news-releases/2015/primary-care-visits-available-to-most-uninsured-but-at-a-high-price.html. Retrieved January 17, 2021.

Santer, J., Singer, S., Solli, A., Trepanier, G., Tyystjärvi, K., and Verheyden, P. (2016). "Correlating Science Center Use with Adult Science Literacy: An International, Cross-Institutional Study." *Science Education* 100(5), 849–76.

Sapolski, R. M. (2004). "Social Status and Health in Humans and Other Animals." *Annual Review of Anthropology* 33, 393–418.

Sartorius, N. (2006). "The Meaning of Health and Its Promotion." *Croatian Medical Journal* 47, 662–64.

Sayin, S., De Backer, J.-F., Siju, K. P., Wosniack, M., Lewis, L., Frisch, L.-M., Gansen, B., Schlegel, P., Edmondson-Stait, A., Sharifi, N., Fisher, C., Calle-Schuler, S., Lauritzen, J. S., Bock, D., Costa, M., Jefferis, G., Gjorgjieva, J., and Kadow, I. G. (2019). "A Neural Circuit Arbitrates between Persistence and Withdrawal in Hungry *Drosophila*." *Neuron*. DOI: 10.1016/j.neuron.2019.07.028.

Scaruffi, A. (2013). *The Nature of Consciousness: The Structures of Life and the Meaning of Matter*. https://www.scaruffi.com/nature/preface.html. Retrieved June 27, 2013.

Schmidt, M. (2021). "Return of Investment Metric ROI Measures Profitability." Solution Matrix, LTD. https://www.business-case-analysis.com/return-on-investment.html. Retrieved March 14, 2021.

Schorch, P. (2013). "The Experience of a Museum Space." *Museum Management and Curatorship* 28(2), 193–208.

Schrodinger E. (1944). *What Is Life?* Cambridge: Cambridge University Press.

Schroeder, S. A., Cornicelli, L., Fulton, D., and Merchant, S. (2019). "The Influence of Motivation Versus Experience on Recreation Satisfaction." *Journal of Leisure Research* 50(2), 107–31.

Schuller, T., Preston, J., Hammond, C., Bassett-Grundy, A., and Bynner, J. (2004). *The Benefits of Learning: The Impacts of Formal and Informal Education on Social Capital, Health and Family Life.* London: Routledge.

Scott, C. (2008). "Using 'Values' to Position and Promote Museums." *International Journal of Arts Management* 11(1), 28–41.

Scott, C. A. (2011). "Measuring the Immeasurable: Capturing Intangible Values." Marketing and Public Relations International Committee of ICOM (International Council of Museums) Conference Keynote Brno, Czech Republic 19th September 2011. https://citeseerx.ist.psu.edu/viewdoc/download?doi=10.1.1.1058.3671&rep=rep1&type=pdf. Retrieved February 18, 2020.

Selwood, S. 2002. "What Difference Do Museums Make? Producing Evidence on the Impact of Museums." *Critical Quarterly* 44 (4), 66–72.

Sernovit, A. (2007). "The Rising Importance of Word of Mouth." Damn, I Wish I'd Thought of That! June 29, 2007. http://www.damniwish.com/2007/06/the-rising-impo.html. Retrieved December 27, 2011.

Service Management Group. (2018). *Five Things We Learned from Talking to More Than 1 Billion People.* https://www.smg.com/resources/detail/five-things-we-learned-from-talking-to-1-billion-people. Retrieved April 12, 2021.

Shepherdson, P. (2014). "Perceptions of Safety and Fear of Crime Research Report." http://saiwa.asn.au/wp-content/uploads/2016/05/Fear-of-Crime-Perceptions-of-Safety-Research-Report-2014-Patrick-She.pdf. Retrieved August 16, 2020.

Sheppard, S. (2014). "Museums in the Neighborhood: The Local Economic Impact of Museums." In F. Giarratani, G. J. D. Hewings, and P. McCann (eds.), *Handbook of Industry Studies and Economic Geography* (pp. 191–204). Cheltenham: Edward Elgar Publishing.

Sidney, J. A., Jones, A., Coberley, C., Pope, J., and Wells, A. (2017). "The Well-Being Valuation Model: A Method for Monetizing the Nonmarket Good of Individual Well-Being." *Health Services Outcomes Research Methods* 17, 84–100.

Siegel, D. (2008). *Mindsight.* Oxford: OneWorld.

Siegel, J. (2005). *The Idea of the Self: Thought and Experience in Western Europe since the Eighteenth Century.* Cambridge: Cambridge University Press.

Siegel, N. (2020). "Europe's Museums Are Open but the Public Isn't Coming." *New York Times.* October 19, 2020. https://www.nytimes.com/2020/10/19/arts/design/europe-museums-covid.html?login=email&auth=login-email&login=email&auth=login-email. Retrieved October 23, 2020.

Simon, N. (2012). "Principles of Participation." In G. Anderson (ed.), *Reinventing the Museum: The Evolving Conversation on the Paradigm Shift,* second edition, 334–55. Lanham, MD: AltaMira Press.

Sims, D. (2020). "Hollywood Is Facing an Existential Crisis." *The Atlantic.* March 24, 2020. https://www.theatlantic.com/culture/archive/2020/03/post-pandemic-future-hollywood/608620/. Retrieved August 30, 2020.

Smith, J. K. (2014). *The Museum Effect.* Lanham, MD: Rowman & Littlefield.

Smith, J. M., and Szathmary, E. (1995). *The Major Transitions in Evolution.* Oxford, UK: Oxford University Press.

Smithsonian Institution (2007, April). *Going Free? Cooper-Hewitt National Design Museum and General Admission Fees.* Technical Report. Washington, DC: Smithsonian Institution Office of Policy and Analysis. https://www.si.edu/Content/opanda/docs/Rpts2007/07.04.Admissions.Final.pdf. Retrieved January 3, 2021.

Spilsbury, J. C., Korbin, J. E., and Coulton, C. E. (2012). "'Subjective' and 'Objective' Views of Neighborhood Danger and Well-Being: The Importance of Multiple Perspectives and Mixed Methods." *Child Indicators Research* 5, 469–82.

Spock, M. (2020). "Museums: Essential or Non-Essential." Wunderkammer. May 7, 2020. https://wunderkammer.blog/2020/05/07/museums-essential-or-non-essential/. Retrieved May 20, 2020.

Staus, N., Falk, J. H., Price, A., Tai, R., and Dierking, L. D. (in press). "Measuring the Long-Term Effects of Informal Education Experiences: Challenges and Potential Solutions." *Disciplinary and Interdisciplinary Research in Science Education.*

Stein, R. (2018a). "Museums and Public Opinion: Exploring Four Key Questions about What Americans Think of Museums." Technical Report. Washington, DC: American Alliance of Museums. January 20, 2018. https://www.aam-us.org/2018/01/20/museums-and-public-opinion/. Retrieved February 18, 2020.

Stein, R. (2018b). "Museums as Economic Engines: A National Report." Technical Report. January 19, 2018. Washington, DC: American Alliance of Museums. https://www.aam-us.org/2018/01/19/museums-as-economic-engines/. Retrieved February 18, 2020.

Steinwald, M., Harding, M., and Piacentini (2014). "Multisensory Engagement with Real Nature Relevant to Real Life." In N. Levent and A. Pascual-Leone (eds.), *The Multisensory Museum*, 45–60. Lanham, MD: Rowman & Littlefield.

Sternberg, R. J. (2012). "Intelligence." *Dialogues in Clinical Neuroscience* 14(1), 19–27.

Stewart, W. P. (1998). "Leisure as Multiphase Experiences: Challenging Traditions." *Journal of Leisure Research* 30(4), 391–400.

Stewart, W. P., and Hull IV, B. R. (1992). "Satisfaction of What? Post Hoc Versus Real-Time Construct Validity." *Leisure Sciences* 14, 195–209.

Stringer, C. (2011). *The Origin of Our Species*. London: Allen Lane.

Stuckey, H. L. and Nobel, J. (2010). "The Connection between Art, Healing, and Public Health: A Review of Current Literature." *American Journal of Public Health* 100(2), 254–63.

Suarez, A. V. and Tsutsui, N. (2004). "The Value of Museum Collections for Research and Society." *BioScience* 54 (1), 66–74.

Sukha. Wikipedia. https://en.wikipedia.org/wiki/Sukha. Retrieved August 2, 2020.

Suttie, J. (2017). "How Does Valuing Money Affect Your Happiness?" *Greater Good Magazine*. October 30, 2017. https://greatergood.berkeley.edu/article/item/how_does_valuing_money_affect_your_happiness. Retrieved March 18, 2021.

Sykes, C. (2020). "Art Therapy at the Manchester Museum." Art Museum Teaching: A Forum for Reflecting on Practice. July 3, 2020. https://artmuseumteaching.com/tag/reflection/. Retrieved February 21, 2021.

Szanto, A. (2020). "People Need Art in Times of Crisis. That's Why Museums Should Be Among the First Institutions to Reopen For Business—Here's How." artnet news. April 14, 2020. https://news-artnet-com.cdn.ampproject.org/c/s/news.artnet.com/opinion/andras-szanto-op-ed-reopening-museums-1832439/amp-page?fbclid=IwAR0G74_QiPefV2c311FSUS9JywuSryV3it6ZHO2L_96DmEmUU58jNJ1pcXs. Retrieved December 21, 2020.

Taoism. Wikipedia. https://en.wikipedia.org/wiki/Taoism. Retrieved August 2, 2020.

Te Papa National Services. (2001). "Valuing Collections." Technical Report. Wellington, NZ: Museum of New Zealand Te Papa Tongarewa. https://www.tepapa.govt.nz/sites/default/files/13-valuing-collections_0.pdf. Retrieved February 18, 2020.

Teasdale, P. (2018). "Go Figure: How to Measure the Value of Museums?" Frieze, 194. March 14, 2018. https://frieze.com/article/how-measure-value-museums. Retrieved February 18, 2020.

Thoreau, H. D. (1854, 1948). *Walden: Or, Life in the Woods.* New York: Rinehart.

Tohmo, T. (2004). "Economic Value of a Local Museum: Factors of Willingness-to-Pay." *Journal of Socio-Economics* 33(2), 229–40.

Torday, J. (2015). "Homeostasis as the Mechanism of Evolution." *Biology* 4, 573–90.

Torday, J. (2016). "The Cell as the First Niche Construction." *Biology* 5, 19–26.

Torday, J. S. (2015). "A Central Theory of Biology." *Medical Hypotheses* 85, 49–57.

Turner, J. H. (2000). *On the Origins of Human Emotions: A Sociological Inquiry into the Evolution of Human Affect*, 59. Stanford, CA: Stanford University Press.

Ulaby, N. (2020). "One-Third of U.S. Museums May Not Survive the Year, Survey Finds." *National Public Radio*. July 22, 2020. https://www.npr.org/sections/coronavirus-live-updates/2020/07/22/894049653/one-third-of-u-s-museums-may-not-survive-the-year-survey-finds. Retrieved July 30, 2020.

van Gulick, R. (2004). "Consciousness." *Stanford Encyclopedia of Philosophy*. Palo Alto, CA: Metaphysics Research Lab, Stanford University.

Van Vugt, M., and Tybur, J. M. (2015). "The Evolutionary Foundations of Status and Hierarchy: Dominance, Prestige, Power, and Leadership." In D. Buss (ed.), *Handbook of Evolutionary Psychology, second edition,* 788–809. New York: Wiley.

Voon, C. (2019). "Museums Are Finally Taking Accessibility for Visitors with Disabilities Seriously." Artsy.net. October 14, 2019. https://www.artsy.net/article/artsy-editorial-museums-finally-accessibility-visitors-disabilities-seriously. Retrieved August 9, 2020.

Wagner, G. P., and Tomlinson, G. (2020). "Extending the Explanatory Scope of Evolutionary Theory: The Origin of Historical Kinds of Biology and Culture." https://doi.org/10.20944/preprints202004.0025.v1. Retrieved June 24, 2020.

Waldinger, R. (2015). "What Makes a Good Life? Lessons from the Longest Study on Happiness." https://www.ted.com/talks/robert_waldinger_what_makes_a_good_life_lessons_from_the_longest_study_on_happiness?language=en. Retrieved March 2, 2016.

Walker, D. (2020). "Extraordinary Times, Extraordinary Measures." Ford Foundation. June 11, 2020. https://www.fordfoundation.org/ideas/equals-change-blog/posts/extraordinary-times-extraordinary-measures/. Retrieved June 11, 2020.

Wambold, S. and Spellerberg, M. (2018). "Identity-Related Motivations Online: Falk's Framework Applied to US Museum Websites." *Journal of Digital and Social Media Marketing* 5(4), 353–69.

Watson, J. D. and Berry, A. (2003). *DNA: The Secret of Life*. New York: Knopf Doubleday.

Webb, R. C. (1996). "Music, Mood, and Museums: A Review of Consumer Literature on Background Music." *Visitor Studies* 8(2), 15–29.

Wegner, D. M. (2002). *The Illusion of Conscious Will.* Cambridge, MA: MIT Press.

Weil, S. (1999). "From Being About Something to Being for Somebody: The Ongoing Transformation of the American Museum." *Daedalus* 128(3), 229–58.

Weil, S. (2002). *Making Museums Matter*. Washington, DC: Smithsonian Institution Press.

Weil, S. (2003). "Beyond Big and Awesome Outcome-Based Evaluation." *Museum News*, November/December, 40–45, 52–53.

Weinschenk, S., and Wise, B. (2013). "Why Having Choices Makes Us Feel Powerful." *Psychology Today*. January 24, 2013. https://www.psychologytoday.com/us/blog/brain-wise/201301/why-having-choices-makes-us-feel-powerful. Retrieved July 22, 2020.

Weinstein, M., and Bradburd, R. (2013). *The Robin Hood Rules for Smart Giving*. New York: Columbia University Press.

Wenger, E. 1998. *Communities of Practice: Learning, Meaning and Identity*. Cambridge: Cambridge University Press.

Whisman, S. A., and Hollenhorst, S. J. (1998). "A Path Model of Whiteriver Boating Satisfaction on the Cheat River of West Virginia." *Environmental Management* 22(1), 109–17.

Wiggins, D. (2001). *Sameness and Substance Renewed*, second edition. Cambridge, Cambridge University Press.

Wikipedia. (2020). "Maslow's Hierarchy of Needs." https://en.wikipedia.org/wiki/Maslow%27s_hierarchy_of_needs. Retrieved July 5, 2020.

Wikipedia. https://en.wikipedia.org/wiki/R/K_selection_theory. Retrieved February 20, 2020.

Wilson, E. O. (1975). *Sociobiology: The New Synthesis*, 38. Cambridge, MA: The Belknap Press.

Woese, C. (1998). "The Universal Ancestor." *Proceedings of the National Academy of Sciences, USA* 95(12), 6854–59.

Wohlleben, P. (2016). *The Hidden Life of Trees*. London: William Collins.

Wohlleben, P. (2017). *The Inner Life of Animals*. Vancouver, CA: Greystone Books.

Wong, J. T. and Hui, E. C. M. (2006). "Power of Expectations." *Property Management* 24, 496–506.

Wood, C., and Leighton, D. (2010). "Measuring Social Value: The Gap between Policy and Practice." Demos. https://www.demos.co.uk/files/Measuring_social_value_-_web.pdf. Retrieved February 18, 2020.

Wood, D. A., and Wills, E. (2012). *Subjective Well-Being and Security*. Dordrecht, NL: Springer.

Yamamoto, M., Naga, S., and Jun Shimizu, J. (2007). "Positive Musical Effects on Two Types of Negative Stressful Conditions." *Psychology of Music* 35(2), 249–75.

Yin, Z., Pascual, C., and Klionsky, D. (2016). "Autophagy: Machinery and Regulation." *Microbial Cell* 3(12), 588–96.

Zahn, R., Moll, J., Paiva, M., Garrido, G., Krueger, F., Huey E. and Grafman, J. (2009). "The Neural Basis of Human Social Values: Evidence from Functional MRI." *Cerebral Cortex* 19, 276–83.

Zakaria, F. (2020). *Ten Lessons for a Post-Pandemic World*. New York: W.W. Norton.

Zimmer, C. (2014). "Secrets of the Brain." *National Geographic* 225(2), 28–57.

Zongker, B. (2020). "U.S. Museums Face Financial Woes, Get More Visitors Says American Association of Museums." Art Daily/Associated Press. https://artdaily.cc/news/46649/U-S--Museums-Face-Financial-Woes--Get-More-Visitors-Says-American-Association-of-Museums-#.XtU2C0FlByx. Retrieved June 1, 2020.

Index

Page references for figures are italicized.

About the Author

John H. Falk is executive director of the Institute for Learning Innovation and Sea Grant Professor Emeritus of Free-Choice Learning at Oregon State University. He is known internationally for his work in the area of free-choice learning, the learning that occurs while visiting museums, science centers, zoos, aquariums, parks, watching educational television, or surfing the Internet for information. His recent research has focused on studying the value and long-term impacts of free-choice learning institutions, understanding why people utilize free-choice learning settings during their leisure time, and helping cultural institutions of all kinds re-think their future positioning and business models in the twenty-first century. Dr. Falk has authored over two hundred scholarly articles and chapters and has published more than two dozen books in this and related areas including *Learning from Museums, Second Edition* (Falk and Dierking, 2019), *Born to Choose* (Falk, 2018), *The Museum Experience Revisited* (Falk and Dierking, 2014), *Identity and the Museum Visitor Experience* (Falk, 2009), and *Thriving in the Knowledge Age* (Falk and Sheppard, 2006).

His awards include the 2010 American Alliance of Museums' John Cotton Dana Award for Leadership, 2013 Council of Scientific Society Presidents Award for Educational Research, and a 2016 NARST Distinguished Contributions to Science Education through Research award for helping to establish the field of free-choice/informal learning research. In 2006, in honor of the American Association of Museums centennial, he was recognized as one of one hundred most influential individuals in the museum community over the preceding one hundred years.